THE
CIVIL WAR
QUIZ BOOK

THE CIVIL WAR QUIZ BOOK

~ 1,600 ~
QUESTIONS AND ANSWERS
TO TEST YOUR **KNOWLEDGE**
OF AMERICA'S MOST
DIVISIVE CONFLICT

BLAKE A. MAGNER

TAYLOR TRADE PUBLISHING
Lanham · New York · Boulder · Toronto · Plymouth, UK

Published by Taylor Trade Publishing
An imprint of The Rowman & Littlefield Publishing Group, Inc.
4501 Forbes Boulevard, Suite 200, Lanham, Maryland 20706
http://www.rlpgtrade.com

Estover Road, Plymouth PL6 7PY, United Kingdom

Distributed by National Book Network

British Library Cataloguing in Publication Information Available

Library of Congress Cataloging-in-Publication Data
Magner, Blake A.
    The Civil War quiz book : 1,600 questions and answers to test your
knowledge of America's most divisive conflict / Blake A. Magner.
        p. cm.
    Includes bibliographical references and index.
    ISBN 978-1-58979-517-4 (pbk. : alk. paper)
    1. United States—History—Civil War, 1861–1865—Miscellanea.
I. Title.
    E468.M14 2010
    973.7—dc22   2010005580

Printed in the United States of America

This volume is dedicated to my grandson
who is the neatest kid I ever met:

Malachy Donald Magner

And a fine Irishman he is, though it will take a
few years for him to realize it.

I love ya, little dude—GG

Abraham Lincoln. USAMHI   Jefferson Davis. USAMHI

CONTENTS

Robert E. Lee. USAMHI   Ulysses S. Grant. USAMHI

FOREWORD

FOR AS LONG as I can remember, I have been blessed with an excellent memory. Thus I have been able to have a lifelong interest in history, geography, politics, and current events. In my junior year in high school in Hardin, Montana, I was introduced to a major network quiz show sponsored by the Mars Candy Co. featuring "Dr. IQ: The Mental Banker." The format was simple. Dr. IQ and his staff traveled about the nation and at prime time on a weeknight presented their program. Dr. IQ's assistants guided him to members of the audience who were then asked a question and if their answer was correct went on to another or if wrong sat down. This would continue until the selected chose to take their money or continue to the next plateau. Dr. IQ and his show even traveled to nearby Billings.

World War II sent me off to the U.S. Marine Corps, but I retained my interest in history, current events, and quiz shows. My friends and I more than sixty-six years later still recall our impromptu quiz shows as we killed time around camp, on humps and in hospitals.

By the mid-1950s, the burgeoning television industry picked up, insofar as it commanded my attention, what radio and Dr. IQ had pioneered. On June 7, 1955, some fourteen weeks before I entered on duty as historian at Vicksburg National Military Park, CBS's Jackson, Mississippi, affiliate premiered *The $64,000 Question*. It took the nation by storm. Families and friends, on Tuesday nights at prime time, gathered in their living rooms to be mesmerized as Hal March hosted the Revlon-sponsored show.

The program became so popular that, prompted by the sponsor, people such as Xavier Cugat and Ralph Newman appeared. The biggest winner was Teddy Nadler, a St. Louis U.S. government employee who netted more than $250,000. Dr. Joyce Brothers became a star attraction because of her encyclopedic knowledge of boxing. The show, because of the approach of the Civil War Centennial, featured, in addition to Newman and Charles Van Doren, several others selecting this subject as their field of expertise.

The public's displeasure with the show came in the late spring of 1958, when it was learned that certain of the more popular contestants were being fed questions prior to the night's program. In June 1958 CBS pulled the plug. In 1994 Hollywood came out with *Quiz Show*, a production directed by Robert Redford. The motion picture drew on the fate of *The $64,000 Question* as its theme.

In the summer of 1963 Revlon sought to reinvent the wheel with another high-stakes quiz program named *100 Grand*. It incorporated a theme introduced in April 1956 as a follow-up to *The $64,000 Question*. Billed as *The $64,000 Challenge*, this program appeared on Sunday nights and was dropped in September 1958.

The format of *100 Grand* pitted an amateur against a professional on a subject selected by the network in cooperation with the sponsor. The amateur, if he/she bested the professional through a series of plateaus, would have an opportunity to pocket "100 grand." The professional could appear only once. If he/she bested the amateur, they got a thousand-dollar U.S. savings bond and $10,000 for a civic project of their choice.

The new programs premiered in mid-September. With the Civil War Centennial at its midpoint, a selected subject was that war. The format was unimaginative, the contestants seated in chairs facing the host inside a Plexiglas bubble. The show was a bust. Fortunately, I participated in the last show held in a New York studio on the final Sunday evening in September.

My opponent was a member of the Madison, Wisconsin, Civil War Round Table, who the previous week had defeated a professional to reach the second plateau. Thanks to my success, the $10,000 that I won helped jump-start "Operation Cairo."

In the years since my introduction to the media and Civil War quiz programs, I have found them invaluable in stimulating interest in what has been referred to as America's *Iliad*. Many of the Civil War roundtables that were organized in the 1950s on the approach of the Civil War Centennial matured in the 1990s and continue into the twenty-first century paying homage to the Civil War quiz element as an important part of the programs in their newsletters where they include such a feature.

This brief journey down memory lane underscores how pleased I was to learn that Blake A. Magner, friend and colleague, had contracted for and was working on his own *Civil War Quiz Book*. My association with Blake goes back more than a score of years. As an editor of the *Gettysburg Magazine*, a subscriber to *Civil War News*, and through my Civil War seminars, I was familiar with Magner's encyclopedic knowledge of the trivia, as well as his mastery of the big picture of "Our War." No one possessed better credentials to undertake such a project. Blake then asked me to write the foreword for his "Quiz Book." My answer was yes, provided I could first see the draft manuscript. Because of numerous requests of this nature, I will not write a foreword or a promotional blurb for a dust jacket unless I have read a draft word-by-word.

Shortly before Thanksgiving 2009, I received in the mail a copy of Magner's manuscript. Touring during the next several weeks, I spent many hours with the draft, reading it line-by-line and checking references. In content, organization, and information, Magner has given his readers a tour de force. The author's graceful writing style will appeal to a broad audience, the generalist as well as the trivia aficionado. Civil War round table quiz masters, such as my friend Charles Crawford of the Atlanta group, will lead the applause.

In closing, thanks, Blake, for giving me the opportunity to read your manuscript. I found it entertaining, enlightening, and educational. I can ask no better way to close out more than seven decades of monitoring quiz shows, be they on radio, television, or in various other venues, as well as on the printed page.

Edwin C. Bearss
Historian Emeritus
National Park Service

PREFACE AND ACKNOWLEDGMENTS

THE REQUEST TO WRITE this book came to me out of the blue. I was contacted by a representative of Taylor Trade Publishing asking me if I'd be interested in writing a "quiz book" on the Civil War. Knowing the number of books that have gone across my *Civil War News* review desk over the last twenty years and how many were "quiz" books I wondered—why do another? Then I thought of a mischievous idea. Do a "quiz" book, but make it one that requires the reader to really know something, and that might, after reading the volume, leave him or her knowing a lot more. Thus I took on the task.

The book is in no way meant to be a scholarly tome on the American Civil War. It is intended to be a fun book. I do not go into great detail on many subjects, just questions that I picked up in my readings. Many battles are covered, but not exhaustively. For those readers wishing to seek more information on a particular question, be it battle, personality, or event, the bibliography will provide excellent sources on all the topics covered. I have in some cases answered the question and given no source. After having spent more than forty-seven years studying the Civil War, there are certain things that I just know and you, the reader, can trust me on the answer. Whenever possible I always double-checked my sources; therefore, if my source was mistaken and I did not pick it up the fault is my own, so blame me.

I have numerous people to thank. Those who helped me with the text and questions include Ted Alexander, historian at Antietam National Battlefield, and Bob English, a drinking and Civil War associate who was kind enough to look through some pages of the original draft and give me a thumbs up. My thanks to Dr. Allen Guelzo, Director of Civil War Era Studies at Gettysburg College and Lincoln Scholar, for some Lincoln questions, and Harold Holzer, a Lincoln scholar who gave me a great source on the dead President Lincoln. My thanks also goes to Jessica Sydnor who, during an offhand conversation, sent me off on a different trail where I came up with some darned good questions—thanks, Jessica. My thanks to Jeffry D. Wert, historian and author, who added a few questions to the list. Thank you, Michael Kauffman, for giving me some good advice on some bad information concerning Mary Surratt's noose. My deepest appreciation goes to Dale Beiver who, just home from a few months in the hospital, provided me with some great artillery/accouterment/weapons questions. Patrick Purcell, the know-all of Vermont generals and now-budding Naval expert, was also most helpful. A wonderful tip on Walt Whitman came from Ronald Funk of Philadelphia; thank you, Ronald. Thanks to John Heiser at Gettysburg for the tidbit of information I asked him for. Thanks also go to Peter Burford. And lastly to Kay Jorgensen, my former editor at *Civil War News*, who two hours after I finished the text sent me another good question—thanks, Kay.

This book would have been much harder to put together without a valuable resource, *Blue & Gray Magazine*. The owner and editor of this publication, David E. Roth, gathers some of the best historians in the field, each of whom puts together fascinating and detailed descriptions of battles, people, places and things. It is a great source for any researcher. I also wish to thank all the other authors whose work I used in creating this volume.

At Taylor Trade Publishing I wish to thank the editing staff, especially Janice Braunstein. (Janice is a trooper, listening to my griping without uttering, "Another know-it-all author.") My thanks also to Flannery Scott, who just couldn't believe that I didn't need a photograph permission slip in some cases.

I personally learned a lot from compiling this volume. I was forced to look at aspects of the Civil War that either did not interest me or that

I had simply overlooked for many years. The one thing that disappointed me was the amount of bad information I came across. I read volumes that were filled with incorrect facts, misidentified photographs with questionable captions, and writing that plainly showed that the authors either did not know what they were talking about or did not care. Thus I warn you, readers—just because it is in print does not mean it is good stuff. In other words, as the old saying goes, buyer beware. Did I make mistakes? Probably—even the Civil War gods make the occasional mistake. I had some of the "gods" read this manuscript, and if the reader checks my source and it doesn't exactly match what I have written it is because I have corrected my sources' mistakes on the advice of those who know better. If you find a mistake, I would appreciate it if you would contact the publisher and have them pass along my errors so that if a second edition of this volume ever comes out the problems can be fixed.

The most important person in the production of this volume has to be Edwin C. Bearss. He was kind enough to write the foreword, but in the process—and I knew he would do this—read and edited the manuscript I sent him. He chewed it to pieces and caught my typos, plus adding in Bearssisms, his little anecdotes and tidbits of really neat information. He then chewed up a lot of my sources. This goes back to my earlier comments on sources: Though Ed is not mentioned very often in the credits, he had a say in almost every one. This book is a much better publication for his input.

And lastly, I wish to thank my wife, Johanna, for giving me peace and much-needed time at my computer, also for occasional help like traveling with me to Carlisle Barracks. She also spent ten hours a day for a week and a half sitting next to me with her laptop while we edited the editing. I am hoping soon to discover once again what month and date it is, as I have completely lost track of time over the last six months—I heard that Thanksgiving, Christmas, and the New Year have come and gone. This volume has not been easy, simply because I had to write so many words and do so much research in so little time, but I hope the reader will enjoy it.

Blake A. Magner
Haddon Township, N.J.
January 2010

∾ CHAPTER 1 ᒧ

PREWAR

PERSONALITIES

Where and when was Abraham Lincoln born?
He was born about three miles south of Hodgenville, Kentucky (this is today's spelling—it was also known as Hodgensville during the early nineteenth century) on February 12, 1809, the first president to be born outside of the original thirteen states. (Henig, 29)

What were Abraham Lincoln's parents' names?
His birth mother was named Nancy Hanks, who died when Lincoln was nine. His father was Thomas Lincoln. Following his wife's death Thomas remarried, taking Sarah Bush Johnston as his wife. (Donald, 19, 23; Faust, 439)

When and where was Jefferson Davis born?
He was born in Christian County, Kentucky, on June 3, 1808, a little over 100 miles from where Abraham Lincoln was later born. However, his family soon moved to Mississippi. (Faust, 20; Henig, 29)

What were the names of Jefferson Davis's parents?
His father's name was Samuel Emory Davis and his mother was Jane Cook. (Davis, 4–5)

Jefferson Davis held what position in the Federal government prior to the Civil War?
Secretary of War from 1853 to 1857. He also served as a U.S. Representative and Senator from Mississippi. During the Mexican War he was the colonel of the 1st Mississippi Rifles.

Where and when was Robert E. Lee born?
Lee was born on January 19, 1807, at Stratford Hall. Lee's home was on the family plantation along the Potomac River near present-day Montross, Virginia. (Weeks, 333)

Who were Robert E. Lee's parents?
Henry "Light Horse Harry" Lee of Revolutionary War fame was Lee's father. At Washington's funeral "Light Horse Harry" coined the phrase about Washington that he was "first in war, first in peace, and first in the hearts of his countrymen." His mother was Ann Carter. (Freeman, 6)

What position did Robert E. Lee hold at the U.S. Military Academy?
Superintendent from 1852–1855. (Faust, 430)

P. T. G. Beauregard was also the superintendent at the U.S. Military Academy. How long did he remain in that position?
Approximately three days. (Faust, 52)

What was Thomas Jonathan Jackson's profession prior to the Civil War?
Professor of artillery and natural philosophy at the Virginia Military Institute.

What was Ulysses S. Grant's real first name?
Hiram.

Confederate general Joseph E. Johnston married Polly Wood. Who was her famous Revolutionary War uncle?
Patrick Henry. (Terdoslavich, 36, 132)

Who was Abraham Lincoln's first vice president?
Hannibal Hamlin. Prior to his being asked to run with Lincoln, Hamlin had been a politician from Maine. He only served one term.

Who was Jefferson Davis's first wife?
Sarah Knox Taylor, the daughter of general and future president Zachary Taylor. She died of malaria three months after their wedding. (Faust, 208)

What was the name of Jefferson Davis's second wife and how many children did they have?
Varina Howell Davis. They wed in 1845. Together they had six children, one of whom died tragically in Richmond during the war. (Faust, 210)

What indiscretion did Daniel Sickles, later a Federal major general, commit on February 27, 1859?
Daniel Sickles entrapped and killed Philip Barton Key (the son of Francis Scott Key) in front of the White House on Lafayette Square for having had an affair with his wife, Teresa Bagioli Sickles. Sickles was tried and found innocent in the first case of "temporary insanity." He was defended by, among others, James T. Brady, John Graham, Thomas Francis Meagher, and Edwin M. Stanton. Sickles's major sin, however, in the eyes of many, was taking his wife back after the affair. (Hessler, 10–17)

Who was perhaps the most celebrated "conductor" on the Underground Railroad?
Harriet Tubman.

What conductor on the Underground Railroad was known as "Moses"?
Harriet Tubman. (Terdoslavich, 39, 135)

Who were the "secret six" who bankrolled John Brown in his raid on Harpers Ferry?
Thomas Wentworth Higginson, Unitarian minister and Transcendentalist; Theodore Parker, Unitarian minister; Samuel Gridley Howe,

physician, freedom fighter and humanitarian; Franklin Sanborn, Massachusetts journalist; George Luther Stearns, Massachusetts businessman; and Gerrit Smith, wealthy New Yorker. (*America's Civil War*, September 2009, 32–33)

Who was the wife of Samuel Gridley Howe (one of the "secret six") and what was she famous for?
Julia Ward Howe, who wrote the poem that would later become the "Battle Hymn of the Republic." (*America's Civil War*, September 2009, 32)

What Virginia governor ordered the execution of John Brown?
Henry A. Wise. (Denney, 49)

What are the names of the four men who ran for president in 1860?
Abraham Lincoln, Stephen Douglas, John C. Breckinridge, and John Bell.

What was the name of the slave who sued for his freedom and whose case ultimately reached the Supreme Court?
Dred Scott.

Who was the chief justice of the Supreme Court during the Dred Scott case and much of the Civil War?
Roger Brooke Taney.

Who was Lincoln's major rival at the Republican National Convention?
New Yorker William Henry Seward. (Henig, 10)

Who was Dennis Hart Mahan?
Mahan was a professor of civil and military engineering at West Point. His students included some of the most important commanders of the Civil War. (Faust, 468)

Where was future Army of the Potomac commander Gen. George Gordon Meade born?
Cadiz, Spain, on December 31, 1815. (Faust, 482)

Who developed the wigwag system of messaging used by the U.S. Army Signal Corps?
Albert J. Myer, who also formed the U.S. Army Signal Corps in 1863. (Catton, 353; Faust, 519)

Who was Andrew Curtin?
Republican war governor of Pennsylvania. (Boatner, 214)

Who was elected Speaker of the House of Representatives in December 1859?
William Pennington, a New Jersey representative and member of the "People's Party." (Henig, 2)

Who was William Henry Herndon?
Lincoln's law partner in Illinois. (Boatner, 397)

Who was Josiah Henson?
He was an African American leader who is thought to be the prototype of Uncle Tom in Harriet Beecher Stowe's *Uncle Tom's Cabin*. He and his family escaped from slavery and fled to Canada. (Boatner, 397)

What British royal visited the United States, arriving on September 18, 1860?
His Royal Highness Albert Edward, Prince of Wales. He became the first heir to the British throne to visit America. Staying for about a month and traveling under the name Baron Renfrew he visited a number of Midwest cities, Washington, D.C., Mount Vernon, Boston, and New York. Prince Albert went on to become Edward VII, which gave rise to the Edwardian Age. (Henig, 13–14)

Who was known as the "Little Giant"?
Senator Stephen A. Douglas of Illinois. His other nickname was "Steam Engine in Britches."

Who was Henry Villard?
Villard, born Ferdinand Heinrich Gustav Hilgard in Rhenish, Bavaria, became the first reporter in American journalism to cover a president-

elect full time. While covering the Lincoln-Douglas debates Villard became friends with Lincoln, who gave him unprecedented access. Reporting for the New York *Herald*, he accompanied Lincoln from Springfield to Washington, D.C. Villard later became a businessman and eventually controlled the Northern Pacific Railroad. (Henig, 22)

Who was Grace Bedell?
She was the eleven-year-old girl who wrote a letter to Lincoln suggesting that he should grow a beard. (Henig, 22)

Who was Abraham Lincoln's business partner in the general store he opened in New Salem, Illinois?
William Berry, who drank himself to death leaving Lincoln in debt for over $1,000. (Henig, 30)

Who was the pastor of Plymouth Church in present-day Brooklyn Heights where many abolitionists' rallies were held?
Rev. Henry Ward Beecher. (Terdoslavich, 38, 134)

Who was Harriet Lane?
She was an orphan who was raised by her uncle James Buchanan. Miss Lane acted as President Buchanan's hostess in London and at the White House. (Boatner, 470)

The minié ball was invented by whom?
Claude Étienne Minié.

Who was the highest-ranking officer to leave the Union Army and side with the Confederacy?
Joseph E. Johnston. (Denney, 50)

What was Frenchman Henri Jomini's impact on the American Civil War?
He wrote the textbook that such notables as Robert E. Lee and George McClellan studied at West Point. Two of his many works were *Traité des grandes operations militaires* and *Précis de l'art de la guerre*. Up until 1832 parts of *Traité* were the only text on strategy available to the

Academy's cadets. Thus during the Civil War much of the strategy used by both the Union and Confederacy was based on the writings of Jomini. (Faust, 401)

Who were five of the most prominent abolitionists?
John Brown, famous for his raid on Harpers Ferry in 1859. Wendell Phillips, of Massachusetts, who not only championed freedom for the slaves but women's rights, prison reform, labor reform, prohibition, and rights for Native Americans. William Lloyd Garrison, also of Massachusetts, a cofounder of the American Anti-Slavery Society. Frederick Douglass, a former slave, who became the most famous black speaker of his time. Gerrit Smith of New York, who went from a great champion of the abolition movement to a critic of the black race. (Flagel, 41–46)

Who were the five most prominent "fire-eaters"?
Robert Barnwell Rhett of South Carolina, who defended slavery early and earnestly. In 1830 he proclaimed secession as the only way to protect slavery. Serving in both the U.S. House and Senate, he fought to repeal the constitutional ban on slave trading. William Lowndes Yancey of Alabama, who served in Congress, where he said that either slavery had to be legal everywhere or the slave states should secede. John C. Calhoun of South Carolina, who eventually became the king of states' rights. Edmund Ruffin of Virginia, who championed secession whenever he could, and was so adamant in his convictions when the South lost the war he committed suicide. And Louis T. Wigfall of South Carolina, who served in the Senate from Texas, where he defended Southern honor and slavery. (Flagel, 51–56)

Abraham Lincoln is the only president to hold one. One what?
A patent. Lincoln received Patent No. 6469 on May 22, 1849, for a device for raising boats off sandbars. The device was never built. (Allen Guelzo, Gettysburg, PA; Smithsonian)

Who was President Lincoln's secretary of the Navy and what was Lincoln's nickname for him?
Gideon Wells, and Lincoln referred to him as "Father Neptune." (Faust, 813; Allen Guelzo, Gettysburg, PA)

What British philosopher's book *On Liberty* did Abraham Lincoln admire?
John Stuart Mill. (Allen Guelzo, Gettysburg, PA)

Who was Lincoln's "beau ideal of a statesman"?
Henry Clay. (Allen Guelzo, Gettysburg, PA)

What foreign correspondent was employed for a time by Horace Greeley's New York *Tribune*?
Karl Marx. (Davis, 200)

Who comprised the "Bohemian Brigade"?
Reporters, mostly Eastern, who kept a common "headquarters" in the field where they shared drink and stories. (Davis, 202)

On May 23, 1856, John Brown led a massacre where?
At Pottawatomie Creek in Kansas, where Brown and six of his followers, including four of his sons, dragged unarmed pro-slavery men and boys out of their homes and "hacked them to death with long-edged swords." (Faust, 83)

Jefferson Davis was in what graduating class at West Point?
Jefferson was a member of the class of 1828. Every year the encampment beginning the new plebes' life at the academy is named after a military leader. The encampment of 1858 was named Camp Jefferson Davis. (Aimone, 14)

Following Abraham Lincoln's election, who was the first Southerner to resign from West Point?
Henry S. Farley (ex–class of 1862) of South Carolina on November 19. By the end of the year he was joined by six other South Carolinians. (Aimone, 22)

At the outbreak of the Civil War who was the Commandant of Cadets at West Point?
Capt., later Maj. Gen. John F. Reynolds. (Aimone, 27)

Who published the most successful ladies' magazine of the period?
Louis Antonie Godey. Born in New York City in 1804, he moved
to Philadelphia in the early 1820s. In 1830, along with a partner he
began publishing the *Ladies Book*, which eventually became *Godey's
Ladies Book*. The magazine reached about 150,000 people, used color
print and had such writers as Oliver Wendell Holmes, Henry Wadsworth Longfellow, Edgar Allan Poe, and Harriet Beecher Stowe as
contributors. In 1836 he began publishing the *Saturday News*, which
eventually evolved into the *Saturday Evening Post*. (Magner, 63)

**What poet, who would later become a volunteer nursing aide and
comforter of many wounded soldiers, reviewed opera prior to the war?**
Walt Whitman. Whitman wrote opera reviews for the *Brooklyn Daily
Eagle* in 1847. One quote about him was, "Opera's greatest contribu-
tion of American culture in the nineteenth century was the poetry of
Walt Whitman. 'But for opera, he said, I never could have written
Leaves of Grass.'" (Ronald Funk, Philadelphia, PA; Dizikes, 184–185)

**The two individuals pictured on page 10 were to become generals
during the Civil War. Who are they?**
Robert E. Lee and his son William Henry Fitzhugh "Rooney" Lee.
The image was taken when Lee was about thirty-eight years of age,
thus making Rooney an eight-year-old. Robert E. Lee was destined to
become a general commanding the Army of Northern Virginia and
was eventually placed in command of all of the Confederate armies.
Rooney became a major general, and from Five Forks to Appomattox
commanded the forces on the right of Lee's retreat. The identity of
Rooney is a bit fuzzy, but due to the time when the photograph was
taken (while Lee was superintendent at West Point) and the look of
the boy, it is a best-guess identification by the staff at the Virginia Historical Society. (VHS; Boatner, 478)

**What happened to Jubal Early in the winter of 1836 while he was
a cadet at West Point?**
One of his classmates, and later, comrade in arms, Lewis "Lo"
Armistead, cracked a plate over his head in the mess hall. (Robbins, 65)

Robert E. Lee and son
"Rooney." VHS

What were the names of Thomas Jonathan Jackson's wives and children?

His first wife was Elinor Junkin, the daughter of the president of Washington College. They were married on August 4, 1853. On October 22, 1854 Ellie gave birth to a stillborn son and shortly thereafter died due to hemorrhaging. Jackson's second wife was Anna Morrison, the daughter of Robert Morrison, the former president of Davidson College. The two were married on July 16, 1857, at the Morrison home. Jackson and Anna had a daughter, Mary Graham, born on April 30, 1858, who died on May 25. The couple had a second daughter, born in November 1862, whom they named Julia Thomas, who survived until 1889. (Robertson, 146–147, 182–183, 645, 649–650)

EVENTS

When and where were Abraham Lincoln and Mary Todd married?
November 4, 1842, in the parlor of her sister Elizabeth Edwards's home in Springfield. Mary was to die in the same house in 1882. (Henig, 312; Craughwell, 166)

What was the first state to secede from the Union?
South Carolina on December 20, 1860.

MISCELLANEOUS

What percentage of the popular vote did Abraham Lincoln receive when he was elected president in 1860?
Approximately 40 percent. He did however, win the Electoral College vote, receiving 180 votes to 72 for Breckinridge, his closest competitor. He received 1,866,452 popular votes over Douglas's 1,376,957 (29 percent). (Catton, 39; Henig 19)

By 1860, 57 percent of the value of all American exports came from what product?
Cotton, totaling $191,000,000. (Catton, 2)

How many African Americans were in the United States in 1860 and how many of them were slaves?
4.5 million, of which 4 million were slaves. (Catton, 2)

What was the main underlying cause of the Civil War?
Though there were many reasons for the Civil War, many of which could have been solved democratically, the one issue that mattered most, and poisoned the idea of compromise, was slavery. (Catton, 7)

What was a "fire-eater"?
"Fire-eaters" were Southern secessionists known for their harsh words and deeds. (Flagel, 51)

After verbally attacking Senator Andrew Butler of South Carolina, which congressman assaulted Senator Charles Sumner?
South Carolina Congressman Preston Brooks, a relative of Senator Butler, caned Sumner senseless on the Senate floor. (Catton, 21; Faust, 732)

What became known as the "Wigwam"?
The building erected in Chicago, Illinois, where the Republican convention was held and where Abraham Lincoln was nominated for president. The two-story building was 180 by 100 feet and could seat 10,000 people. (Catton, 38; Henig, 8)

How many ballots did it take to nominate Lincoln at the Republican National Convention and how many votes did he get?
Three ballots, with Lincoln getting 235½ votes (233 were needed to win). (Henig, 10)

Why is the yacht *America* famous?
The *America* won the America's Cup in 1851. During the first part of the Civil War she became a Confederate dispatch boat and was scuttled in 1862. Raised by Union forces, the *America* then became part of the South Atlantic Blockading Squadron. Following the war she unsuccessfully defended her Cup in 1870. In 1873 the yacht was bought by former Maj. Gen. Ben Butler, who changed her so much that twenty years later she would be unrecognizable. She was eventually sent to the Naval Academy where she fell into disrepair. Basically destroyed during a snow storm in 1942, she was scrapped and burned in 1945. (Boatner, 11; History Central)

Who commanded the *America* while she was a Confederate blockade-runner?
From 1860 to December 1861 she was owned and operated by Henry Edward Decie. During that time she cruised the West Indies and then made a trip to Europe. Decie sold the yacht to the Confederate States Navy but she was soon destroyed. (History Central)

What was unusual about Stephen Douglas's method of campaigning for the presidency?
He was the first presidential candidate in history to campaign on his own behalf. (Henig)

What was a Sibley Tent and who invented it?
Henry Hopkins Sibley, later a brigadier general in the Confederate service, invented the tent prior to the war. It was conical and light, and was erected on a tripod holding a single pole. It could accommodate twelve soldiers. When a fire was made in the center of the tent the men could all sleep with their feet toward the heat. (Boatner, 760)

Where and what is Wilkes Land?
Wilkes Land is a place in Antarctica named for Charles Wilkes, who led a squadron of six ships to the continent in 1838. During the Civil War he commanded the Navy ship USS *San Jacinto* that captured the *Trent*, beginning the Trent Affair. (Boatner, 925)

What American at the Harpers Ferry Arsenal improved on Claude Minié's projectile, and how?
James H. Burton. He developed a bullet that would expand from the gas of the powder's explosion, thus eliminating the need for a wooden plug. (Henig, 69)

What was the primary asset of having a rifle-musket using minié balls?
It greatly increased the accuracy and effective range of the weapon. Old smoothbores were accurate only up to eighty yards or so, while the rifle-musket was accurate to three hundred yards.

What was the Crittenden Compromise?
A bill concerning slavery that John Jordan Crittenden introduced in Congress in December 1860. It included six constitutional amendments, the first being that it prohibited slavery north of the 36° 30' line. The second provision prohibited Congress from abolishing slavery and the third

forbade emancipation in the District of Columbia. The fourth provision protected the interstate transportation of slaves and the fifth provided for compensation by the U.S. government for any "rescued" slave. The sixth provision stated that no future amendments could change these guarantees. The compromise did not make it through Congress. (Faust, 193)

What manual did future Confederate Lt. Gen. William J. Hardee write in 1853–1854?
He penned *Rifle and Light Infantry Tactics,* soon to become simply known as "Hardee's *Tactics.*" It became popular at West Point and was used by thousands of officers, North and South, during the course of the war. There were new editions printed in 1860 and 1861 and the Confederates printed versions of the book, though no major changes were made to the text. The text was based on an 1848 French manual focusing on speed and small unit tactics. (Faust, 338)

What two states had the largest population of slaves?
South Carolina and Mississippi. South Carolina's slave population was 57 percent. For every three whites in the state there were four slaves, numbering 402,000. Mississippi's slave population was 55 percent. Eleven of every twenty Mississippians were slaves, approximately 437,000. (Flagel, 26–28)

What city was the first capital of the Confederacy?
Montgomery, Alabama, but after four months the capital was moved to Richmond, Virginia.

Of the 20 percent of the emigrant soldiers who served the Union, what two countries were most of them from?
Ireland and Germany. Almost one in every eight Union soldiers was of German background. There were 150,000 Irish who wore blue, while almost 200,000 Germans did. (Davis, 169, 172, 178)

What was the Fenian Brotherhood?
Irishmen who joined the Union army to get training so that they could return to Ireland and free it from British rule. Many Confederate Irish were also of this thought. (Davis, 172–173)

What was the Declaration of Immediate Causes?
Drafted during the South Carolina secession convention by Christopher G. Menninger, the declaration justified the state's right to secede from the Union on the grounds that the North had violated the Constitution. Because the North encouraged abolition and attempted to limit slavery they were in violation of the Constitution, thus making it null and void. (Faust, 213)

In the 1820s what did Henry Deringer invent that would later impact American history?
Deringer was a gunsmith who produced a compact large-caliber pocket pistol. By the 1850s the weapon, with a change in spelling to *derringer*, was extremely popular, being carried by both men and women. John Wilkes Booth used one of Mr. Deringer's weapons to assassinate President Lincoln at Ford's Theater. (Magner, 61)

What were the two most populous states, one Union, one Confederate?
New York and Virginia.

Why was July 15 a special day for West Point plebes?
On that day all previously acquired demerits were forgiven. (Aimone, 14)

Until he was called to active service in 1861, what did Lt. Oliver Otis Howard lead twice a week at the Military Academy?
Lt. Howard, a mathematics instructor, held twice weekly evening prayer meetings. There were usually ten to thirty cadets who attended the Bible reading, hymn singing, and prayer sessions. The meetings continued even after Howard's departure. (Aimone, 17)

Who were the prominent instructors at West Point during the Civil War?
Dennis Hart Mahan (Department of Civil and Military Engineering); William H. Bartlett (Department of Natural and Experimental Philosophy); Albert E. Church (Department of Mathematics); Henry L. Kendrick (Department of Chemistry, Mineralogy and

Geology); John W. French (Department of Geography, History and Ethics); Robert W. Weir (Professor of Drawing); Patrice de Janon (Spanish) and Hyacinth R. Agnel (French). Of all the instructors, only Kendrick had seen active military service, on the frontier and in Mexico. (Aimone, 18)

Which graduate of the West Point class of 1861 had to change his wedding plans?
Judson Kilpatrick. No leaves were granted following graduation so his fiancée went to the Academy for his graduation and stayed to be married at the West Point Hotel. (Aimone, 28)

BATTLES

How many men accompanied John Brown on his raid into Harpers Ferry?
Twenty one—sixteen whites, four African Americans and one runaway slave. (Catton, 37)

What were the names of the men who followed Brown to Harpers Ferry and what were their fates?
Jeremiah Anderson (mortally wounded), Osbourne Perry Anderson (African American; escaped to Canada), Oliver Brown (John Brown's youngest son; mortally wounded), Owen Brown (survived the raid and later moved to California), Watson Brown (mortally wounded), John E. Cook (executed in Charles Town on December 16), John Anthony Copeland Jr. (African American; executed in Charles Town on December 16), Barclay Coppoc (escaped and later joined the 3rd Kansas Infantry where he was killed in a train accident), Edwin Coppoc (executed in Charles Town on December 16), Shields Green (escaped slave; executed in Charles Town on December 16), Albert Hazlett (escaped, captured, and executed in Charles Town on March 16, 1860), John Henry Kagi (shot and killed while attempting to escape), Lewis Leary (African American; killed while trying to escape), William Leeman (killed while attempting to escape), Francis Jackson Meriam (escaped), Dangerfield Newby (African American; the first

raider killed), Aaron Stevens (executed on March 16, 1860), Stewart Taylor (killed), Dauphin Thompson (killed), William Thompson (killed), and Charles Plummer Tidd (escaped). (Frye, 31)

Where was the staging area for Brown's Harpers Ferry Raid?
The Kennedy farm, located along the Harpers Ferry Road north of Harpers Ferry.

Who was the first victim of John Brown's raid?
A free black and baggage man for the B&O railroad, Hayward Shepherd. (*America's Civil War*, September 2009, 33)

Who commanded the detachment of Marines sent to Harpers Ferry to capture John Brown and what was the name of his subordinate who led the Marines who stormed the engine-house?
Lt. Col. Robert E. Lee and Lt. J. E. B. Stuart.

What was the name of the judge who presided over John Brown's trial?
Judge Richard E. Parker. (Patchan, 10)

When and where was John Brown executed?
About 11:30 a.m. on December 2, 1859, in Charles Town, Virginia (now West Virginia). Brown was taken from the county jail and moved about five blocks to some open ground where the scaffold had been built. He rode on his black walnut coffin. Maj. Thomas Jackson described Brown as being dressed "in carpet slippers of predominating red, white socks, black pants, black frock coat, black vest, black slouch hat. Nothing around his neck beside his shirt collar." (Robertson, 198–199)

Who made up the majority of the spectators at John Brown's execution?
There were very few civilians in attendance. Because there had been so many rumors of attempts to rescue Brown, Virginia Governor Henry A. Wise opted to increase security. There were more than 650 soldiers in

Charles Town, with 300 more at the execution site and 300 more in various surrounding towns in case they were needed. (Robertson, 198)

What person who would later become important in American history was in the crowd and witnessed Brown's hanging?
John Wilkes Booth. (Kauffman, 106)

What were Maj. Thomas J. Jackson's duties at the hanging of John Brown?
He commanded twenty-one VMI cadets who manned two howitzers. At the hanging Jackson's detachment was placed along the pathway leading to the gallows, one gun on either side, about forty yards from the scaffold. (Robertson, 298)

Who accompanied Mrs. John Brown to see her condemned husband and to retrieve his body?
Philadelphian Hector Tyndale, who took on the task out of a sense of duty and chivalry. During the course of his duties he was insulted, threatened, and, on the morning of the execution, shot at. After the hanging Tyndale demanded that the coffin be opened to positively identify Brown's corpse. During the war Tyndale rose to the rank of brigadier general. (Magner, 56)

On what date did Maj. Robert Anderson and his garrison abandon Ft. Moultrie?
The garrison secretly abandoned the fort on December 26, 1860, after spiking all the guns and cutting down the flagstaff to impede the Southerners from raising their colors on United States property. (Catton, 48)

How many men were in Anderson's command at Ft. Sumter?
Sixty-eight.

What event do some consider to be the first overt action of the Civil War?
The raising of the Palmetto State flag over Castle Pinckney in Charleston Harbor on December 27, 1860. (Catton, 51)

UNITS

What was the first "real" Zouave unit formed in the United States?
In 1859 the United States Zouave Cadets was organized by a twenty-three-year-old Chicago lawyer, Elmer Ephraim Ellsworth. To be a member of the unit the recruit could not drink, gamble, play billiards or patronize brothels. They were an excellent drill team. In 1860 Ellsworth took his men on a tour of the Midwest and Northeast. They were a hit wherever they performed and ultimately spawned dozens of other Zouave companies. (Davis, 144–145)

~⊃ CHAPTER 2 C~

1861

PERSONALITIES

What was William Tecumseh Sherman's position at the beginning of the Civil War?
He was the head of the Louisiana State Seminary of Learning and Military Academy, at Pineville (known today as LSU). (Denney, 19)

Who commanded the *Star of the West* on its journey to Ft. Sumter?
The ship's master was a civilian by the name of John McGowan. The soldiers on board were commanded by Lt. Charles R. Woods. (Faust, 714)

Who commanded the garrison at Ft. Moultrie and Ft. Sumter and where did he hail from?
Maj. Robert Anderson, who, like Lincoln and Davis, was born in Kentucky, on June 14, 1805. Raised in a slave-owning family, he sympathized with the South but remained loyal to the Union. (Faust, 15; Henig, 33)

What were the names of the three Confederate emissaries who visited Ft. Sumter on April 11?
Col. James Chesnut, Capt. Stephen D. Lee, and Lt. Col. A. R. Chisolm. (Denney, 34)

Where did Col. Chesnut's wife gain her fame?
A noted Confederate diarist, she was educated and articulate and knew the leaders of the Confederate government. She wrote *A Diary from Dixie,* which today is best known as *Mary Chesnut's Civil War.* (Faust, 36)

Who was the senior brigadier general in the Union army at the beginning of the war?
Brig. Gen. John Ellis Wool. He expected to replace Winfield Scott on his retirement but instead was placed in command of the Department of Virginia. Appointed major general, he retired in July 1863. (Faust, 842)

Who took over command of the Washington Navy Yard when Capt. Franklin Buchanan resigned and went to serve the Confederacy?
Capt. John A. Dahlgren. (Denney, 37)

Who were Gen. Robert Patterson's two sons who served in the Union Army?
Brevet Brig. Gen. Robert Emmet Patterson and Brig. Gen. Francis Engle Patterson, who was "killed by the accidental discharge of his own weapon" on November 22, 1862. (Magner, 39, 41)

Who was the first general officer, Union or Confederate, killed in the Civil War?
Robert Selden Garnett, at Corrick's Ford following the battle of Rich Mountain in northwestern Virginia, on July 13, 1861. Garnett's cousin, Richard B. Garnett, was killed during the Pickett-Pettigrew-Trimble Assault on July 3, 1863, at Gettysburg. (Faust, 300)

What Union general had the nom de guerre "Old Fuss and Feathers"?
Gen. Winfield Scott.

Who replaced Winfield Scott as the commander of all Union forces?
Maj. Gen. George McClellan.

In what position did Lincoln place Maj. Anderson following his return from Ft. Sumter?
Anderson was given the rank of brigadier general and placed in command of the Department of Kentucky which later became the Department of the Cumberland. Due to ill health, Anderson was forced to retire in 1863. (Faust, 15)

Of Jefferson Davis's appointments to his cabinet, who were the only two who would remain until the end of the war?
Secretary of the Navy Steven R. Mallory and Postmaster General J. H. Regan. (Denney, 27)

Who designed the "Stars and Bars," the first official Confederate flag?
Nichola Marschall. The flag contained two wide red bars separated by one white one. It also contained a field of blue in the upper left corner with seven stars. (Denney, 30)

What future Confederate general swore in Hannibal Hamlin as the new vice president?
Vice President John C. Breckinridge. (Denney, 29)

Who was the quartermaster general of the U.S. Army?
Brig. Gen. Montgomery Cunningham Meigs, who served from May 15, 1861, until the end of the war. (Faust, 485)

Who was Abraham Lincoln's first secretary of the treasury?
Salmon Portland Chase. A former governor of Ohio, Chase took up his post despite having no professional training in finance. (Faust, 132)

Who was Lincoln's secretary of state?
William H. Seward. (Faust, 669)

Who were Abraham Lincoln's private secretaries?
John Hay and John George Nicolay.

Who was Jefferson Davis's first secretary of war?
Leroy Pope Walker. Walker served for only a short time, resigning on September 16, 1861, following which time he became a brigadier general.

Who was Jefferson Davis's secretary of the Navy?
Stephen Russell Mallory.

Who was the vice president of the Confederate States of America and where did he hail from?
Alexander Hamilton Stephens of Georgia.

Whom did Jefferson Davis place in overall command of the Western Theater?
General Albert Sydney Johnston. (Catton, 109)

Who commanded the Union forces in the Western Theater?
Maj. Gen. Henry W. Halleck, as of March 11, 1862, including the troops in Brig. Gen. Don Carlos Buell's Department of the Ohio who assumed command of the Department of the Mississippi. (Catton, 110)

Who was Lincoln's American Minister to England?
Charles Francis Adams Sr., son of President John Quincy Adams. (Faust, 2)

Who was the superintendent of the Old Capital Prison in Washington, D.C.?
William P. Wood.

Who were two of the most famous female inmates at the Old Capital Prison?
Belle Boyd and Rose O'Neal Greenhow. (Faust, 544)

Who was Princess Agnes Elisabeth Winona Leclerq Joy Salm-Salm?
She was the wife of Prince Salm-Salm, a colonel of the 8th and later 68th New York. Princess Salm-Salm lived in the field with her hus-

band and worked as a nurse and with various soldiers' relief organizations. She was a high-spirited woman who became a favorite among both officers and enlisted men. (Faust, 653)

Who wrote the poem "The Picket Guard," also known as "All Quiet Along the Potomac"?
Mrs. Ethelind Eliot Beers. (Boatner, 10)

Who was "Crazy Bet" Van Lew?
Elizabeth "Crazy Bet" Van Lew was a Union spy who lived in Richmond, Virginia. As she was known for her odd behavior, Richmond residents never suspected her of espionage. She aided Union prisoners escaping from Libby Prison and sent valuable information north. She was especially helpful to U. S. Grant during his Overland Campaign. Following the war, Grant appointed her postmistress of Richmond. (Faust, 778)

By what other name is Frederick Augustus Washington Bailey better known?
Frederick Douglass. (Boatner, 245)

Who was Kate Warne?
She was the first professional detective in U.S. history, working for the Pinkerton Agency. She also became the first woman to guard a president-elect, accompanying Lincoln from Philadelphia through the train change in Baltimore. (Henig, 23, 25)

What dubious event is Capt. John Q. Marr known for?
His death. In a skirmish with Federal cavalry near Fairfax Court House on June 1, 1861, he was shot in the chest and the impact of the bullet, although it did not break the skin, caused his heart to stop. Thus he became one of the first Confederate casualties of the war. (Denney, 47)

What prominent politician died on June 3, 1861, at the age of forty-eight?
The "Little Giant," Stephen A. Douglas. (Denney, 48)

When Lincoln placed McClellan in command of the Federal forces around Washington, who took over command of the Department of the Ohio?
Maj. Gen. William S. Rosecrans. (Denney, 60)

Who did John J. Crittenden's sons fight for?
One son, George B., became a Confederate major general; his brother, Thomas L., became a Union brigadier general. (Boatner, 208)

Because of the failing health of Brig. Gen. Robert Anderson, who was assigned as his second in command in his new post in the West?
Brig. Gen. William T. Sherman. (Denney, 63)

On Saturday, August 3, 1861, the White House held a state dinner for what visiting dignitary?
Prince Napoleon of France. (Denney, 63)

In August 1861, who replaced John Rodgers as the commander of the river forces in the Western Theater?
Capt. Andrew Foote. (Denney, 70)

Whom did Lincoln send west to rein in Frémont and assist him in running his department?
Maj. Gen. David Hunter. (Denney, 73)

Who took over command of the Union Department of the Cumberland when Brig. Gen. Anderson stepped down due to ill health?
Brig. Gen. William T. Sherman. (Denney, 86)

How did John C. Frémont learn of his removal from command?
He had cut off all access to himself so he could not get the order. Brig. Gen. R. S. Curtis, who was delivering the order, got a captain to disguise himself as a local farmer and sent him to Frémont saying he had a problem. Upon seeing the general, the captain gave him the order, whereupon Frémont arrested the captain so that the news would not leak out. (Denney, 91)

When did Frémont finally resign?
On November 2, 1861. He sent a farewell address to his command and then took his wife to St. Louis. (Denney, 92)

Who finally replaced Frémont?
Maj. Gen. David Hunter. (Denney, 93)

Who replaced William T. Sherman as commander of the Department of the Cumberland?
Brig. Gen. Don Carlos Buell. (Denney, 94)

Who became Davis's secretary of war on November 21, 1861?
Judah P. Benjamin. (Denney, 97)

By a vote of 36 to 0, who was expelled from the U.S. Senate on December 4, 1861?
Senator John C. Breckinridge of Kentucky. Breckinridge had remained in the Senate hoping to find some peaceful way to end the conflict. He returned to Kentucky and was placed in command of the 1st Kentucky Brigade. (Denney, 99)

Who was the most famous photographer of the Civil War?
Mathew B. Brady. Though known for his photography, the man himself is an enigma. It is not really known what the B of his middle name stands for. It is not known whether he was born in Ireland or New York or even the date of his birth. (Henig, 247)

At the height of his popularity, how many photographers did Mathew Brady have working for him?
Twenty. Some of the more famous included Alexander Gardner, Timothy O'Sullivan and George Barnard. (Henig, 249)

Who was Rufus King?
Brig. Gen. Rufus King helped to organize the Iron Brigade in the fall of 1861 and became the unit's first commander. King commanded King's Division, the First Division, Third Corps, of the Army of Virginia during the Second Manassas Campaign. The division, including

the Iron Brigade, was surprised at the battle of Brawner's Farm. He then missed the battle of Second Manassas due to an epileptic attack. He was court-martialed, found guilty, and given minor duties until he retired in October 1863. During this period he sat on the court-martial of Brig. Gen. Fitz John Porter. After his resignation he became minister to the Papal States. (Faust, 418)

What is Julia Ward Howe famous for?
Mrs. Howe was an abolitionist, suffragette, and peace activist. She is best known for being the author of the poem "Battle Hymn of the Republic," which when set to the tune of "John Brown's Body" became the best remembered Civil War song. (Faust, 373)

What position did Rufus Ingalls hold through most of his military career?
Quartermaster. He became chief quartermaster of the Army of the Potomac in September 1861 and in June 1864 Grant placed him in charge of supplying the two armies operating against Richmond, where he built up the supply depot at City Point, Virginia. He retired in 1883 as quartermaster general. (Faust, 383)

Who was appointed the first quartermaster general of the Confederacy?
Lt. Col. Abraham C. Myers, in December 1861. He held this position until April 1863, when he was replaced by Brig. Gen. A. R. Lawton. Refusing to serve under Lawton, Myers resigned his commission and left the army, living the rest of his life believing that Jefferson Davis had wronged him by making the change. (Faust, 519)

Who replaced Maj. Henry H. Sibley as commander of the Department of New Mexico Territory?
Maj. Edward R. S. Canby. (Klinger, 11)

Who commanded the newly formed "Army of New Mexico"?
Brig. Gen. Henry H. Sibley. (Klinger, 13)

What frontiersman commanded the 1st New Mexico Volunteers of Col. Canby's command at Ft. Craig, New Mexico Territory?
Col. Christopher "Kit" Carson. (Klinger, 14)

Who headed the U.S. Sanitary Commission?
Rev. Dr. Henry W. Bellows, pastor of All Souls Unitarian Church in New York City. (Faust, 656)

Who was Gilbert Moxley Sorrel?
Savannahian Gilbert Moxley Sorrel became a member of Brig. Gen. James Longstreet's staff at First Manassas and remained with the general until 1864, eventually becoming the First Corps' chief of staff. He was promoted to brigadier general and led troops in Mahone's Division. He was wounded at Petersburg and again at Hatcher's Run. (Faust, 702)

Who was William Howard Russell?
Russell was a British journalist who came to the United States to cover the first few months of the Civil War. A member of the British aristocracy, he had covered wars in Denmark, the Crimea, and India, which brought him a knighthood. He arrived in New York in March 1861 and went south, where he traveled for two months, writing and angering the people over his criticism of slavery. He then came back north, where he covered First Manassas. His reporting on the Federals as severe as it had been of the Southerners, he again angered many people. He angered so many people, in fact, that he was sent back to England in the spring of 1862. He is known for two works on the Civil War: *The Civil War in America* (1861) and *My Diary North and South* (1863). (Faust, 649)

What was Abraham Lincoln's favorite Shakespeare play?
Macbeth. (Allen Guelzo, Gettysburg, PA)

Who was Hiram Berdan?
A New Yorker, Berdan had been the top amateur rifle shot in the country since 1846. In 1861 he organized two regiments of sharpshooters

that served throughout the Civil War, one of which Berdan commanded as a colonel. He was not the most reliable of men, often sending his troops into action while he had other things to do in the rear. Many called him "unscrupulous," "totally unfit for command," and a liar. Though brevetted major general after Gettysburg he resigned his commission in January 1864 to pursue other interests. (Faust, 56)

Who was Dr. Samuel Preston Moore?
He was a U.S. Army doctor who resigned his commission in 1861 to become the Confederacy's surgeon general. (Davis, 414)

Who was the oldest and most senior U.S. Army officer to resign and pledge his loyalty to the Confederacy?
Brig. Gen. David Emanuel Twiggs, sometimes known as "Old Davy," "The Bengal Tiger," and "The Horse." He surrendered Texas and all the Union forces it contained, including their supplies, in February 1861. According to Mark Mayo Boatner III, "This is the only such dishonorable incident among those Regular Army officers who resigned to go with the South." (Faust, 767; Boatner, 854)

Who was placed in the position to oversee the Federal prisoner of war facilities?
Lt. Col. William H. Hoffman. He ran the prisons as inexpensively as possible, reducing the rations and rarely issuing clothing. Every month he returned unspent funds to the Federal government and at the end of the war returned $1.8 million in unused monies. (Davis, 439, 440)

Who was placed in command of the Confederate prisons during the war?
An actual commander of prison camps was not appointed until 1864; however, because most of the prisons were around Richmond, Virginia, the city's provost marshal, Brig. Gen. John H. Winder, was placed in charge of them. In 1864 he was placed in command of the Andersonville prison and later became commissary general of all prisons east of the Mississippi. (Davis, 440; Faust, 836)

Who was Daniel Ammen and what was his major claim to fame?
A Union naval officer who once saved Ulysses S. Grant from drowning.

Who was Harry McCarthy?
He penned the tune "The Bonnie Blue Flag."

Who was William Lewis Dayton?
In 1860 Dayton became a presidential candidate on the Republican ticket but only made it through three ballots, withdrawing when it became evident that Abraham Lincoln would win. On election day, Lincoln appointed Dayton to the post of minister to France. Arriving in France with no diplomatic training or any knowledge of the language, Dayton still managed to do a credible job. He stopped the French from supporting the Confederacy, the Confederate purchasing agents from operating in France, the French from building Confederate ships, and prevented French ports from giving sanctuary to Confederate raiders. He died in France on December 1, 1864. (Faust, 212)

What early-war noms de guerre were given to Robert E. Lee by his men?
"King of Spades," because he always had them digging entrenchments. He was also known as "Granny Lee" because of his lack of luster in oversight of military operations in Western Virginia during the period August 12–23, 1861. (Terdoslavich, 123)

Who was John Trout Grebiel?
He was the first regular army officer to die in the Civil War. A graduate of West Point, he became an artillery officer and was killed at the battle of Big Bethel. (Sifakis, 162)

At the outbreak of the war, who was the governor of Texas?
The "Father of Texas," Sam Houston. When he refused to support the Confederacy his office was declared vacant and the lieutenant governor succeeded him. Houston then retired to his Huntsville, Texas, farm. (Sifakis, 201)

Who was Anna Maria Ross?
Ross established the Cooper's Shop Saloon in Philadelphia. The saloon provided soldiers with rooms, food, clothing, and medical treatment. She died in December 1863, and was sorely missed. (Sifakis, 343)

In 1861 Thomas J. Jackson advocated a black flag policy—what was it?
"Take no prisoners, kill all Yankees, scourge the land in order to make peace with God." (Robertson, 17)

Who was the mayor of New York City at the outbreak of the war?
Fernando Wood. He was antiwar and anti-Lincoln. He felt that the war would disrupt the city's income because of the loss of Southern customers. He even advocated the city's secession from the Union and the state of New York. (Livingston, 10, 15)

Who was the U.S. Navy's ranking officer at the beginning of the war?
By a specific congressional act on April 20, 1859, Charles Stewart was named Senior Flag Officer of the Navy. A native of Philadelphia, Stewart had commanded the USS *Constitution* during part of the War of 1812, capturing two British frigates. He retired in December 1861, and was named a rear admiral on the retired list, but continued in an advisory capacity. When he died he was credited with seventy-one years of naval service. (Patrick Purcell, Wayne, PA)

BATTLES

What event have some called "the first true Union military action of the war"?
The occupation of Alexandria, Virginia, by Ellsworth's Fire Zouaves and a naval landing force from the sloop-of-war USS *Pawnee*. (Davis, 147)

What was the name of the proprietor of the Marshall House Hotel in Alexandria, Virginia, who on May 24, 1861, killed Col. Elmer

Ephraim Ellsworth, and who was the soldier who avenged Ellsworth's killing?
The proprietor was James T. Jackson and the avenger was Pvt. Francis E. Brownell. (Faust, 240)

What did Pvt. Brownell receive for becoming "Ellsworth's Avenger"?
He was given a lieutenant's commission in the 11th U.S. Regular Infantry and in 1877 he was awarded the Medal of Honor for killing Jackson. (Davis, 151)

Who commanded the cannons inside Ft. Moultrie and the guns and mortars on Sullivan's Island during the bombardment of Ft. Sumter?
Lt. Col. Roswell Sabine Ripley. (Faust, 635)

Who pulled the lanyard, firing the first Confederate shot on Ft. Sumter?
Reputedly, Lt. Henry S. Farley, manning a 10-inch mortar on James Island, fired the first shot of the Civil War at 4:30 a.m. on April 12, 1861. (Faust, 260)

When the American flag flying over Ft. Sumter fell, who raised it again?
Peter Hart. Hart had served with the New York City Police Department before being asked by Maj. Robert Anderson's wife to accompany her to Charleston. He had been an orderly to Anderson. Being a civilian, he was not allowed to join the garrison, so he volunteered to go as a laborer. During the bombardment when the colors fell, Hart nailed the colors back up, attaching them to a gun carriage. When the colors were once again raised over the fort after the war ended, Hart was there. (Sifakis, 181)

Which Confederate general ordered the firing on Ft. Sumter?
Brig. Gen. Pierre Gustave Toutant Beauregard.

Interior of Ft. Sumter, April 1861. USAMHI

Who aimed and fired the first Union gun in response to the Confederates firing on Ft. Sumter?
Capt. Abner Doubleday, around 7:00 a.m., April 12, 1861.

What happened during the fort's surrender on April 13, 1861?
Anderson ordered a one hundred–gun salute to the American flag before hauling it down. On the fiftieth shot the cartridge exploded prematurely and the sparks detonated a pile of nearby cartridges, killing one soldier and mortally wounding another. (Faust, 280)

What were the names of the two casualties at Ft. Sumter on April 13, 1861?
Killed outright was Pvt. Daniel Hough, and Pvt. Edward Galloway was wounded so badly that he died a few days later. These two soldiers became the war's first casualties. (Barnes, 24; Sifakis, 147)

FIRST MANASSAS

What action took place during the First Manassas Campaign on July 18, 1861?

About two miles southwest of Centreville, along Bull Run Creek, lay Blackburn's and Mitchell's fords. Manning the two fords on the morning of July 18 were the Confederates of Brig. Gen. Millege L. Bonham at Mitchell's and Brig. Gen. James Longstreet at Blackburn's. Brig. Gen. Daniel Tyler sent Col. Israel Richardson's Federal brigade forward in a reconnaissance toward the creek. Soon there was artillery fire between the two sides before Richardson sent his infantry forward. Early in the afternoon Col. William T. Sherman brought up his brigade and placed it next to Richardson. The Federals were eventually repulsed, suffering eighty-three casualties while the Confederates lost sixty-eight. (Boatner, 99; Davis, 112–131)

Who commanded the Federal troops at First Manassas and what was his plan?

Brig. Gen. Irvin McDowell. His plan was to march the majority of his command on a circuitous route to Sudley Ford. The Federals would then deploy and attack south toward Henry Hill. At first the Federals were successful but Confederate reinforcements from the unthreatened right were brought up and the Union troops were pushed back. (Boatner, 100)

What was the outcome of the First Battle of Manassas?

The Federals began an orderly withdrawal around 4:00 p.m., which turned into a rout that didn't stop until many of the troops were safely back in Washington. The Federal casualties were 3,334 while the Confederates suffered 1,982. (Fox, 543, 549)

Who commanded the Confederate forces at the battle of First Bull Run?

Brig. Gen. P. T. G. Beauregard and Brig. Gen. Joseph E. Johnston.

At First Manassas, who shouted, "There stands Jackson and his men, like a stone wall"?

Brig. Gen. Barnard Bee. There are two stories behind what Bee meant, if he made the statement at all. One story goes that he was insulting Jackson and his men for not moving. The other was a compliment meaning that Jackson and his men were bravely defending their position.

What Philadelphia general failed in his mission to keep Joseph E. Johnston's troops in Harpers Ferry, thus denying them the ability to move to Manassas in support of P. T. G. Beauregard?
Maj. Gen. Robert Patterson.

Who led the 79th New York Highlanders at First Bull Run?
Col. James Cameron, the younger brother of Lincoln's first secretary of war, Simon Cameron. While leading an attack up Henry Hill, Cameron was hit in the chest and killed. Carried to the rear, his body was abandoned and later buried. His remains were recovered in March 1862, taken to Lewisburg, Pennsylvania, and placed in the family plot. (Heidler and Heidler, 341)

What happened to McDowell following First Manassas?
He commanded McDowell's Division from October 1861 to March 1862 before being named major general. He then commanded the First Corps of the Army of the Potomac and then led the Army of the Rappahannock. He was criticized for his leadership of the Third Corps, Army of Virginia, for his actions at Rappahannock Station, Cedar Mountain, and Second Manassas. Though relieved of command, he was eventually exonerated. After he served for a time on boards in Washington he went on to command the Department of the Pacific. He remained in the Regular Army until his retirement in 1882. (Boatner, 531)

Where did the first serious land battle of the war take place on June 10, 1861?
Big Bethel, Virginia. (Denney, 50)

What Zouave regiment was part of the Union forces at Big Bethel?
The 5th New York, or Duryée's Zouaves, organized by Abram Duryée, a rich mahogany importer from Manhattan. (Davis, 150)

What was the outcome of the battle of Big Bethel?
It was a Confederate victory. The Federals had 2,500 men engaged and had eighteen killed, fifty-three wounded and five missing. The Confederates, on the other hand, fielded 1,200 men and had only one killed and seven wounded. (Faust, 59)

Who was the first regular army officer wounded in the war?
Capt. Hugh Judson Kilpatrick, when he was struck in the left thigh by a piece of shrapnel at the battle of Big Bethel. (Venter, 7)

Whose home did the Confederates use as their headquarters at First Manassas?
Wilmer McLean.

Who was the highest-ranking Confederate officer to be killed at First Manassas?
Brig. Gen. Barnard Bee. (Catton, 87)

Who commanded the Union and Confederate forces at the battle of Ball's Bluff?
Union—Brig. Gen. Charles P. Stone. Confederate—Brig. Gen. Nathan G. Evans. (Faust, 36)

Which U.S. senator was killed at Ball's Bluff?
Col. Edward D. Baker of Oregon, whose brigade was caught in the open and with their backs to the river by the Confederates. Besides Baker, the Union troops suffered 49 killed, 158 wounded, and 714 missing. (Faust, 36–37)

What Union officer was blamed for the Federal loss at Ball's Bluff?
Brig. Gen. Charles Stone, who was arrested on the orders of the Committee on the Conduct of the War, thrown into prison at Ft. Lafayette and Ft. Hamilton, and served 189 days without knowing the charges against him. (Faust, 720)

What naval officer commanded the ironclads that pounded Ft. Henry into submission?
Flag Officer Andrew H. Foote. (Faust, 274)

Who commanded and ultimately surrendered Ft. Henry?
Brig. Gen. Lloyd Tilghman. (Faust, 274)

What three Confederate generals commanded Ft. Donelson?
Brig. Gen. John B. Floyd, Brig. Gen. Gideon J. Pillow, and Brig. Gen. Simon B. Buckner. (Faust, 272)

Which Confederate general ultimately surrendered Ft. Donelson?
Gen. Simon Buckner. Floyd, with about 2,500 men, escaped in boats while Pillow and his staff crossed the Cumberland River in a flatboat. Lt. Col. Nathan Bedford Forrest sneaked his men out of the fort and forded Lick Creek. (Faust, 272)

What were the terms U. S. Grant gave General Buckner concerning the surrender?
"No terms except an immediate and unconditional surrender can be accepted." (Catton, 115)

Who commanded the two armies that clashed at Wilson's Creek, Missouri?
Brig. Gen. Nathaniel Lyon commanded the Union forces, while Brig. Gen. Ben McCulloch led the Confederates. (Faust, 833)

What was the outcome of the battle of Wilson's Creek?
When the Confederates broke off the fighting, Maj. Samuel D. Sturgis, then in command of the Federals, withdrew the Union troops toward Springfield. The Northern troops suffered 1,300 casualties while the Confederates had 1,200. (Faust, 833–834)

What happened to Brig. Gen. Lyon during the battle?
Close to the end of the engagement, after having been wounded twice, he was killed. (Boatner, 934)

What was the first successful invasion of Southern territory?
When Maj. Gen. Ben Butler took eight ships and 900 men and attacked Fts. Hatteras and Clark near Cape Hatteras. After two days the forts were shelled into submission and Butler managed to get some of his troops ashore. The action effectively closed Hatteras Inlet to passage by ships running the blockade and stopped ships from bringing in much needed supplies for the Confederacy. (Denney, 70)

Where was Zagonyi's Charge?
North of Springfield, Missouri, on October 25, 1861. An ambush had been set up to spring on a Union column moving north of the city. Discovering the trap, Maj. Charles Zagonyi led a charge of Union cavalry, driving off the Confederates. (Weeks, 47)

Who commanded Ft. Pulaski on the Savannah River near Savannah, Georgia, and how many men did he have?
Col. Charles Olmstead. The garrison consisted of 385 men. (Weeks, 199)

What new technology helped Federal troops take Ft. Pulaski?
Rifled cannon. It was thought that smoothbore cannons could not seriously damage the fort from their position on Tybee Island some 1,650 yards away. Therefore, Brig. Gen. Quincy A. Gillmore believed that the use of the rifled pieces would be more accurate, and brought up ten James rifled cannon to be used in the bombardment. (Weeks, 200)

What was the first ironclad to see action in the Civil War?
The CSS *Manassas*, a steam ram with one-inch plate iron, led an attack that scattered Union warships on the lower Mississippi River at Head of Passes, Louisiana, on the night of October 12, 1861. (Patrick Purcell, Wayne, PA)

What small action occurred near Dranesville, Virginia, on December 20, 1861?
Elements of Johnston's Confederate army and those of McClellan's Federals met in a short skirmish while attempting to collect food and

rations for the soldiers and forage for their animals. The Confederates, led by J. E. B. Stuart, tangled with Pennsylvania troops led by Brig. Gen. E. O. C. Ord. The engagement only lasted a few hours, with Stuart pulling his men off the field around 3:00 p.m. The Confederates lost about 194 men while Federal losses were around 68. By the next day the two forces were back in their respective camps. (Faust, 226)

EVENTS

What was the second state to leave the Union?
Mississippi, on January 9, 1861. (Denney, 21)

With a vote of 62 to 7, what was the third state to secede from the Union?
Florida, on January 10, 1861. (Denney, 22)

What was the fourth state to secede from the Union?
Alabama, on January 11, 1861. (Faust, 3)

When did the Confederacy get a Constitution?
The provisional Confederate Congress approved a Constitution on March 11, 1861. The document had been in the works for about five weeks. The Constitution was then sent to the states, all of which ratified it. (Faust, 161)

What is the Confederate Constitution based on?
The U.S. Constitution. The first twelve amendments are the same. Where the differences occur are with the relationship between the executive and legislative branches and between the states and the central government. (Faust, 161)

What state was admitted to the Union as the thirty-fourth state on January 29, 1861?
Kansas. (Denney, 24)

What is the significance of February 9, 1861?
Jefferson Davis was elected provisional president of the Confederacy. Alexander Stephens was elected as the provisional vice president. (Denney, 25)

On what date was Jefferson Davis sworn in as the provisional Confederate president?
Monday, February 18, 1861. (Denney, 26)

On what day did Abraham Lincoln become the sixteenth president of the United Sates?
March 4, 1861. (Denney, 29)

What was the eleventh and last state to secede from the Union?
Tennessee, on June 8, 1861. (Denney, 46)

What happened to the 6th Massachusetts Infantry as it marched through Baltimore on April 19, 1861?
At this time in the war, Baltimoreans had a definite Southern slant. Unfortunately, Federal troops were forced to go through the city on their way to the seat of the war. Trains coming into the city were forced to stop at the President Street Station and passengers continuing south had to transfer to the Camden Street Station, either by trolley or by walking. On April 19, the 6th Massachusetts reached the first station and had to march to the second station, all along the way taunted by Southern sympathizers. Rocks were thrown and shots fired. Eventually, shots were returned by the soldiers. Before the troops finally left the city, four soldiers had been killed and thirty-nine wounded. Civilian casualties totaled twelve killed and an unknown number of wounded. (Faust, 37; Boatner, 42)

MISCELLANEOUS

Who was the first Union officer killed in the Civil War?
Col. Elmer Ellsworth. (Davis, 149)

Whose home near Manassas did P. T. G. Beauregard use as his headquarters during the summer of 1861?
The home of William Weir, "Liberia." (Hennessy, 16)

At the outbreak of the Civil War, how large was the Regular Army?
It consisted of 1,105 officers and 15,259 enlisted men. Most of the army was on outpost duty in the West. (Henig, 37)

Name the states that ultimately made up the Confederate States of America?
Alabama, Arkansas, Florida, Georgia, Louisiana, Mississippi, North Carolina, South Carolina, Tennessee, Texas, and Virginia. Also there were Missouri and Kentucky by a vote of rump legislatures from these two states who were admitted to the Confederacy and were represented in the Confederate Congress. (Boatner, 171)

Of the approximately 1,100 U.S. Army officers, how many resigned to join the Confederacy?
There were 286, the highest ranking of which was Joseph E. Johnson. (Gallman, 52; Henig, 37)

To what city did the U.S. Naval Academy move in May 1861?
Newport, Rhode Island. The USS *Constitution* also took up her station there. (Denney, 42)

What was the name of the Confederate prisoner-of-war camp located in the middle of the James River in Richmond?
Belle Isle. The site became a prison after the battle of First Manassas and at one time later in the war held as many as 10,000 prisoners. (Faust, 54)

What committee did Congress set up after the Union disaster at Ball's Bluff?
Joint Committee on the Conduct of the War, led by Republican senators Benjamin F. Wade and Zachariah Chandler and in the House by representatives D. W. Gooch and George W. Julian. (Catton, 99)

What were "Quaker guns"?
Fake cannons. Confederates would take logs that were shaped to look like cannons and paint the "firing" end black. These would be placed behind defenses in hopes of making the Federals think the Confederates were better armed than they were. (Faust, 606)

At what battle were Signal Corps flags and towers first used?
The battle of First Manassas, by E. P. Alexander and his new Confederate Signal Corps. Alexander sent a message warning Confederate forces of approaching Union troops, allowing them time to react. (Henig, 92)

What is the typical alignment of an attacking infantry regiment?
First to advance are one or two companies of skirmishers. Five hundred yards behind this line are six or seven companies in line of battle. Three hundred yards behind the main battle line are one or two reserve companies. (Coggins, 23)

What comment did Abraham Lincoln make about U. S. Grant when a prominent Republican demanded his removal?
"I can't spare this man, he fights." (Catton, 116)

What was the name of the Union prisoner-of-war site on Pea Patch Island located in the Delaware River off of New Jersey?
Ft. Delaware, which at times held up to 8,000 Confederate prisoners. The last Confederates were not released from the prison until mid-July 1865. (Faust, 272)

Who commanded the USS *San Jacinto* that removed James M. Mason and John Slidell from the British mail steamer, causing the *Trent* Affair?
Capt. Charles Wilkes. He was relieved of duty in 1863, court-martialed and received a public reprimand. (Faust, 827, 828)

What happened to Mason and Slidell after they were captured?
They were placed in Ft. Warren in Boston Harbor. They were soon released, in part due to the uproar the affair caused in Great Britain,

and continued on their missions, Mason going to England and Slidell to France. (Catton, 243)

What was "Old Abe"?
"Old Abe" was an eagle, the mascot of the 8th Wisconsin. During battles "Old Abe" would be carried into battle alongside the color guard. Contrary to the stories of "Old Abe" soaring around over the fighting and then returning to his perch, he was always chained to his roost. (Faust, 543)

Who made the first balloon ascent from the deck of a ship?
John LaMountain, from the deck of the *Fanny*. He took the balloon ride in Hampton Roads to observe a Confederate battery on Sewell's Point. (Denney, 63)

What village did Brig. Gen. "Price John" Magruder burn to prevent Maj. Gen. Ben Butler from using it as a holding point for runaway slaves?
Hampton, Virginia. (Denney, 64)

What were the "Stone Fleets"?
Derelict ships, many of them old whaling vessels that were filled with stones and sunk at the entrances to Southern harbors. The ploy did not work, as the timbers were soon eaten by marine worms and the stones settled into the mud. (Boatner, 801)

What was the "Crittenden Resolution" passed by the U.S. House of Representatives on July 22, 1861?
Named for John J. Crittenden of Kentucky, it stated that the war was being waged "to defend and maintain the supremacy of the Constitution and to preserve the Union." It said the war was not being waged to interfere with slavery or to subjugate the South. It was also known as the Crittenden-Johnson Resolution. (Denney, 60)

What event happened in Missouri that Lincoln termed "dictatorial"?
Maj. Gen. John C. Frémont declared martial law throughout the state and confiscated the property of anyone who might take up

arms against the United States. He also issued his own emancipation proclamation on August 30, 1861, and an order of confiscation. Frémont later issued a proclamation freeing the slaves of owners who fought for the South, confiscating their property, and assigning death penalties to the owners. Lincoln ordered Frémont to modify the order. (Denney, 71)

Who were the first five Confederate officers who were appointed to full general and what was their order of rank?
Samuel Cooper, Albert Sydney Johnston, Robert E. Lee, Joseph E. Johnston, and P. T. G. Beauregard. (Denney, 71)

What are the three states that in late 1861 had two governments, one Confederate, one Union?
Missouri, North Carolina, and Kentucky. (Denney, 97)

What were "Ladies' Gunboat Societies"?
Popular in 1861 and 1862, these societies were established by patriotic Southern women to raise funds for the construction of Confederate ironclads. The ladies held auctions, raffles, concerts, and "gunboat fairs" in their attempts to raise money. Three boats, the *Charleston*, *Fredericksburg*, and *Georgia*, were referred to as "ladies gunboats" as most of the monies used to build them came from the societies. Because of the loss of major Confederate ports and also the loss of many ironclads, interest in the societies waned, and by 1863 donations had ceased. (Faust, 422)

What was the Department of Key West, Florida, and who commanded it?
Throughout the war, Key West and Ft. Taylor remained in Union hands, though surrounded by and mostly made up of staunch secessionists. The navy controlled the Key West Naval Base, keeping gunboats and an artillery force there. The War Department turned Key West, the Dry Tortugas and the Florida mainland extending to Apalachicola on the west coast and Cape Canaveral on the east coast, into the Department of the South and on March 15, 1861, placed Maj. Gen. David Hunter in command. (Faust, 416)

What was the goal of Gen. Sibley and his army when they began their campaign to New Mexico Territory on December 14, 1861?
To move up the Rio Grande Valley and capture Santa Fe and Ft. Union. The campaign would then continue on into the Colorado mining fields near Denver and then on to Utah Territory and California. By doing this they hoped to set up a Confederacy extending from the Atlantic to the Pacific. (Klinger, 9)

By whom and when was the U.S. Christian Commission organized?
It was formed on November 15, 1861, by the Young Men's Christian Association. (Faust, 140)

What was the function of the Christian Commission?
The commission worked in conjunction with the U.S. Sanitary Commission, bringing relief to the soldiers at the front. They provided free box lunches and coffee wagons and a special diet kitchen for the sick and wounded. Female members volunteered as nurses in hospitals. Reading rooms were provided for the soldiers as were free writing materials and stamps. (Faust, 140)

When was the U.S. Sanitary Commission founded?
June 9, 1861. Its purpose was to assist the army by providing care for the sick and wounded and to protect their dependent families. (Faust, 656)

What was Castle Pinckney?
Castle Pinckney was a fort in Charleston Harbor named for Revolutionary War patriot Charles C. Pinckney. Following the first battle of Manassas the fort became a prison housing soldiers of the 79th and 69th New York, 8th Michigan, and 11th Fire Zouaves (New York), along with a number of casualties. The relationship between captives and guards was peaceful and the quarters were kept in excellent condition. There were no reported escapes from the fort. (Faust, 119–120)

How wide was a six-gun Union battery?
As per regulations the linear space occupied by a battery was fourteen yards between each piece and because each piece was two yards in width the total would have been eighty-four yards. (Coggins, 71)

How many horses or mules made up a cannon's gun team?
Six. Hitched to a limber there was, from front to back, the Lead pair, the Swing pair, and the Wheel pair. (Coggins, 72–73)

Each artillery piece carried what other equipment besides ammunition?
A sponge and rammer staff, worm, thumb stall, grease bucket, vent pick, prolong, rope, muzzle sight, lanyard, friction primers, sponge bucket, and pendulum sight. (Coggins, 74)

Where was one of the first prisons in the Confederacy?
In the Alamo in San Antonio, Texas. (Davis, 438)

Where were the first prisoners of war captured?
In Texas, when Brig. Gen. David E. Twiggs surrendered his troops, supplies, forts, outposts, equipment, and army funds to Texas troops commander Col. Ben McCulloch on February 18, 1861. (Faust, 767)

What was an aide-de-camp?
An officer who was a member of the staff of a general officer and whose job it was to write orders and deliver them if necessary and be knowledgeable about troop positions, maneuvers, column orders of battle, routes, and the locations of officers' quarters. (Faust, 3)

What was the Augusta Powder Works and who commanded it?
Commanded and designed by Col. George W. Rains, the powder works were built on the Savannah River at Augusta, Georgia. It was erected between September 1861 and May 1863 and consisted of a two-mile-long factory complex. The facility was able to produce 5,000 pounds of powder per day and was estimated to have made 2,750,000 pounds by the end of the war. (Faust, 31)

What Northern state, though it remained loyal to the Union, was officially a slave state until 1865, counting 1,900 slaves in 1860?
Delaware. Though Lincoln offered to compensate owners for freeing their slaves the proposal did not pass in the state legislature. So while

fighting gallantly for the Union, Delaware remained a slave state until passage of the Thirteenth Amendment. (Faust, 214)

How many stars were on the First National Confederate flag?
Seven. (Dale Beiver, Boyertown, PA)

What were the "90-Day Gunboats"?
Ordered by the U.S. Navy as an emergency measure, twenty-three wooden, 507-ton screw gunboats were built at various shipyards on the North Atlantic coast in late 1861. Known as the *Unadilla* class, the vessels were very successful in coastal and river warfare. Fleet Officer David Farragut had ten on the lower Mississippi River and used them in the capture of New Orleans and the thrust up the Mississippi River to Vicksburg, followed by the move on Baton Rouge before returning to New Orleans. (Patrick Purcell, Wayne, PA)

What was the Anaconda Plan?
The first military strategy plan devised by General-in-Chief Winfield Scott that was presented to President Lincoln. The plan was for a blockade of Southern ports and a thrust down the Mississippi Valley, including the forming of a line of Federal positions there. It was thought that this would isolate the Confederates and that calmer heads would ultimately prevail, leading to surrender. McClellan called it the "boa-constrictor" plan and it was never adopted. The press, using McClellan's description, changed boa constrictor to anaconda and the name stuck. Surprisingly, a similar plan took place in 1864 when Grant's armies fought the war on fronts in Virginia and Tennessee while Sherman marched from Atlanta to the sea, squeezing the South into a military death. (Faust, 12–13)

What was the CSS *Arkansas*?
The keel of the *Arkansas* was laid down at Memphis, Tennessee, in October 1861. When Memphis was threatened by the Federals, the *Arkansas* was towed first to Green Wood and then to Yazoo City, Mississippi, where she was completed and commissioned in early July 1862. She was a twin screw ram, 165 feet long with a 35-foot beam and a draft of 11–12 feet. She carried ten guns and a 200-man crew. She was destroyed by her crew on August 6, 1862. (Faust, 22)

What was the *Enchantress* Affair?
On July 6, 1861, the Confederate privateer *Jefferson Davis* took the merchant schooner *Enchantress* off the coast of Delaware. Five members of the *Jefferson Davis*, led by Walter W. Smith, were put aboard the *Enchantress* where they took the crew prisoner and confiscated $13,000 worth of cargo. Sixteen days later the USS *Albatross* recaptured the *Enchantress,* sent her to North Carolina, and placed the Confederate captors in irons. The men were sent to the Philadelphia Navy Yard where they were held for trial. In an October trial, the raiders were convicted of piracy and sentenced to hang. In response Gen. John H. Winder, under the orders of Confederate Secretary of War Judah P. Benjamin, chose by lottery fifteen Union officer prisoners, including Col. Michael Corcoran of the 69th New York, to suffer the same fate as the *Enchantress*'s crew. The U.S. War Department suspended the hanging sentence and held the men as prisoners of war. It was a small but significant diplomatic victory for the Confederacy. (Faust, 243)

UNITS

What nom de guerre was given to the 13th Pennsylvania Reserves?
"Bucktails," named for the buck (deer) tails they sported on their hats. Members of the regiment had to be crack shots. They served from 1861 to 1864. Later in the war the 150th Pennsylvania, who served gallantly at Gettysburg, was raised and they also wore a buck's tail on their hats, however, they were referred to as the "Bogus Bucktails." (Boatner, 637)

Who raised then commanded the 6th Pennsylvania Cavalry?
Colonel Richard H. Rush. The unit was also known as Rush's Lancers due to the nine-foot lances they carried until 1863, when they were replaced with more appropriate weapons.

Name the six Federal regiments that were at one time or another part of Meagher's Irish Brigade?
63rd New York, 69th New York, 88th New York, 29th Massachusetts, 28th Massachusetts, and 116th Pennsylvania. The 29th Massachusetts was not an Irish regiment and was replaced with the 28th Massachusetts following the battle of Antietam.

What was the only brigade in the Army of the Potomac solely made up of regiments from the West?
The Iron Brigade, which was comprised of the 2nd, 6th and 7th Wisconsin, the 19th Indiana, and the 24th Michigan.

What five regiments comprised the Excelsior Brigade, and what major general later commanded it at Seven Pines?
The brigade was comprised of the 1st, 2nd, 3rd, 4th and 5th Excelsior, later re-designated the 70th, 71st, 72nd, 73rd, and 74th New York. The brigade was raised by Daniel Sickles and though always associated with his name he only commanded it at Seven Pines and during the Seven Days' Battles. (Faust, 250)

What was the name of the Georgia militia company raised by John Brown Gordon, who would later become a Confederate general?
The Raccoon Roughs.

What was the nom de guerre of the 1st Kentucky Brigade?
The "Orphan Brigade." Though rooted in Kentucky, most of the men were forced to train and organize in Tennessee. When the Confederate army left Kentucky in late October 1862 the "Orphan Brigade" went with it, never to return to the state during the war. (Faust, 548–549)

What New York regiment marched off to war wearing trues and kilts?
The 79th New York Volunteers. They took their name from the 79th (Cameron) Highlanders of the British army. The regiment was made up mostly of Scottish, Irish, and English New Yorkers with a smattering of other nationalities. The regiment fought at First Manassas, where its commander, Col. James Cameron, was killed. During the course of the war the distinctive Scottish uniform gradually gave way to regulation Union blue. (Haythornthewaite, 150)

What controversy surrounded the 79th New York following First Bull Run?
After its colonel was killed, Col. Isaac Ingalls Stevens was placed in command of the regiment, causing a mutiny. As punishment, the

regimental colors were taken away from the unit. Stevens eventually became very popular with the regiment. The colors were returned to the regiment after Second Manassas, where the regiment showed valiant conduct in its service. (Haythornthwaite, 150)

Who were Berdan's Sharpshooters?
They were an organization of marksmen put together by Hiram G. Berdan in 1861. There were eventually two regiments: the 1st U.S. Sharpshooters, led by Col. Berdan; and the 2nd U.S. Sharpshooters, led by Col. Henry A. V. Post and then Col. Homer R. Stoughton. They carried .52-caliber Sharps rifles, some with telescopic sights. They also wore a distinctive green uniform. The two regiments claimed to have inflicted more Confederate casualties that any other unit of comparable size. During the course of the war they lost 1,008 of the 2,570 men who enlisted with the unit. (Faust, 57)

What was the origin of the Zouaves?
The legacy and uniform came from a North African tribe, the Zouaoua, which had been pacified by the French and then brought into the French army that invaded Algeria in the 1830s. The uniform, associated with Algeria and Tunisia, was comprised of baggy red trousers, short blue jackets with red piping, and a tasseled fez. (Davis, 141)

What was the second Zouave unit, organized by Elmer Ellsworth?
The Fire Zouaves, made up of men from the New York City Fire Department. The regiment was also known as the 11th New York Volunteers. Ellsworth and his men arrived in Washington on May 2, 1861. (Davis, 146)

What did the rowdy and undisciplined Fire Zouaves do to gain the respect of Washingtonians?
On May 9, 1861, the Willard Hotel, one of Washington's leading hotels, caught fire. The Zouaves rushed to the scene and, after a two-hour battle, managed to put out the fire and save the building. For their effort, the regiment got a free breakfast and $500 that was collected and given to them. (Davis, 146–147)

What differentiated the uniforms of Ellsworth's Fire Zouaves and Duryée's Zouaves?
Whereas the Fire Zouaves wore a uniform of gray pants and jacket, red shirts, and caps, the 5th New York wore a more traditional Zouave uniform with billowing red pantaloons, short blue jackets with red trim, and red fezzes with tassels. They were also different in make up: the Fire Zouaves were known for their rowdiness, while the 5th New York had experienced officers, even some West Pointers who enforced discipline. (Davis, 150–151)

Who were the Woodis Rifles?
A militia company raised in Norfolk, Virginia, in 1858. They were named after the mayor of Norfolk, Hunter Woodis. In April 1861 they became Co. C, 6th Virginia Infantry. They were in continual action from the Seven Days to Appomattox Court House. Their original uniform consisted of a "hunting green" frock-coat with black velvet facings, gilt buttons, and gold lace. (Haythornthwaite, 176)

Mustered in on October 30, 1861, what was the 60th New York Infantry known as?
The St. Lawrence Regiment. The regiment participated in the Second Manassas Campaign, Fredericksburg, Burnside's "Mud March," Chancellorsville, Gettysburg, Chattanooga, Lookout Mountain, Missionary Ridge, the Atlanta Campaign, the March to the Sea, and the Carolina Campaign. (Raus, 64; Fox, 1427)

What name was given to the 66th New York?
The Governor's Guard. The regiment was mustered into service on November 4, 1861. It was commanded by Col. Orland Harriman Morris until Cold Harbor, where he was killed on June 3, 1864. The regiment participated in the Peninsula Campaign, Antietam, the "Mud March," Chancellorsville, the Overland Campaign, Petersburg actions, and the Appomattox Campaign. (Raus, 67; Fox, 1429–1430)

~∽ CHAPTER 3 ᗡ~

1862

PERSONALITIES

Who was the first medical director of the Army of the Potomac?
Dr. Charles S. Tripper. Overwhelmed by the job, he was replaced on July 1, 1862, by Dr. Jonathan Letterman. (Davis, 414)

Who established the ambulance corps in the Army of the Potomac?
Dr. Jonathan Letterman. (Davis, 420)

Who was George Frederick Root?
Root was a composer who wrote twenty-eight Civil War songs, the most famous of which was "The Battle Cry of Freedom." Released in August 1862, sheet music for the song was estimated to have reached 350,000 copies by 1864. Root also wrote "Tramp, Tramp, Tramp, The Boys Are Marching," "Just Before the Battle, Mother" and "The Vacant Chair." (Faust, 642)

In Washington, Secretary of War Simon Cameron resigned on January 11, 1862. Who did Lincoln replace him with two days later on January 13, 1862?
Edwin M. Stanton. (Denney, 111)

What sad event occurred at the White House on February 20, 1862?
William Wallace "Willie" Lincoln died at the age of twelve from typhoid fever. (Denney, 131)

Why was February 22, 1862, a major day in Confederate history?
Jefferson Davis was inaugurated as the first president of the Confederacy. (Denney, 132)

By January 1862, who was in command of the Springfield Arsenal in Springfield, Massachusetts, and how many weapons were they producing per month?
Maj. Alexander B. Dyer, and the arsenal turned out 10,000 muskets per month. (Denney, 62)

What Union general almost flew into Confederate lines when the mooring line broke on the Thaddeus Lowe balloon he was riding in?
Brig. Gen. Fitz John Porter. (Catton, 130)

In March 1862, Jefferson Davis replaced Judah Benjamin as secretary of war with whom?
George W. Randolph. Benjamin was made the new secretary of state. (Denney, 143)

Who commanded the Federal troops that reoccupied Norfolk and Portsmouth when the Confederates left in May 1862?
Brig. Gen. John E. Wool. (Denney, 168)

Who was the leader of the African American crew that stole the steamer *Planter*?
Robert Smalls. (Denney, 169)

Who was the first Marine to be awarded the Medal of Honor for his actions on the *Galena* during its May 15, 1862, fight before Drewry's Bluff?
Cpl. John B. Mackie, who was a member of the ship's Marine guard. (Denney, 171)

Who was Armistead Lindsay Long?

Maj. Long became part of Gen. Robert E. Lee's staff while he was in Charleston, South Carolina, in the fall of 1861. When Lee took over command of the Army of Northern Virginia on June 1, 1862, he made Long his military secretary. Long was experienced in the artillery branch of the military so Lee eventually appointed him commander of the Second Corps artillery. Promoted to brigadier general on September 21, 1863, Long served with the Second Corps until the end of the war. (Faust, 444)

On July 16, 1862, what happened to David G. Farragut?

He became the first rear admiral in Naval history. (Denney, 194)

Who was Mansfield Lovell?

Early in the war, Maj. Gen. Mansfield Lovell commanded the defenses of New Orleans, where he supervised the arming of the area's forts and batteries. He also played a part in creating the Confederate River Defense Fleet. When Flag Officer David G. Farragut attacked New Orleans in April 1862 Mansfield and his command were driven from the city. (Faust, 450, 451)

Who was Stonewall Jackson's map maker?

New York–born Jedediah Hotchkiss. (Faust, 370)

What were the two nicknames given to Gen. George McClellan?

"Little Mac" and "The Young Napoleon."

Who was the oldest Union corps commander in the Civil War?

Edwin Vose "Bull" Sumner. At the start of the war Sumner was sixty-four years old. He did not survive the war, dying on March 21, 1863, of pneumonia. (Faust, 733)

Who was Edwin V. Sumner's son-in-law?

Armistead Long, Lee's military secretary during the Maryland Campaign. (Frye, 91)

Why was Gen. Edwin V. Sumner sometimes referred to as "Bull Head"?

While serving in the old army during the Mexican War a musket ball supposedly bounced off his head. (Warner, 490)

What was Lee's first position with the new Confederacy after his refusal to remain loyal to the Union?
He was designated the commander-in-chief of the military and naval forces of Virginia, a position given to him by Virginia governor Letcher. (Warner, 181)

In what capacity was Lee acting when Jefferson Davis placed him in command after Johnston's wounding?
He was the military adviser to President Davis. During this time Lee helped formulate the plan carried out by Stonewall Jackson in the Shenandoah Valley that prevented Federal reinforcements from reaching McClellan on the Peninsula. (Warner, 182)

Who was Confederate cavalry commander J. E. B. Stuart's father-in-law?
Brig. Gen. Philip St. George Cooke, who led a Federal cavalry division during the Peninsula Campaign. (Faust, 184)

Name the Confederate soldier who became known as the "Angel of Marye's Heights" following the Federal fiasco at Fredericksburg?
Sgt. Richard Rowland Kirkland. Kirkland was a nineteen-year-old South Carolinian who spent the night of December 13 listening to the cries of the Union soldiers in front of the stone wall asking for help and water. After getting permission from his commander, Brig. Gen. Joseph B. Kershaw, Kirkland took a number of canteens and went over the wall where he spent close to an hour giving water and succor to the wounded. He was later killed at the battle of Chickamauga on September 20, 1863. (Faust, 18)

Whom did Abraham Lincoln name as his general-in-chief replacing Gen. George McClellan on July 4, 1862?
Maj. Gen. Henry Wager Halleck.

What was Maj. Gen. Henry Halleck's nom de guerre?
"Old Brains."

Who designed the USS *Monitor*?
Swedish-born John Ericsson. (Faust, 246)

What was the name of the Federal major general who went on to write the classic novel *Ben Hur*?
Maj. Gen. Lew Wallace.

Who was Abraham Lincoln's second secretary of war?
Edwin McMasters Stanton. His nomination to that post was confirmed on January 15, 1862.

Who commanded the Department of Norfolk when it was abandoned on May 10, 1862?
Maj. Gen. Benjamin Huger (pronounced U-gee). When the Federals approached Norfolk, Huger dismantled his works, torched the navy yard, and ordered the CSS *Virginia* to be destroyed. Huger later commanded troops during the Seven Days' Battles, but his leadership was less than stellar. He was eventually reduced to artillery and ordnance-inspection duties, at which he was much more efficient. (Faust, 374)

Who was Lee's chief of artillery?
Brig. Gen. William Nelson Pendleton, who was also an Episcopal minister. (Faust, 570)

Who was the last Union general to die from his Antietam wounds?
Maj. Gen. Israel B. Richardson, who died at the Philip Pry house on November 3, 1862. (Frye, 145)

What did Gen. Stonewall Jackson and Maj. Gen. Daniel Harvey Hill have in common?
They were brothers-in-law. (Frye, 100)

How did a Union musket ball save Col. John B. Gordon's life?
Gordon was wounded five times at Antietam. Upon receiving the final wound in the side of the face, he fell, unconscious, landing facedown

in his kepi. Luckily the hat had been hit by an enemy minié ball, allowing the blood to drain out so that Gordon did not drown. (Frye, 109)

Who replaced George McClellan as commander of the Army of the Potomac on November 10, 1862?
Maj. Gen. Ambrose Burnside. (Warner, 57)

What future Supreme Court justice was seriously wounded when shot in the neck at Antietam?
Oliver Wendell Holmes, Jr.

Who became the Army of the Potomac's provost marshal general in October 1862?
Brig. Gen. Marsena R. Patrick. He held the position for the rest of the war. (Faust, 561)

Who replaced Maj. Gen. Don Carlos Buell on October 30, 1862, as commander following the battle of Perryville?
Maj. Gen. William S. Rosecrans. (Warner, 52)

Who was John Franklin Farnsworth?
A politician who raised the 8th Illinois Cavalry in 1861 and led it until severely injured following the action at Antietam. In 1863 he took up the congressional seat he had won the previous fall. He supported emancipation and the Thirteenth Amendment and was a leader in the impeachment of Andrew Johnson. His nephew was Elon Farnsworth. (Boatner, 275)

Who replaced Maj. Gen. Earl Van Dorn in the defense of Vicksburg on October 14, 1862?
Maj. Gen. John C. Pemberton. (Denney, 220)

Who was appointed to the post of commissioner for the exchange of prisoners in November 1862?
Maj. Gen. Ethan Allen Hitchcock. Prior to being appointed to this position it is said that he was slated to replace Maj. Gen. George McClellan as general-in-chief of the Union army, a position "Little Mac" had been relieved of on March 11, 1862. (Faust, 363)

During McClellan's Peninsula campaign, who was the chief quartermaster of the Army of the Potomac?
Brig. Gen. Stewart Van Vliet. (Boatner, 867)

Who was the only soldier killed during Stuart's ride around McClellan and where was he killed?
Capt. William Latané of Co. F, 9th Virginia Cavalry. He was killed on June 13, 1862, near Old Church, which is located near the confluence of Totopotomoy Creek and the Pamunkey River. (Mewborn, 14)

What artist painted *The Burial of Latané*?
William D. Washington completed the painting in 1864 and it was used as a fundraiser for the Confederacy. (Mewborn, 53)

Where is William Latané buried?
Latané lies in an unmarked grave in a small cemetery located on the privately owned Grainfield Farm off the River Road, near where he died. (Mewborn, 15)

Who commanded the Federal cavalry in its poorly coordinated pursuit of Stuart in his ride around McClellan?
Brig. Gen. Philip St. George Cooke. (Mewborn, 50)

Who commanded Ft. Union in New Mexico Territory during Sibley's 1862 campaign?
Col. Gabriel René Paul who, as a brigade commander, was wounded at the battle of Gettysburg on July 1, 1863. (Kliger, 20)

Because of seniority, but in spite of little military experience, who took over command of Ft. Union upon his arrival there?
Col. John P. Slough. (Kliger, 20)

Whom did Maj. Gen. William Rosecrans make the chief engineer of the Army of the Cumberland in December 1862 and what happened to him?
Capt. James St. Clair Morton. Morton formed a Pioneer Brigade whose task it was to build bridges, roads, and fortifications. He was

commissioned a brigadier general on April 4, 1863, but then reverted to a major in the Corps of Engineers. He participated in the construction of the defensive works around Chattanooga and Nashville, including Forts Negley and Casino. He eventually became the chief engineer in Burnside's Ninth Corps and was killed while reconnoitering near Petersburg on June 17, 1864. He is buried in Laurel Hill Cemetery in Philadelphia. (Kelly, 11; Magner, 33, 34)

Who was Kady Brownell?
Kady Brownell was the wife of Robert Brownell, who enlisted in the 1st Rhode Island Infantry in 1861. Following her husband off to war, Kady carried the colors of her husband's company in a charge at First Bull Run. When the regiment was mustered out of service in August 1861 the husband and wife enlisted in the 5th Rhode Island. As part of Burnside's North Carolina Expedition the regiment fought at New Bern, North Carolina, where Kady once again carried the colors. In the latter battle her husband was seriously wounded and Kady acted as a nurse, not only for her husband but for others, including Confederates. When her husband was discharged as being unfit for duty, Kady ended her military career and returned to Rhode Island with him. (Faust, 85; civilwarwomen)

Who was Franklin Buchanan?
Buchanan commanded the CSS *Virginia* on its first sortie on March 8, 1862, against the Federals, destroying the USS *Congress* and the USS *Cumberland*. Wounded during this action, Buchanan was not present for the *Virginia*'s fight with the USS *Monitor*. He was later promoted to admiral and placed in command of the Confederate naval forces at Mobile, Alabama. Here he fought gallantly from his flagship, CSS *Tennessee*, against the Federal attack in August 5, 1864. Wounded again, he was taken prisoner and not exchanged until February 1865. (Faust, 86)

Who was Matthew Fontaine Maury?
Maury served in the Confederate Navy and was "in charge of devising and placing submarine batteries in the James River." He had an international reputation, so in late 1862 he was sent to Great Britain as a

Confederate naval agent. His mission was to buy ships and supplies. He finished the war living in London. (Faust, 481)

Who was Zebulon Vance?
After service as colonel of the 26th North Carolina at New Bern, Vance was elected to the first of two terms as governor of North Carolina in September 1862. He worked hard at keeping up the fighting spirit of his state and helped maintain munitions and clothing factories. He maintained the troops the state supplied to the Confederacy. Using overseas supply purchases he relieved the Confederate government of having to supply North Carolina troops and he often shared these purchases with other states. He was briefly imprisoned after the war. (Faust, 777)

When U. S. Grant was temporarily removed from command in early March 1862 and accused of indulging in his old habits, who took over his command?
Maj. Gen. Charles Ferguson Smith, who took the army upriver to Savannah and to Pittsburg Landing. Unfortunately, Smith, while jumping into a small boat on March 15, badly scraped his shin. The wound became septic and Smith became quite ill. Taken to Savannah, Tennessee, he grew worse and died on April 25, 1862. (Faust, 695)

What soldier who fought at Shiloh with the 6th Arkansas would later be knighted by Queen Victoria?
Henry Morton Stanley, who became a journalist and African explorer. During one exploration he located Dr. David Livingston and in later expeditions he traced the course of the Congo River. He was later knighted. (Jell, 115, 215, 457)

Who was the highest-ranking general officer of either army to be killed in action during the Civil War?
Gen. Albert Sydney Johnston. (Allen, 53)

Who commanded the 12th Massachusetts at the Second battle of Manassas?
Col. Fletcher Webster, the son of orator and senator Daniel Webster. The colonel was killed during the action of August 30, 1862. (Hennessy, 55)

Who was Maj. C. Roberdeau Wheat?
Wheat organized a Zouave unit in New Orleans that later became known as Wheat's Tigers. Wheat had been a soldier of fortune before the war, at one point becoming an officer in the Mexican army. He later fought with Garibaldi in Italy. He stood six feet four inches tall and tipped the scales at 300 pounds. During the attack of his men at First Manassas, Wheat was shot through both lungs. The surgeon told him he was dying, but Wheat replied, "I don't feel like dying just yet," and recovered. He was killed a year later during the fighting at Gaines's Mill on June 27, 1862. Upon his death no one could control the men of his battalion, so it was broken up and the men were placed in other Louisiana regiments, one becoming a brigade known as the Louisiana Tigers. (Davis, 156, 157)

What later "hero" of Gettysburg served for a time as colonel of the 5th New York Infantry, Duryée's Zouaves?
Brig. Gen. Gouverneur K. Warren. (Faust, 803)

Who was the most famous Irish Confederate general?
Patrick Cleburne. Cleburne enlisted as a private in the 15th Arkansas at the start of the war but was soon elected colonel of his regiment. By the battle of Shiloh he was a brigadier general. (Faust, 145)

Who was appointed the Union surgeon general on August 25, 1862?
William Alexander Hammond, with the rank of brigadier general. He established the Army Medical Museum and collected data that eventually became the basis for the *Medical and Surgical History of the War of the Rebellion*. He clashed with Secretary of War Stanton and was court-martialed on a petty charge in 1864. After the war he was vindicated and restored to brigadier general. (Faust, 334)

Who was known as the "Nurse with the Bottle"?
Louisa May Alcott, who for a short time was a nurse during the war. She used to carry a bottle of lavender water that she sprinkled on herself and her surroundings in order to cover the smells of sickness and

bad sanitation. She left nursing in 1862 due to ill health and devoted the rest of her life to writing. (Faust, 5)

Who was Turner Ashby?
Ashby initially commanded the 7th Virginia Cavalry and performed scouting duties in the Shenandoah Valley. In the spring of 1862 Maj. Gen. "Stonewall" Jackson placed Ashby in command of all the Confederate cavalry in the valley. His career was unfortunately cut short when he was killed, many say by friendly fire, during a rear-guard action near Harrisonburg, Virginia, on June 6, 1862. (Faust, 26)

Who was Kate Cumming?
A Confederate nurse whose family had tried to stop her from joining that profession because it was unladylike. Despite this she became one of the best-known nurses in the western Confederacy. She was at Shiloh, Corinth, Okolona, and Chattanooga. Following the war she was active in the United Daughters of the Confederacy and the United Confederate Veterans. (Faust, 197)

What make of pistol did Jeb Stuart and P. G. T. Beauregard carry?
A LeMat revolver. The LeMat was a nine-shot pistol that also had an 18-gauge shotgun load in a separate barrel. Designed by Dr. Jean LeMat of New Orleans, the weapon was manufactured in France. The revolver was not very well made and did not become popular. (Faust, 433)

Sgt. Oliver Hardy, wounded at Antietam, was whose father?
The famous comedian Oliver Hardy. (Ted Alexander, Antietam National Battlefield)

Who was Mary S. Quantrill?
As Confederates were passing through Frederick, Maryland, on September 6, 1862, she and her daughter waved United States flags at them. However, in John Greenleaf Whittier's poem the credit goes to Barbara Fritchie, who waved U.S. flags as "Stonewall" Jackson's troops passed through town on September 10. (Sifikas, 324)

Who was a cavalry instructor and commandant of cadets at West Point while waiting to be exchanged?
Kenner Garrard. He had been captured in San Antonio by Southern sympathizers on April 12, 1861. He was a very popular commandant and, after exchange, went on to be colonel of the 146th New York and commanded Stephen Weed's brigade after Weed was killed at Gettysburg. He was promoted to brigadier general and led a cavalry division under Sherman and then a Sixteenth Corps Division at the battle of Nashville and in the Mobile Campaign. (Aimone, 55; Boatner, 325)

In 1862 who was the librarian at West Point?
Capt. Stephen Vincent Benét—father of the Pulitzer Prize–winning poet of the same name. (Aimone, 55)

In late 1861 New York mayor Fernando Wood was voted out of office. Who replaced him?
The Republican candidate George Opdyke. (Livingston, 15)

Who was Captain Nathaniel Gordon and what happened to him?
Gordon was the captain of the ship *Erie*. The *Erie* was in fact a slave ship that was captured off the coast of Africa by the USS *Mohican*. When taken, the ship was carrying 897 men, women, and children. Gordon was taken to New York City where he was put on trial, found guilty, and sentenced to death. Despite pleas to the president for mercy and an attempted suicide, Gordon went to the gallows on February 21, 1862. (Livingston, 15)

Who was Francis Preston Blair Jr.?
Many Civil War political generals were considered overrated. They had little knowledge of military affairs and were most often serving to impress others and enhance their political future. One exception to this was Maj. Gen. Blair. The brother of Lincoln's first postmaster general, Montgomery Blair, he proved to be a competent military leader. During the war he recruited seven regiments of infantry and rose to the rank of major general. He won praise from Ulysses S. Grant and William T. Sherman. He served in the Vicksburg Campaign, the Atlanta Campaign, and Sherman's March to the Sea. At

various points he commanded the Fifteenth Corps and Seventeenth Corps. (Faust, 65)

Why did John Bankhead Magruder get the nickname "Prince John"?

Because he was "[p]ompous, egotistical, and given to theatrical behavior, he thrived on recognition." (Faust, 468)

Who was George Norman Barnard?

A photographer who in 1862 became the official photographer of the Military Division of the Mississippi. His most famous photographs were taken during the Atlanta Campaign, the March to the Sea, and the Carolina Campaign. (Heidler and Heidler, 179, 180)

BATTLES

Who commanded the Confederate troops at the battle of Mill Springs, Kentucky, on January 19, 1862?

Maj. Gen. George Crittenden. (Faust, 850)

What happened to Brig. Gen. Felix Kirk Zollicoffer at the battle of Mill Springs?

Nearsighted and riding in advance of his troops, he was killed by a Federal volley. (Faust, 850)

What was the first action of the Civil War in northwest Arkansas?

Potts' Hill, about a mile south of the Missouri state line, on February 16, 1862. The Confederates had set an ambush, but after a Union cavalry charge and the actions of dismounted cavalry, Sterling Price's rear guard was forced back. (Hughes, 12)

Pea Ridge (Elkhorn Tavern)

When Brig. Gen. Samuel R. Curtis (Commander of the Union Army of the Southwest) began his campaign toward Pea Ridge, who were his division commanders?

The First Division was commanded by Brig. Gen. Franz Sigel. Since Sigel was second in command of the army, Col. Peter J. Osterhaus was the de facto commander of the First Division. The Second Division was led by Brig. Gen. Alexander S. Asboth; the Third Division was under Brig. Gen. Jefferson C. Davis; and the Fourth Division was led by Col. Eugene Asa Carr (in total around 12,000 men). (Hughes, 12)

What was the first significant action of the Pea Ridge Campaign?
A fight between Asa Carr's Division and the Confederates at Little Sugar Creek on February 17, 1862. The action was mostly between Rebel artillery and Federal cavalry. The Confederate guns would fire, then disappear. The Federal cavalry would follow until they found the Rebel guns again, only to be fired on. The action finally ended up as a running fight with one of Carr's brigades, backed up by the Union troopers down the Telegraph Wire Road (the major road in the area running through both the Wilson's Creek and Pea Ridge battlefields). The Federals suffered thirteen dead and fifteen wounded. (Hughes, 12, 13)

Who was in command of the Confederate Army of the West and who were his three subordinates?
Maj. Gen. Earl Van Dorn. Under him, commanding McCulloch's Division, was Brig. Gen. Ben McCulloch; Pike's Indian Territory Command, led by Brig. Gen. Albert Pike; and the Missouri Troops of Maj. Gen. Sterling Price (around 16,000 men total). (Hughes, 15, 36)

The battle of Pea Ridge was fought on what two fronts?
The Elkhorn Tavern front, along the Telegraph Wire Road; and Cross Timber Hollow, just to the north of Leetown. (Hughes, 20)

After participating in the fighting at Pea Ridge, what unfortunate duty did Union Col. Julius White have to perform six months later?
White performed well during the battle and in June was promoted to brigadier general and sent east. Unfortunately, he found himself at Harpers Ferry at the same time that "Stonewall" Jackson surrounded the town. On September 15, following the wounding of Col. Dixon Miles, White would find himself in the position of having to surrender the garrison and its 12,000 men. (Sears, 153; Boatner, 914; Hughes, 22)

What was the outcome of the fighting around Leetown?
With two of its major commanders dead and those who should have taken command riding off in search of Van Dorn, the Confederates slowly began to withdraw back over the Bentonville Detour toward Elkhorn Tavern. At the same time, fresh Federal troops began deploying in the area and started following the retreating Confederates north. (Hughes, 22, 23)

Who was the not-so-successful Confederate brigadier general who led Cherokee warriors at the battle of Pea Ridge, Arkansas, on March 7, 1862?
Brig. Gen. Albert Pike. Though a poet of some recognition as well as a successful lawyer, planter, and newspaper publisher, his career as a soldier was less than stellar. Though Pike's Indians successfully attacked a Federal battery on the first day of the battle, they stopped to celebrate and were routed by a Union counterattack. Pike was unable to round up his men, which contributed to the Confederate defeat. Federal authorities claimed that some of Pike's men scalped a number of the dead and wounded soldiers. Later, charges of mishandling money were leveled against Pike, leading to his arrest and later resignation on November 11, 1862. (Faust, 585)

Who were the only two Federals to receive the Medal of Honor at Pea Ridge?
Col. Eugene A. Carr and Col. Francis J. Herron. (Hughes, 24, 26)

What three Confederate generals were killed at Pea Ridge?
Brig. Gen. William Slack, Brig. Gen. Benjamin McCulloch and Brig. Gen. James M. McIntosh. The deaths of these officers meant that the Confederate army at Pea Ridge "suffered the highest loss ratio of general officers, in proportion to the size, of any army engaged in any battle of the war." (Hughes, 24)

What were the names of the two newspaper correspondents at the battle of Pea Ridge?
Thomas W. Knox of the *New York Herald* and William Fayel of the (Missouri) *Democrat*. (Hughes, 28)

What was the outcome of the fighting at Pea Ridge?
Though the Confederates seemed to be winning, Van Dorn chose to withdraw to the southeast, ultimately putting the White River between them and the Federals. The ultimate result of the battle, however, was that Van Dorn's army was driven south of the Boston Mountains and major units of Van Dorn's Army of the West redeployed east of the Mississippi River. (Hughes, 31, 32)

Shenandoah Valley 1862

What were the major battles of Stonewall Jackson's Shenandoah Valley Campaign in 1862?
Front Royal (May 23); Kernstown (March 23); McDowell (May 8); First Winchester (May 25); Cross Keys (June 8) and Port Republic (June 9). (Heidler and Heidler, 1749)

What happened at Front Royal on May 23, 1862?
"Stonewall" Jackson with a force of about 17,000 men chased Col. John R. Kenly's 1,000-man detachment out of the town, capturing many of them near Cedarville. At the end of the action the Federals had suffered 904 casualties to the Confederates' fifty. A major source of information prior to the battle was Confederate spy Belle Boyd, who gave Jackson the strength and location of the Federal force. (Faust, 293)

What was the outcome of the fighting at First Winchester?
Jackson sent the "Stonewall" Brigade plus Col. John A. Campbell's brigade against the Federals. Initially finding light resistance, the attacking force soon came upon Maj. Gen. Nathaniel Bank's Federals in force. The Federals made a gallant stand, but with the addition of Richard Ewell's division and Brig. Gen. Richard Taylor's brigade the Union troops eventually broke and retreated. (Faust, 834)

What happened at Cross Keys and Port Republic?
Little came of the fighting at Cross Keys except casualties. The next day at Port Republic Jackson attacked prematurely. The fighting was perhaps the most severe of the campaign but the arrival of Richard Taylor's Louisianans sealed a victory for the Confederates. (Robertson, 26)

What was the ultimate outcome of Jackson's 1862 Valley Campaign?

He ensured the safety of the Shenandoah Valley, inflicted 7,000 casualties (at a cost of a little over 2,000 Confederate casualties), and captured tons of arms and supplies. (Robertson, 26)

The Peninsula and Seven Days

What did "Prince John" Magruder do along his line extending from the mouth of the Warwick River to Yorktown to slow McClellan's advance up the Peninsula?

Put on a show for the Yankees. He marched a number of his troops up and down the line, making the enemy think they were arriving reinforcements. A member of one regiment, the 14th Louisiana, said that by the time they stopped marching they had gone from Yorktown to the James and back six times. Magruder also added sound effects: drum rolls, bugle calls, shouting of marching orders and occasional firing along the entrenchments. (Sears, 37, 38)

How did Winfield Scott Hancock get the title "Hancock the Superb"?

During the fighting at Williamsburg Hancock "foiled a Confederate rear guard action by first feigning retreat, then counterattacking the Rebels, turning a badly mismanaged battle for the Federals into a complete victory for himself." McClellan termed what Hancock did "brilliant" and later said to his wife, "Hancock was superb yesterday." The press picked up on this and thus Hancock got his nom de guerre. (Venter, 42)

Where was Gen. Fitz John Porter's headquarters at Gaines' Mill?

The Watt House.

Where was Gen. George McClellan's headquarters during much of the Seven Days' Battles?

The Trent House, located about halfway between Fair Oaks Station and the Chickahominy. (Catton, 146)

What were the five major battles of the Seven Days' Campaign?
Mechanicsville (Beaver Dam Creek) (June 26, 1862); Gaines' Mill (June 27, 1862); Savage's Station (June 29, 1862); Glendale (June 30, 1862); and Malvern Hill (July 1, 1862).

What was the "Land Merrimack"?
It was a 32-pounder Brook naval rifle placed on a railroad flatcar that was shielded by a sloping casemate of railroad iron. (Sears, 269–272)

What was the outcome of the fight at Savage's Station?
"Bull" Sumner's Second Corps fought only ten of its twenty-six regiments while "Prince John" Magruder only used two and a half of his six brigades. The day's final tally, including a skirmish in the morning, was 1,038 Federal casualties against just 473 for the Confederates. Gen. Lee was very disappointed in Magruder's handling of his troops during the battle and told him so. (Sears, 273–274)

What future Army of the Potomac commander was badly wounded during the fighting at Glendale?
George Gordon Meade. (Sears, 299)

Who made the comment following the action at Malvern Hill, "It was not war—it was murder"?
Confederate Brig. Gen. D. H. Hill. (Sears, 335)

Who was Willie Johnston?
At the tender age of twelve, Johnston was the youngest person to be awarded the Medal of Honor for his action during the fighting of the Seven Days' actions. He was a drummer with Co. D., 3rd Vermont, a unit that also had Johnston's father as a member. (Sifakis, 213)

Who replaced Joseph E. Johnston as commander of the Confederate forces when he was wounded at Seven Pines on May 31?
Gen. Robert E. Lee. For a brief period of eighteen hours, Maj. Gen. Gustavis W. Smith commanded on the early afternoon of June 1.

When Smith suffered a nervous breakdown, Robert E. Lee replaced him.

From where did Jeb Stuart start his ride around McClellan on June 12, 1862?

The Mordecai farm and Kilby Station on the Richmond, Fredericksburg and Potomac Railroad just north of Richmond. (Mewborn, 10)

How many men did Stuart take on his ride around McClellan?

Approximately 1,200. (Mewborn, 10)

What two Robert E. Lee relatives accompanied Stuart on his ride?

His son Col. William Henry Fitzhugh "Rooney" Lee and nephew Col. Fitzhugh "Fitz" Lee. (Mewborn, 10)

What was Lee's failure on June 26, 1862?

At the battle of Beaver Dam Creek (Mechanicsville), five brigades of A. P. Hill's division attacked a well-entrenched line of Maj. Gen. Fitz John Porter's corps. Met by heavy Federal fire, the attack failed, only to be followed by an attempted flank attack, which again met failure. At the end of the fighting the Confederates had suffered 1,484 casualties to only 361 for the Federals. (Faust, 484)

Shiloh (Pittsburg Landing)

Who commanded the three armies at the battle of Shiloh?

Union (Army of the Tennessee) Maj. Gen. Ulysses S. Grant; (Army of the Ohio) Maj. Gen. Don Carlos Buell. Confederate (The Army of the Mississippi): Gen. Albert Sydney Johnston. The use of the name Army of the Tennessee was only semiofficial as of April 21, 1862. The Department (and Army) of the Tennessee did not become official until October 1862. (Allen, 13)

Where was the Army of the Mississippi concentrated prior to the Shiloh Campaign?

Around Corinth, Mississippi, more than twenty-two miles southwest of Pittsburg Landing. (Faust, 684)

Who were the four corps commanders of the Army of the Mississippi who would go on to greater things?
First Corps: Maj. Gen. Leonidas Polk; Second Corps: Maj. Gen. Braxton Bragg; Third Corps: Maj. Gen. William J. Hardee; Reserve Corps: Brig. Gen. John C. Breckinridge. (Allen, 10)

What was the first major Union force to occupy Pittsburg Landing?
The Sixth Division of the Army of the Tennessee, commanded by Brig. Gen. Benjamin M. Prentiss. (Bearss)

When did Johnston begin his movement against Grant?
His troops began the one-day march north on April 3, but rain, terrain, and inexperience turned the one-and-a-half days into three. They did not reach a position to attack until the afternoon of April 5. (Faust, 684)

Where was Grant's army positioned prior to the Confederate attack?
His right (Sherman's Fifth Division) was near Owl Creek. It then extended east, south of Shiloh Church. On the far left was the brigade of Col. David Stuart, detached from Sherman's main line near Lick Creek. Behind Sherman was the First Division of Maj. Gen. John A. McClernand. Brig. Gen. William H. L. Wallace's Second Division lay just west of Snake Creek north of Pittsburg Landing and the Sixth Division of Brig. Gen. Benjamin M. Prentiss was near Crumps Landing and Adamsville between Sherman's left and Stuart's right. Finally, Lew Wallace's Third Division was kept north of Snake Creek. In all, before the fighting started Grant had 39,830 men and 112 guns. (Allen, 16, 47)

Where was Grant's headquarters during the buildup prior to the battle of Shiloh?
In the home of William H. Cherry in Savannah, Tennessee. Grant would daily board a steamer and visit the camps of his army. (Allen, 16)

What was Maj. Gen. Don Carlos Buell doing while Grant was building up his army at Pittsburg Landing?
Buell was ordered to march cross-country from Nashville to Savannah, repairing roads and bridges en route. (Allen, 13)

What was the opening action of the battle of Shiloh?
Brigade commander Col. Everett Peabody sent a five-company patrol led by Maj. James Powell on a reconnaissance of a suspected Confederate position. Just before 5:00 a.m. the patrol was fired upon by some Confederate cavalry vedettes. Powell deployed his men into a skirmish line and took them forward. He exchanged shots with some Mississippi pickets, then looking across J. C. Fraley's cotton field, Powell saw the blast of a Confederate volley. This skirmish lasted about an hour before Powell started to pull his men back. The Confederates faded back into the woodline, but then seconds later Hardee's corps emerged in a battle line extending a mile. Hardee was followed by Bragg, then Polk and Breckinridge. (Allen, 19–20)

When did Grant learn of the fighting near Pittsburg Landing?
Around 7:15 a.m., while he was eating breakfast at the Cherry Mansion, he received a report that there was artillery fire upriver from Savannah. Going outside he could distinctly hear the cannon fire. He immediately sent orders to Brig. Gen. William "Bull" Nelson of Buell's army to march up the east side of the river to Pittsburg Landing where they would be ferried across the Tennessee River. He himself then boarded the steamer *Tigress* and headed upriver. (Allen, 46–47)

When did Grant arrive at the Landing?
About 9:00 a.m. He was assisted onto a horse (he had been injured two days before when his horse had fallen on his leg) and rode to the fighting, first meeting with Gen. William H. L. Wallace, who indicated to him that the army was under a full-scale attack. (Allen, 47)

What was the "Hornets' Nest"?
As the Confederates attacked, routing Brig. Gen. Benjamin M. Prentiss's Federals, the Yanks threw up a battle line extending along a

sunken road from Duncan Field past Sarah Bell's Peach Orchard to the Savannah-Hamburg Road. Despite repeated attacks, the line held for almost six hours until it was surrounded and crushed. Saying the minié balls flew like angry hornets, the Confederates dubbed the site the "Hornets' Nest." (Faust, 370)

What was the Peach Orchard?
The Peach Orchard fronted the "Hornets' Nest," and as the Federals were pushed back toward the landing the fighting moved through it. Finally the Confederates managed to surround the Union soldiers, forcing Gen. Prentiss to surrender rather than suffer any more casualties. (Cunningham, 302–303)

What is Shiloh's "Bloody Pond"?
Just northwest of the Peach Orchard was a shallow pond, the only water in the immediate area. Wounded men and animals from both sides crawled to the pond to quench their thirst and ease their pain. So many men bled into the pond that it was said that the water became the color of blood, thus becoming known as "Bloody Pond." (Allen, 54)

What happened to the Confederate commander around 2:00 p.m.?
Gen. Albert Sydney Johnston was shot in the right leg just below the knee. The round was a .577-caliber ball from an Enfield rifle-musket, which means he could have been shot by his own men. The ball had torn the popliteal artery, causing extensive bleeding. Because the wound either bled internally or because Johnston wore knee-high boots, the bleeding took some time to be noticed. The general was taken to a ravine about fifty yards south of where he was wounded and taken off his horse, already unconscious. One of Johnston's staff officers, William Preston, who was also his brother-in-law, comforted the general, but he never regained consciousness, dying about 2:45 p.m. He may have been helped had he not left his personal physician in a Union camp to attend to Confederate and Federal wounded. He might also have been saved if someone had found the field tourniquet that was in his coat pocket. (Faust, 399; Allen, 53)

Who took over command of the Confederate forces at the battle of Shiloh after Gen. Albert Sydney Johnston's wounding?
Gen. Pierre G. T. Beauregard.

What was "Grant's Last Line"?
About 2:30 p.m. Grant ordered his chief of staff, Col. Joseph D. Webster, to establish a defensive line for the Federals. Webster commandeered any artillery he could find and placed it on the far left of the line. The left of the line was anchored on the river, protected by the *Lexington* and *Tyler*; it then extended west for a mile to the Hamburg-Savannah Road. Above the Landing the colonel placed fifty more cannon. The line was about 2,200 yards long and contained nearly seventy cannon. By 5:30 p.m. approximately 20,000 infantry had taken their places among the cannons. (Allen, 61)

What was the day's outcome for the Federals?
The Federal line had been driven two miles north of its original position. Four of the five division camps had been captured and plundered by the Confederates. Gen. William H. L. Wallace had been mortally wounded and Gen. Prentiss captured. Forty cannon had been captured along with supplies and ammunition. Casualties were estimated to be around 8,500, while thousands hugged the riverbank utterly demoralized. (Allen, 62–63)

What was the day's outcome for the Confederates?
They had won a partial victory, though the Federals were still on the field. They retired south to the first line of Union camps. They were disorganized and exhausted. Many were hungry, not having eaten in two days. (Allen, 63)

Where did Gen. Grant spend the night of April 6?
Because his headquarters had been made into a field hospital, he spent the night sleeping in the mud under a tree on a bluff overlooking the Landing. (Allen, 7)

When did Maj. Gen. Lew Wallace's Division reach the battlefield?
After nightfall on April 6. From his position at Crump's Landing, Wallace should have marched his men over a six-mile route, taking about two hours. Instead he took the division on a circuitous route of fifteen miles that took seven hours. Finally reaching the field after 7:00 p.m., he took up a position on the right of Sherman's and McClernand's divisions. (Allen, 10, 16)

Where were Buell's troops deployed?
On Grant's left and center near the Landing. (Allen, 16)

What were Grant's orders on the morning of April 7?
There were no instructions as to deployment of combat assignments. The only "command decision" understood by Grant and his generals was that the two combined Union armies would attack at dawn and recover the original camps of April 6. (Allen, 16)

Which army "opened the ball" on April 7?
Grant ordered his men forward before dawn. The entire Federal line, spearheaded by Lew Wallace's division on the right and "Bull" Nelson's on the left, along a two-mile front and some 40,000 men strong, attacked south toward the badly disorganized Confederates. (Allen, 17)

What comprised Gen. Beauregard's reconstructed line?
The only semi-organized unit was Breckinridge's, with Hardee, Bragg, and Polk all commanding commingled commands (in all, around 28,000 men and eighty cannon). The Confederate line was about three miles long, about a mile and a half south of the Landing, though it was 10:00 a.m. before they were able to piece this line together. (Allen, 19)

When did Beauregard issue orders to retreat back to Corinth?
About 2:00 p.m. (Allen, 46)

Whose troops were the last Confederates to retire from the field?
Breckinridge's, at about 5:00 p.m., who were acting as rear guard of the army. (Allen, 46)

Who led the Federal "reconnaissance in force" on the morning of April 8?
Sherman led two infantry brigades and two cavalry battalions south from the Shiloh Church on the Corinth Road. He ultimately met Wood's division of Buell's army. These troops had passed through abandoned Confederate camps and past field hospitals, encountering no resistance. (Allen, 47)

Where was Sherman almost captured?
Sherman continued his reconnaissance, moving south on the Ridge Road until he got about six miles southwest of Pittsburg Landing, where there was an open field and beyond it, an area covered with fallen timbers. On the opposite ridge Sherman observed a Confederate camp and a field hospital protected by Confederate cavalry (about 300 in all). This group of cavalry was commanded by Col. Nathan Bedford Forrest. Sherman advanced the 77th Ohio and the 4th Illinois cavalry. Seeing these advancing troops Forrest attacked, driving the Yankees back and almost capturing Sherman. The action became known as "Fallen Timbers." When the Confederate cavalry retired, Sherman eventually captured the field hospital. (Allen, 47–48)

What was the final cost of the battle of Shiloh (Pittsburg Landing)?
It is estimated that 110,000 soldiers participated in the battle, 65,000 Union and 45,000 Confederate. The number of killed, wounded and missing totaled 10,699 Confederate and 13,047 Federals. To that date Shiloh was the largest and most costly battle of the war. (Allen, 48)

Where was Ft. Pulaski?
It was located on Cockspur Island at the entrance to the Savannah River near Savannah, Georgia.

Who commanded the Federal troops that captured Ft. Pulaski?
Acting Brig. Gen. Quincy Adams Gillmore. (Boatner, 296)

When did Ft. Pulaski fall?
Gillmore began pounding the fort with his artillery on April 11, 1862, which knocked out a number of the Confederate guns and weakened

the walls of the fort. During the night the men managed to remount a number of the guns but they were quickly knocked out again on April 12. Eventually a breach was hammered in the southeast angle of the scarp wall which gave the Federals a clear shot at the northwest angle powder magazine, causing Confederate commander Col. Charles Olmstead to run up the white flag and surrender. (Weeks, 200–201)

What was the number of casualties in Ft. Pulaski's surrender?
The Federals had one killed and several wounded; the Confederates had one killed and 384 prisoners of war. (Denney, 159)

When the CSS *Arkansas* sailed down the Yazoo River on July 15, 1862, what happened to her?
She met the *Carondelet, Tyler,* and *Queen of the West.* In the ensuing action the *Carondelet* was disabled and the other two ships, a timberclad and a ram, retired down the river with the *Arkansas* in hot pursuit. Upon reaching the Mississippi River she found thirty Union warships commanded by flag officers Charles H. Davis and David G. Farragut. Steaming slowly through the Union fleet, she was hit by shot and shell but returned fire, damaging several vessels but only the *Lancaster* seriously. She continued on to Vicksburg, where that night she once again came under fire as Farragut's ships headed downstream. After repairs were made she steamed south, again heading for Baton Rouge. On August 26 the *Arkansas*'s engines began giving her trouble. Finally, as she came within sight of Baton Rouge and the Union fleet, her engines totally broke down. Her crew abandoned her, setting her on fire. She then drifted down the river before exploding and sinking. (Faust, 22–23)

Who commanded the CSS *Arkansas*?
Lt. Henry K. Stevens. (Faust, 22)

Second Manassas (Bull Run)

What was the name of the army John Pope commanded at the battle of Second Manassas?
The Army of Virginia.

What were Brig. Gen. Samuel Sturgis's feelings toward Maj. Gen. John Pope during the Second Manassas Campaign in August 1862?
He commented, "I don't care for John Pope one pinch of owl dung!" (Faust, 730)

Who were Pope's corps commanders in his new army?
The First Corps was under Maj. Gen. Franz Sigel; the Second Corps was led by Maj. Gen. Nathaniel Prentiss Banks; and lastly Maj. Gen. Irvin McDowell commanded the Third Corps. The army had 51,000 men. During the course of the campaign, however, various units of the Army of the Potomac began augmenting Pope's army. (Hennessy, 12)

The battle of Slaughter Mountain on August 9, 1862, is known by what other name?
The battle of Cedar Mountain. James Edwin Slaughter owned the property around and including the mountain, which is really little more than an isolated hill commanding the Culpeper & Orange Turnpike. Slaughter became a brigadier general and served on the staffs of such notables at Albert Sydney Johnston, P. T. G. Beauregard, Braxton Bragg, and John B. Magruder. After the war he fled to Mexico before returning to Mobile, Alabama, and then New Orleans.

What was the first major battle between elements of Pope's army and troops from the Army of Northern Virginia?
The battle of Cedar Mountain on August 9, 1862. A force of 24,000 Confederates under "Stonewall" Jackson attacked Nathaniel Banks's corps near Cedar (Slaughter) Mountain. Though technically a Confederate victory, Banks was reinforced by other elements of Pope's army, forcing Jackson to retire south of the Rapidan River. (Hennessy, 12)

What was Lee's plan for dealing with Pope?
He ordered Longstreet to join Jackson in Gordonsville. Pope's army was positioned in a V formed by the valleys of the Rapidan and Rappahannock rivers. Jackson and Longstreet would cross the Rapidan and attack Pope's right while the Confederate cavalry would cross the Rapidan below Pope's left and, speeding ahead around Pope, burn the

bridge at Rappahannock Station. With Pope trapped, Lee would be able to destroy the Union army. (Hennessy, 12)

What is the tale of the captured order?
Jeb Stuart had moved most of his cavalry to Verdiersville. Hearing the noise of an approaching column on the morning of August 18, Stuart walked out of his headquarters only to find 1,000 Federal troops bearing down on him. Quickly mounting their horses, Stuart and his staff took to the woods, where they watched as the Yankees pillaged and tore the house apart. Among the things the Federals got was Stuart's cloak and plumed hat, much to the chagrin of the general. Far more important, however, was a satchel that contained an order from Lee to Stuart. In it was a description of Lee's plan to attack Pope. From this, Pope decided that remaining in his V position was not advantageous, so he sent orders for the army to retreat across the Rappahannock. A similar incident would happen a month later near Sharpsburg, Maryland. (Hennessy, 12–13)

How did Stuart get revenge for the theft of his cloak and hat?
On August 22 Stuart took 1,500 of his men into Catlett's Station along the Orange & Alexandria Railroad. He had two objectives: first, capture Pope's headquarters train; and second, to burn the bridge over Cedar Run. Because the rain was coming down in buckets, Stuart's men could not burn the bridge, though they did unsuccessfully try to chop it down. They were much luckier with the headquarters train: the men looted it, rifling stores and breaking into anything that looked valuable. When Stuart left Catlett's Station he took with him several hundred prisoners, 500 horses and mules, important papers from Pope's headquarters wagon giving invaluable information concerning the Union troop movements, and a payroll chest with thousands of dollars in it. The most prized capture, however, was Pope's dress uniform coat. Stuart sent Pope a note suggesting an exchange, but he never heard from the Union general. (Hennessy, 14)

On August 24, 1863, what plan did Lee improvise to get Pope off his Rappahannock line?
Lee decided to keep Longstreet, with his 30,000 men, along the Rappahannock while "Stonewall" Jackson would take his 24,000 men,

cross the Hedgeman's River at Hinson's Mill, turn east at Salem, and make an arcing movement to the Union rear, hitting the Orange & Alexandria Railroad, Pope's supply line. (Hennessy, 17)

Where did Jackson end up during his movement?
Jackson marched his men north on Pope's right, passing through Thoroughfare Gap and Haymarket, finally reaching Gainesville on August 26. Jackson was now in Pope's rear. Back south of the Rappahannock, Lee told Longstreet to leave a token force, then march the rest of his men to join Jackson. While this was going on, Jackson was busy taking Bristoe Station. After destroying track and capturing two Federal trains, he then set his eye on Manassas Junction, a main Union supply depot. (Hennessy, 18)

Who were the first Confederate troops to enter Manassas Junction?
The 21st North Carolina and the 21st Georgia of Brig. Gen. Isaac R. Trimble's brigade, using some of Stuart's cavalry as a screen. Moving up the railroad, the Confederates got to within a few yards of the Union line before charging. It was all over in a few minutes, with Trimble's men, on the night of August 26–27, capturing three hundred prisoners, dozens of horses and eight cannon. (Hennessy, 18)

What did Pope do in response to Jackson's raid on Manassas Junction?
He pulled his men off the Rappahannock line and headed them eastward on an arc from the Warrenton Turnpike to the Orange & Alexandria Railroad. By nightfall of August 27, Sigel's corps had reached Gainesville, with McDowell's right behind. At Greenwich, a few miles southwest of Gainesville, was Jesse Reno's Ninth Corps; just behind him was part of Heintzelman's corps. Hooker was at Bristoe Station. Pope issued orders that the next day McDowell would approach Manassas Junction from the north, Sigel from the northwest, and Reno, Kearny, Hooker and Porter from the west. (Hennessy, 20)

Knowing that Pope was coming, what did Jackson do on August 28?
He marched his troops out of Manassas Junction and into a position north of the Warrenton Turnpike near Groveton. In this position

his men would be concealed, Longstreet could get to him when he had passed through Thoroughfare Gap, and if needed, he would have direct and safe retreat routes. (Hennessy, 20)

What kind of delicacies did the Confederates feast on at Manassas Junction and what did they do with the remaining stores when they left?
They had wine, canned ham, lobster salad, candy, coffee, fruit, oysters, and every other sort of repast imaginable, especially to tattered, barefoot, hungry soldiers. When the men set out that night, what they didn't steal, they burned. (Hennessy, 20)

What surprise did Lee and Longstreet find waiting for them when they reached Thoroughfare Gap?
Brig. Gen. James B. Ricketts's division. Pope had sent Ricketts to hold up Longstreet's movement, spearheaded by G. T. "Tige" Anderson's brigades through the gap. Unfortunately for the Rebels, Longstreet sent two brigades over the mountain toward Ricketts's position. Law's brigade hit Ricketts's right and Bennings's brigade hit his left, driving him back. Ricketts's deployment did nothing to hold up the Confederate advance. (Hennessy, 21)

What was the bloody action preceding the major battle at Second Bull Run?
The battle of Brawner's Farm (Groveton) on August 28, 1862, between elements of Stonewall Jackson's wing and the unit destined to become known as the Iron Brigade.

What brigade of Brig. Gen. Rufus King's division "opened the ball" at the battle of Second Manassas?
The Fourth Brigade of Brig. Gen. John Gibbon, later to become famous as the Iron Brigade.

What was the line of march for King's division on August 28, 1862?
Brig. Gen. John P. Hatch's brigade led the column, followed by Brig. Gen. John Gibbon's brigade, Brig. Gen. Abner Doubleday and finally Brig. Gen. Marsena Patrick. (Hennessy, 22, 24)

When Gibbon's column was fired on by Confederate artillery, which regiment did he send to capture the guns and who did they meet?

He sent the 2nd Wisconsin across the fields toward Brawner's Woods. The artillery limbered and left but as the infantry neared the wood line they saw a Confederate battle line emerge. It was the Stonewall Brigade commanded by Col. William S. Baylor. The Confederates moved forward to a fence-line about seventy yards from the Wisconsin boys and then the two sides started to throw lead at each other. Gibbon sent forward the 19th Indiana, which took up a position on the left of the Wisconsin regiment, and the two sides continued the fight. After about thirty minutes the Stonewall Brigade was finally reinforced by elements of Brig. Gen. A. R. Lawton's Georgia brigade. (Hennessy, 22)

The fighting at Brawner Farm was done by what units?

Union: Gibbon's Brigade, 2nd Wisconsin, 19th Indiana, 7th Wisconsin, and 6th Wisconsin; and Doubleday's 76th New York, 56th Pennsylvania and Co. B, 4th U.S. Artillery. Confederate: The Stonewall Brigade as well as elements of Lawton's Brigade and Trimble's Brigade, and, late in the action, Col. Alexander G. Taliaferro's Brigade. (Hennessy, 23–24)

Who was the most notable casualty of the battle of Brawner's Farm?

Maj. Gen. Richard S. Ewell, who received a wound shattering his right kneecap and tibia. The wound was serious enough to require the leg to be amputated, putting the general out of action until just before the Gettysburg Campaign. (Hennessy, 24)

Who was Edgar O'Connor?

O'Connor, a West Point graduate, was the colonel of the 2nd Wisconsin and the only regimental commander from the Iron Brigade killed at Brawner's Farm. (Sifakis, 291)

What was the outcome of the battle of Brawner's Farm?

As darkness came on the fighting stopped, ending in a stalemate. The casualties were high; the Stonewall Brigade lost 40 percent of the men engaged, while the 2nd Wisconsin lost more than half its numbers. Two Georgia regiments took 70 percent casualties. When it was learned that all of Jackson's command were on their front, the Federals decided the best thing to do would be to retire, so at midnight the men left their battle lines and headed for Manassas Junction. (Hennessy, 25)

By noon of August 29 what was the Confederate line?

Longstreet had passed through Thoroughfare Gap and reached the field, extending Jackson's right flank. When Longstreet got into position the Confederate line stretched almost three miles from its right on the Manassas-Gainesville Road, across the Warrenton Pike, then northeast to Sudley Church. (Hennessy, 25)

What was the Federal army's first movement against Jackson's line on August 29?

Franz Sigel lined up his division facing where he thought Jackson might be. Other Federals lined up on Sigel's left. Around 7:00 a.m. Federal artillery on Chinn Ridge opened up and the Federals surged forward. Within an hour the two forces had found each other and were engaged. (Hennessy, 26)

What was the outcome of the first day's battle?

Despite attacking the Confederate line and being repulsed three times Pope was pleased with the day's outcome. The Army of Virginia had held its own against the enemy and was basically in its original position at the end of the day. (Hennessy, 46)

During the day's fighting what happened between Pope and Fifth Corps commander Maj. Gen. Fitz John Porter?

Porter was not a fan of John Pope, at one point having called him an "ass." On the morning of August 29 Pope sent Porter some confusing orders, telling him to take his corps and part of McDowell's to Gainesville and get between Jackson and Longstreet. Porter moved, but when he met some of Longstreet's troops along the Manassas-Gainesville Road, he chose to stop. Pope spent the day waiting for Porter to attack and Porter spent the day doing nothing, not knowing he was supposed to attack. By nightfall Pope was convinced that Porter had disobeyed his orders and even started to write up an arrest order. Instead, he sent orders for Porter to march to the battlefield on the morning of August 30. Porter was probably correct in not attacking, having no clear access to Jackson's right due to the position of Longstreet. For not attacking, Porter might be given credit for not sacrificing his men and perhaps the army. Pope didn't see it this way. This was to come back and haunt Porter, and he would spend many years of his life striving for vindication. (Hennessy, 17, 46)

What was Pope's attack plan of August 30?
Porter was to attack along the Warrenton Pike against Jackson's right with the help of Hatch's division as support. Pope also provided a few artillery batteries, but most of these were ineffectual. Porter's task was daunting. Most of the ground he was to attack across was open and some of his men had to cross 600 yards of ground in order to reach the Confederate line. The unfinished railroad angled away from his front. In addition, S. D. Lee's artillery covered every inch of his left front. Despite this, the attack began at 3:00 p.m. (Hennessy, 48–49)

What was the result of Porter's attack?
It was a slaughter. At least one-third of the attackers became casualties. Many of the Federals made it to the railroad cut, but Confederate reinforcements soon pushed them back. At one point, out of ammunition, Confederates started heaving rocks at the Yankees. The Yanks, in response, started throwing them back, and for a couple minutes it was a rock-throwing battle. As the Feds were working their way back through the fields, Longstreet sent forward his men. (Hennessy, 50–51)

While the Federals were falling back, where did Pope set up his final defensive line?
From Henry Hill along the Sudley Road. The line was about 700 yards long and defended by four brigades. It was also directly in front of Longstreet's advancing Confederates. (Hennessy, 54)

What happened to Pope's last line?
They managed to hold their ground from 6:00 p.m. until 8:00 p.m., in part because the Confederates ran out of steam. As happened in

other battles under Lee's command, the Confederates were on the verge of victory but simply ran out of manpower. Finally, at 8:00 p.m. Pope issued orders for his army to retreat. (Hennessy, 56–57)

What did Maj. Gen. John Pope receive for having commanded the Army of Virginia?
First, he was relieved of command and replaced by Maj. Gen. George B. McClellan. Second, he was sent west to head the Department of the Northwest and cope with the Great Sioux uprising then raging in Minnesota. (Hennessy, 58)

Who was George W. Roosevelt?
At the battle of Second Manassas, Roosevelt was the first sergeant of Co. K, 26th Pennsylvania. During the fighting he recaptured his regiment's colors. At the battle of Gettysburg he captured a Confederate flag and was wounded while falling back with it. His left leg was amputated due to the wound. For these two actions he was later awarded the Medal of Honor. Roosevelt was the third cousin of future President Franklin D. Roosevelt. (Sifakis, 340)

Which two Federal generals were killed at the battle of Chantilly (Ox Hill)?
Maj. Gen. Philip Kearny and Brig. Gen. Isaac Ingalls Stevens. (Faust, 408, 718)

Where is Harrison's Landing and why is it significant in Civil War history?
Harrison's Landing lies along the James River on the Peninsula, twenty-two miles southeast of Richmond. George McClellan withdrew his army to this area following the Peninsula Campaign. (Boatner, 379)

Who commanded the USS *Monitor* during its March 9, 1862, fight with the CSS *Virginia*?
Lt. John L. Worden. (Faust, 504)

Who commanded the CSS *Virginia* during the March 9 battle of Hampton Roads?
Lt. Cmdr. Catesby ap R. Jones. (Faust, 401)

On March 8, 1862, what three Federal ships did the CSS *Virginia* set its sights on?
The USS *Cumberland,* which the *Virginia* rammed, causing a large hole below its waterline; and the USS *Congress,* which was run aground by its crew but nevertheless was destroyed by the *Virginia's* guns. She also drove the USS *Minnesota* aground. (Faust, 335; Catton, 175)

What was the fate of Col. Dixon Miles after he surrendered the Federal garrison at Harpers Ferry to Stonewall Jackson?
He was hit by one of the final shots fired by the Confederate artillery and died the following day.

South Mountain

What were the names of the three gaps that were attacked by the Army of the Potomac on September 14, 1862?
To the north was Turner's Gap, which had the National Road running through it. Just to the south of Turner's Gap was Fox's Gap, and the southernmost gap was Crampton's Gap.

What Federal units attacked the South Mountain gaps?
Maj. Gen. William Buel Franklin's Sixth Corps moved against Crampton's Gap. Maj. Gen. Jesse L. Reno led the Ninth Corps against Fox's Gap. Finally, Maj. Gen. Joseph Hooker placed his men from the National Road north facing Turner's Gap. (Frye, 47, 52–54)

What was the only Federal brigade to attack up the National Road toward Turner's Gap?
The brigade of western troops under the command of Brig. Gen. John Gibbon. The 6th and 7th Wisconsin attacked north of the road

while the 19th Indiana and 2nd Wisconsin attacked south of the road. (Frye, 57)

What Confederate troops initially defended South Mountain?
Five brigades, totaling about 5,000 men, under Maj. Gen. Daniel Harvey Hill. (Frye, 46)

What was the name of the Confederate general killed while inspecting his line near Fox's Gap?
Brig. Gen. Samuel Garland. (Faust, 706)

What was the name of the Union general mortally wounded in Wise's Field during the fighting at South Mountain?
Maj. Gen. Jesse L. Reno. (Frye, 54)

What was the outcome of the battle of South Mountain?
McClellan claimed victory but he was technically incorrect. His forces did manage to take Crampton's Gap, but did not occupy Turner's Gap until after dark and the day's fighting was over; they could not hold Fox's Gap. (Frye, 58)

Antietam

When Gen. Lee and Gen. Longstreet entered Maryland during the Antietam Campaign, what was unusual about their appearance?
Gen. Lee, in a freak accident, had broken a bone in his right hand and severely sprained the left. Thus he was forced to ride into Maryland in an ambulance. Gen. Longstreet had a badly blistered heel, forcing him to give up a boot and use an old carpet slipper instead. (Sears, 72)

Before the battle of Antietam, what was today's Burnside's Bridge named?
Rohrbach's Bridge. It was a three-arch, 125-foot limestone structure built in 1836 that spanned Antietam Creek a short distance from the farm of Henry Rohrbach. (Frye, 115)

Who commanded the Georgia troops overlooking the Rohrbach Bridge?
Brig. Gen. Robert A. Toombs. His force consisted of the 2nd, 20th, and 50th Georgia, somewhere around 400 men. (Frye, 116)

What happened to the Mumma farmstead on the early morning of the battle?
It was torched by D. H. Hill's men so that it would not be used by Yankee sharpshooters. Smoke still rose from the fire when the battle began. (Sears, 282)

What did Brig. Gen. Alfred Colquitt's brigade meet when it attacked toward the Mumma farm?
A stampede of six cows. One Georgia soldier said he was more afraid of being run over by a cow than being hit by a bullet. (Sears, 208)

What was the name of the fifty-nine-year-old major general who had been in command of the Twelfth Corps for only two days when he was mortally wounded at Antietam?
Maj. Gen. Joseph K. E. Mansfield. It was Mansfield's first infantry command in the war. Prior to this he had been serving as an engineer for the defenses of Washington. (Catton, 221; Frye, 86)

What were the names of the three 27th Indiana soldiers who found a copy of Lee's Special Orders 191 in a clover field near the B&O railroad's Monocacy Junction?
Sgt. John Bloss, Cpl. Barton Mitchell, and Pvt. David Vance. All three men would be wounded during the fighting on the morning of September 17; however, all would survive. (Frye, 18, 87)

Who penned the Special Orders 191 for Lee?
His chief of staff, Robert Hall Chilton. (Faust, 139)

What is one of the greatest mysteries of the American Civil War?
What Confederate lost Gen. Lee's Special Orders 191, which outlined the disposition of the Army of Northern Virginia during the 1862 Maryland Campaign. (Frye, 19)

What is the bloodiest day in American military history?
September 17, 1862, the battle of Antietam, where almost 23,000 men became casualties.

Where was Gen. McClellan's headquarters at Antietam?
The Philip Pry house. The large two-and-a-half-story brick house was located on the high ground east of Antietam Creek, about two miles from the Miller Cornfield where Hooker opened the battle. The site was later a hospital and Maj. Gen. Israel Richardson died in the home on November 3, 1862. (Sears, 195)

What were the three phases of the battle of Antietam?
The early morning phase, with fighting occurring on the northern part of the battlefield around the Cornfield, East and West Woods, Dunker Church and Hagerstown Road; the late morning–early afternoon phase, that took place in the center of the battlefield with attacks on the Sunken Road, and the late afternoon phase, focusing on Burnside's Bridge and the heights south of Sharpsburg.

Where did Jeb Stuart and his artillerist set up fourteen guns to fire on Hooker's advance toward Jackson?
Nicodemus Heights, the high ground west of the Hagerstown Pike. The Nicodemus Farm lies on the eastern base of the heights; reputedly, Oliver Wendell Holmes went to the house after he was wounded, for medical attention. (Howe, 65, note 1)

With more than 500 cannons engaged, the artillery fire was so intense that Col. Stephen D. Lee referred to the Antietam battlefield as what?
"Artillery hell." (Antietam)

Who were the two "51sts" who finally captured Burnside's Bridge?
The 51st New York, led by Col. Robert Potter, and the 51st Pennsylvania of Col. John Hartranft. Potter went on to be brevetted major general before being seriously wounded on April 2, 1865, in the assault on Petersburg. Hartranft was awarded a Medal of Honor for his actions at

First Bull Run and later became a two-term governor of Pennsylvania. (Frye, 121; Faust, 347, 559)

Who saved Lee's right at Antietam by marching his troops in from Harpers Ferry, reaching the battlefield just in time?
Maj. Gen. Ambrose Powell Hill.

How many field hospitals did Dr. Jonathan Letterman set up around Sharpsburg?
Seventy-one, at eight different sites.

How many doctors were killed at the battle of Antietam?
Four; three Federal and one Confederate. One of the Union doctors killed was Dr. Edward Revere of the 20th Massachusetts. Revere was the great-grandson of Massachusetts patriot Paul Revere. (Davis, 423)

Who was George Smalley and why did his presence at the battle of Antietam become important?
Smalley was a newspaper correspondent for the *New York Tribune*. During the fighting on September 17 Smalley found himself with Gen. Joseph Hooker, who asked the correspondent who he was and what he was doing. When Smalley explained his presence Hooker asked him to carry a message for him as the rest of his staff was busy. Smalley agreed and spent the remainder of the day acting as a messenger for the general. Hooker later praised Smalley for his work. (Davis, 219)

Where was the Army of the Potomac camped when Burnside took over command?
Near Warrenton, Virginia. (Catton, 255)

Where was the Army of Northern Virginia camped in November 1862?
Winchester and Culpeper. (Catton, 255)

Who was the youngest soldier from either side to die due to wounds received during combat?
Charles E. King, who enlisted in Co. F of the 49th Pennsylvania Volunteers as a drummer on September 9, 1861. The next year at the

Confederate dead gathered for burial. USAMHI

battle of Antietam Charley was hit "through the body" by a shell fragment. Carried to the rear by his mates, he died three days later, on September 20, 1862, at the tender age of thirteen. (Frassanito, 192–195)

**The above photograph was taken at Antietam by whom, and why
was it important?**
Alexander Gardner. His photographs were the first-ever images that
showed dead soldiers on the battlefield. (Antietam)

Perryville

**The Perryville Campaign began when the Union Army of the Ohio
under Maj. Gen. Don Carlos Buell was directed to take what city?**
Chattanooga, Tennessee. The city was a vital rail junction and if the
city was under Federal control a move on Atlanta might be possible.

The area also held resources vital to the Confederate war effort such as coal, saltpeter, and lead. (Sanders, 7)

To combat Buell's movement, what did Confederate authorities do to meet it?
Gen. Braxton Bragg, after reorganizing his Confederate Army of the Mississippi, took his men to East Tennessee. It was a logistical feat, as the 30,000 infantry traveled by rail from Tupelo, Mississippi, to Montgomery, Alabama, and then northeast via Atlanta to Chattanooga, in total a 776-mile trip. Meanwhile the cavalry, artillery, and baggage moved across northern Alabama. By July 24, 1862, the lead elements of Bragg's army reached Chattanooga. (Sanders, 7)

As Bragg moved into Chattanooga, where were Buell and his army?
Parts were about thirty miles from Chattanooga, while a majority were in Nashville or scattered through middle Tennessee. (Sanders, 7)

What did Maj. Gen. E. Kirby Smith decide to do rather than hook up with Bragg and fight Buell at Nashville?
Invade Kentucky. Though Kentucky was primarily pro-Union, Smith thought that his move into the state would put a permanent presence there and that recruits would rally to the Confederate cause. Also, there were ample supplies of forage and horses, and if Lexington could be taken, there was a major supply depot there. (Sanders, 7)

Who was in overall command of the Confederate invasion?
No one. Bragg decided that he would also move into Kentucky, fearing that Smith might be cut off and destroyed. Though Bragg outranked Smith, President Davis refused to put him in overall command, so the two armies, Bragg's and Smith's, operated as independent commands. (Sanders, 8)

What did Buell do to counteract the Confederate movement into the Bluegrass State?
He also headed for Kentucky. Leaving Brig. Gen. James S. Nagley to guard Nashville, Buell moved north toward Bowling Green. He

wanted to protect the Louisville depot. Once in Louisville he added troops to his army and then sent 55,000 men after Bragg and another 20,000 against Smith. (Sanders, 8)

Whom did Braxton Bragg appoint the provisional governor of Kentucky at Frankfort on October 4?
Richard Hawes. (Sanders, 8)

Who were Bragg's two wing commanders?
Maj. Gen. William J. Hardee and Maj. Gen. Leonidas Polk. (Sanders, 9)

What were the opening shots of the battle of Perryville?
Col. Daniel McCook's brigade, trying to take Peter's Hill east of and overlooking Doctor's Fork, ran into an advance unit of Arkansas troops. After a sharp skirmish, the Confederates were pushed back and the green-scummed water of the creek was made available to the Yankees. (Sanders, 10)

What was the first major fighting at Perryville?
About 2:00 p.m., when Brig. Gen Daniel S. Donelson's Confederates attacked McCook's corps. Bragg had shifted his line north in an attempt to strike the Union left flank; unfortunately, Union reinforcements had also arrived, extending that line farther north. Thus when Donelson attacked, thinking he was going in on the flank of the Federals, he was moving more toward McCook's center. The result was that he got trapped in a crossfire. (Sanders, 14)

What relative of Robert E. Lee and Jeb Stuart was leading a Union infantry brigade that was protecting a rookie artillery battery?
Brig. Gen. William R. Terrill. A native Virginian, he had attended West Point, where he got in a fight with cadet Phil Sheridan when Sheridan attacked him with a bayonet. At the beginning of the war he remained loyal to the Union and was disowned by his family, his ex-relatives telling him that his name would be removed from the records. His brother was Confederate Brig. Gen. James B. Terrill. Late in the afternoon at Perryville, Terrill was wounded by a Confederate shell fragment and died later that night. (Sanders, 15; Faust, 748)

How did Bragg send his men into the battle?

En echelon. The first troops in were from "hard drinking fighting" Maj. Gen. B. Frank Cheatham's Division and included Tennessee and Georgia troops under Brig. Gen. Daniel S. Donelson, Brig. Gen. George E. Maney and Brig. Gen. Alexander Stewart. These Confederates attacked McCook's corps, going up against Terrill's and Col. John C. Starkweather's brigades. During the second phase of the Confederate attack, two brigades from Brig. Gen. Patton Anderson's division hit the Union brigades of Col. Leonard Harris and Col. William H. Lytle in the Federal center. The first brigade in was that of Col. Thomas Marshall Jones. Jones's men were followed by Col. John Calvin Brown's brigade and Brig. Gen. Sterling A. M. Wood. Finally, the Confederates attacked McCook's right with Maj. Gen. Simon B. Buckner's division. The first brigade to move forward was that of Brig. Gen. Bushrod R. Johnson, followed by those of Brig. Gen. Patrick R. Cleburne and Brig. Gen. Daniel W. Adams. Finally, the Confederate brigades of Brig. Gen. John R. Liddell and Brig. Gen. Sterling A. M. Wood moved against the Union brigade of Col. George P. Webster north of Cleburne's position. (Sanders, 20, 44–46)

What Union division had its entire upper-level command killed on the field?

The Tenth Division of the First Corps. This included the division commander, Brig. Gen. James S. Jackson, 33rd Brigade commander, Brig. Gen. William R. Terrill, and 34th Brigade commander, Col. George P. Webster. (Sanders, 21)

Why didn't the majority of the Federal troops participate in the battle of Perryville?

The phenomenon called an "acoustic shadow." Buell, sitting at his headquarters just a few miles from the fighting, only heard a few scattered shots, not the roar of nearly 40,000 men fighting for their lives. (Sanders, 47)

Who won the battle of Perryville?

Bragg and his Confederate Army of the Mississippi essentially won a tactical victory. Unfortunately, during the late evening of the battle, fresh

Union troops began reaching the battlefield; seeing that he was outnumbered, Bragg chose to abandon the field, thus giving the Union a strategic success. Then Bragg and Kirby Smith abandoned the Kentucky Bluegrass region, retreating and returning to Tennessee. (Sanders, 48)

What was the most lopsided Confederate victory of the Civil War?
The battle of Richmond, Kentucky, on August 29–30, 1862. The lead element of Maj. Gen. E. Kirby Smith's advance into Kentucky was Brig. Gen. Patrick Cleburne. Over the course of two days, Cleburne's men, later supported by more of Smith's column, fought Union troops commanded by Brig. Gen. Mahlon Dickerson Manson. The battle was in three stages, culminating in the fighting in Richmond, the Federal troops now under command of Maj. Gen. William Nelson. When the fighting ended, the Federals had been routed, suffering 206 killed, 844 wounded and 4,303 missing (most of them captured). Confederate casualties amounted to 78 killed, 372 wounded, and one missing. (Faust, 629–630; Sanders, 7–8)

Prairie Grove

Who commanded the opposing forces at the battle of Prairie Grove?
The Army of the Frontier (U.S.) was commanded by Brig. Gen. James G. Blunt in place of Maj. Gen. John M. Schofield, who was absent. The First Corps, Confederate Army of the Trans-Mississippi, was led by Maj. Gen. Thomas C. Hyndman. (Sallee, 25)

What were the opening shots of the battle?
Troops of the 7th and 8th Missouri Union cavalry were feeding their horses just south of Prairie Grove Church when they were attacked by Confederate partisans dressed in blue uniforms. The Confederates were led by Lt. William Gregg, who was commanding Quantrill's Guerrilla Company. (Sallee, 20)

What later outlaw rode with Gregg in the first attack at Prairie Grove?
Frank James, who later, with his brother Jesse, would become a legendary outlaw. (Sallee, 20)

What was the outcome of the battle?
It was tactically a draw; however, Hindman was forced to retreat because his supply trains were thirty miles south and he was out of ammunition, thus giving the Union a strategic success. (Sallee, 45)

Fredericksburg

What was Burnside's plan concerning the Army of Northern Virginia?
Move the Army of the Potomac to Fredericksburg, cross the Rappahannock River on pontoon bridges, and attack Lee's army somewhere between Fredericksburg and Richmond before moving on to the Confederate capital. (Catton, 255)

What happened to Burnside's plan?
It failed because the pontoons were late in arriving, and after they did reach Fredericksburg, Burnside did not immediately position them and cross the river. This allowed Lee to bring his army to the western outskirts of town.

A pontoon train was comprised of what?
Typically, thirty-four pontoon wagons carrying a pontoon and equipment such as ropes, oars, rowlock, boat hooks and an anchor. In other wagons were timbers, and those wagons also carried chains, cables, and cross planks. Four tool wagons carried such items as entrenching tools, carpenter's tools, and cordage. There would also be traveling forges with ironworking tools and spare iron. Lastly, there would also be supply wagons. (Coggins, 104)

When did Burnside start building his bridges across the Rappahannock River in front of Fredericksburg?
During the early morning hours of December 11, 1862. Two bridges would be thrown across opposite the city. It was the job of the 50th New York Engineers to build these. A third would be on the south end of town, near the city docks. A fourth span was to be erected about two miles south of the city, and this fell to the engineers of the 15th New York. Overlooking the river and Fredericksburg was Stafford Heights,

on which the Federals placed 147 cannon, then bumped the number up to 183. (O'Reilly, 9)

What Confederate units were in Fredericksburg, and who commanded them when Burnside started his crossing?
The Mississippi Brigade of Brig. Gen. William Barksdale. The general spread his men out instead of concentrating them, taking over houses that overlooked the crossing sites. The 17th Mississippi covered both the upper bridges. The 18th and 21st Mississippi guarded the basements of the middle crossing. The 13th Mississippi readied itself to help at the upper crossings. Later, the 8th Florida also became part of the defense, though their contributions were scant. At 5:00 a.m. the 17th fired its first volley at the 50th New York Engineers, clearing them off the half-completed bridge. This precipitated a flurry of artillery fire from Stafford Heights, but as soon as the guns stopped firing and the engineers returned to their work, the Confederate fire started again. Through much of the morning and early afternoon, this scenario was repeated several times. (O'Reilly, 9, 20)

Whose idea was it to put infantry in the pontoons and send them across the river to secure both sides so that the bridge-building could continue?
It may have been the engineers' idea, but it was Brig. Gen. Henry Hunt who suggested it to Burnside. Because such a maneuver had never been attempted, Burnside was hesitant but eventually he deferred to Hunt. (O'Reilly, 19)

What Union regiments were ferried across the Rappahannock to stop the Confederate fire?
The 89th New York crossed near the Middle Bridge while the 7th Michigan crossed at the upper bridges. Once they reached the town the Confederate fire slackened, and as more Federal troops crossed to back up the two regiments, the fighting became street to street and house to house. (O'Reilly, 20)

What was the Confederate defensive position west of Fredericksburg?
A series of hills and ridges extended south for eight miles above and below Fredericksburg. In the north directly behind the city was Mar-

ye's Heights. James Longstreet placed his First Corps along the first six miles of the ridges including Marye's Heights and Willis' Hill. Below the town was Prospect Hill. Here Stonewall Jackson placed his men along the last two miles of heights. While Jackson had to stack his troops into a defensive position, Longstreet's line was thinner but had the advantage of being naturally more defensible. (O'Reilly, 22)

What was Burnside's main focus in his attack on December 13?
The main assault would be on the Federal left, sending Burnside's Left Grand Division against Jackson. The Right Grand Division would attack Marye's Heights and Willis' Hill, but it was simply to keep Longstreet busy so that he would not reinforce Jackson. (O'Reilly, 22, 23)

How did Jackson align his men prior to the Federal attack on December 13, 1862?
His right flank was near Hamilton's Crossing and was manned by the division of Maj. Gen. A. P. Hill. To Hill's rear was the division of Maj. Gen. Daniel Harvey Hill. Ewell's division, under the command of Brig. Gen. Jubal Early, was to the northwest of A. P. Hill. Jackson's division, commanded by Brig. Gen. William B. Taliaferro, was on Early's left. Beginning at the Lansdowne Valley Road on Jackson's left was Longstreet's Corps. (O'Reilly, 132)

The 12-pounder Napoleon that Maj. John Pelham used to harass the Federal left flank near Hamilton's Crossing came from whose battery?
Capt. Mathis Henry's horse battery. They kept up their fire for almost an hour before falling back. (O'Reilly, 143, 148)

What name was given to Prospect Hill by many veterans?
"Dead Horse Hill." When R. Lindsay Walker brought his guns into action he sent his horses back into the woods for protection. Unfortunately, most of the Union shells missed the Confederate artillery line and sailed into the ravine containing the horses, many of which were killed. (O'Reilly, 155)

What Federal unit spearheaded the attack on Jackson's front?
Maj. Gen. George G. Meade's Third Division, comprising the Pennsylvania Reserves. Though hit by artillery fire from Pelham and a

14-gun battery on their front, the Reserves were eventually able to pierce Jackson's line. Luckily, they had hit a 600-yard gap in the Confederate line, an area of boggy forest that was poorly defended. Their stay there was short-lived, however, as Jackson brought up his reserves who hit the Pennsylvanians, driving them back across the railroad to the Richmond Stage Road. (Fredericksburg)

What was Gen. Lee's comment on the slaughter of Meade's and Gibbon's men in front of Prospect Hill?
Watching the carnage from Telegraph Hill, he commented to Gen. Longstreet, "It is well that war is so terrible, or we would grow too fond of it." (O'Reilly, 237)

Who commanded Burnside's Grand Divisions?
Maj. Gen. William B. Franklin commanded the Left Grand Division while Maj. Gen. Edwin V. "Bull" Sumner commanded the Right. The Center Grand Division was led by Maj. Gen. Joseph Hooker. (O'Reilly, 23)

What obstacles did Sumner's troops face in attacking Marye's Heights and Willis' Hill?
The area between the city and the heights was largely open. Centered in the attacking area was the town's fairgrounds, which was surrounded by a heavy plank fence. Though the Confederates had removed the western end of the fencing, the remaining three sides still stood in the attackers' way. On the extreme western side of the fields and at the base of Marye's Heights and Willis' Hill was a sunken road and stone wall. On the northern end of the city was a slack-water canal, which prohibited movement in that direction. To the south of the attack field was Hazel Run. These two boundaries left the attacking forces a narrow front. On the western side of the city there was also a sluiceway, fifteen feet wide and five feet deep, which was filled with three feet of water. Over this obstacle were the remnants of two bridges where attacking forces would tend to bunch up. Added to this there were only three streets exiting the city that attacking troops could use; William, Hanover, and Frederick. (O'Reilly, 23)

What was E. P. Alexander's comment to Gen. Longstreet when he questioned the number of guns on the Confederates' heights?
"A chicken could not live on that field when we open on it." (O'Reilly, 42)

Who were the first Federals to attack Marye's Heights?
The brigade of Brig. Gen. Nathan Kimball, of Brig. Gen. William H. French's Division, of Maj. Gen. Darius N. Couch's Second Corps. They were followed by Col. John W. Andrews's brigade and finally Col. Oliver H. Palmer's brigade, likewise of French's Division. (O'Reilly, 23)

Who commanded the Confederate troops shielded by the stone wall at Fredericksburg?
Col. Thomas R. R. Cobb. Late in the day, Cobb was hit in the thigh by a musket ball and bled to death despite medical help. (Faust, 147)

What was the result of French's attack?
It was doomed from the start, lasted less than one hour, and caused a 25 percent loss in killed and wounded. (O'Reilly, 43)

What troops followed French in the attack against the heights?
Brig. Gen. Winfield Scott Hancock's Division. The first brigade forward was that of Col. Samuel K. Zook and they followed directly in French's path. When Zook was repulsed, Hancock shifted the rest of the division north to George Street. Brig. Gen. Thomas F. Meagher's Irish Brigade was the next unit to attack, followed by Brig. Gen. John C. Caldwell.

What did Brig. Gen. Thomas Meagher do with the boxwood he took from a Fredericksburg house's garden?
He distributed it to the members of his Irish Brigade. Each man took a sprig of the boxwood and placed it in his hat to denote his Irish heritage and membership in the Irish Brigade.

What regiment reputedly made it closest to the stone wall in front of Marye's Heights and Willis' Hill at Fredericksburg?
One of the regiments of the Irish Brigade (probably the 88th New York). Some sources indicate that it could have been Maj. William

Horgan and his adjutant John R. Young, who were killed within yards of the wall. Exactly which Irish regiment made it closest will probably never be known, but men with boxwood sprigs in their hats got very near it. Other sources say that the men of Humphreys' Division got as close to the wall as any other Union soldiers. (O'Reilly, 45, 48)

What was the outcome of Hancock's attack?
It was the same as that of French. Hancock lost 2,000 of his 5,500 men. Meagher's Irish brigade alone lost 545 out of 1,200.

Who followed Hancock into the tempest?
Brig. Gen. O. O. Howard's Division, supported by Brig. Gen. Samuel D. Sturgis's Division of the Ninth Corps. (O'Reilly, 45)

Once the Second Corps and that portion of the Ninth Corps involved had basically ceased to exist as effective combat units, what commands did Burnside throw against the stone wall?
Hooker's Grand Division, composed of the Third and Fifth Corps. Only one brigade of the Third Corps, Col. Samuel Sprigg Carroll's, would attack Marye's Heights and Willis' Hill. The First Division of the Fifth Corps, Brig, Gen. Charles Griffin, sent in his three brigades, Col. James Barnes, Col. Jacob Sweitzer and Col. Thomas B. W. Stockton. (O'Reilly, 47)

Who was the highest-ranking Federal officer wounded in the attacks on Marye's Heights?
Brig. Gen. Charles Griffin received a slight wound. (O'Reilly, 47)

Who followed Griffin's Division into the fighting?
The green Third Division of Brig. Gen. A. A. Humphreys. (O'Reilly, 47)

Who led the final assault on the stone wall on December 13?
Col. Rush C. Hawkins, leading the First Brigade, Third Division of the Ninth Corps. (O'Reilly, 48)

What did Burnside gain by attacking Marye's Heights and Willis' Hill?
Nothing. Over the course of six hours he had sent close to 35,000 men against the heights, who suffered 8,000 casualties. As one Pennsylvanian commented, "The ground, as far as the eye could reach, was thickly strewn with the dead and dying. . . ." On the Confederate side, Longstreet engaged some 5,000 men and took only 1,000 casualties. (O'Reilly, 48)

A Confederate soldier entering what city commented, "It seems very strange to see a deserted town, with nothing but corpses of the dead men and horses for inhabitants"?
Fredericksburg, Virginia, following the battle. (Catton, 264)

What did one lone 88th New York soldier say to his division commander during an inspection following the battle of Fredericksburg, when told to join his company?
"I am my company." (Davis, 175)

What happened to the USS *Cairo* on December 12, 1862?
It became the first warship to be sunk by a mine during combat. Steaming up the Yazoo River, the ship struck two torpedoes and went down in twelve minutes, with no loss of life. (Henig, 119–120)

Who was in command of the USS *Cairo* when she was sunk?
Lt. Cmdr. Thomas Selfridge. (Henig, 119)

What were the four major battles fought in Kentucky during the war?
Mill Springs (January 19, 1862); Munfordville (September 14–17, 1862); Richmond (August 30, 1862); and Perryville (October 8, 1862).

What two ships did Jeb Stuart's men destroy during his ride around McClellan?
The *Island City* and *Whitman Phillips* at Garlick's Landing along the Pamunkey River. The *D. A. Berry*, which was also tied up at the landing,

managed to cut her mooring lines and drift out into the river at the approach of the Confederates. (Mewborn, 19)

What battle, fought on April 15, 1862, was the only Civil War engagement in the present-day state of Arizona?
Picacho Pass. Troops of the Confederate Army of New Mexico under Capt. Sherod Hunter clashed with Unionist California cavalry. (Kliger, 13)

What hollow victory was won by Brig. Gen. Sibley on February 21, 1862?
The battle of Valverde, New Mexico Territory. Union commander Edward Canby attacked the Confederate position north of Ft. Craig. Though it seemed initially to be a Union victory, an attack from the Confederate left captured a Federal battery. New Mexico and U.S. Regular troops under Canby fled and forced the colonel to take his men back to the fort. Unfortunately, the Confederates had lost over 200 casualties and a number of wagons and supplies as well as their beef cattle. (Kliger, 18)

Who commanded the Union and Confederate forces at the battle of Apache Canyon, the opening action of the battle of Glorieta Pass?
Confederate: Maj. Charles L. Pyron. Union: Maj. John M. Chivington. (Kliger, 49)

What was the outcome of the battle of Apache Canyon?
The Union forces under Chivington managed to push the Confederates back with a loss of only nineteen men. The Confederates, on the other hand, suffered ninety-four casualties. (Kliger, 50)

Who commanded the two forces at the battle of Glorieta Pass?
Union: Col. John P. Slough. Confederate: Col. William R. "Dirty Shirt" Scurry. (Kliger, 52)

What was the outcome of the battle of Glorieta Pass?
The Confederates initially were successful, pushing Slough's troops back; however, the Union colonel had sent Chivington and his men

around to the rear of the Confederate line where they fell on the Rebel supply wagons at Johnson's Ranch. Chivington's men burned the supplies and the wagons. Some sources indicate that the men also destroyed 500 to 600 horses and mules, but there is no direct evidence of this. Because of the loss of their supplies, the Confederates were forced to retreat, eventually moving back to Texas. (Kliger, 52–56: Faust, 422–423)

When and where did the battle of Secessionville take place?
On June 16, 1862, on James Island, south of Charleston, South Carolina. (Faust, 664)

Who were the army commanders at the battle of Secessionville?
Brig. Gen. Henry W. Benham commanded the Union troops while Brig. Gen. Nathan G. Evans led the Confederates. Ft. Lamar at Secessionville, which was the focus of the Union attack, was defended by Col. Thomas G. Lamar. (Faust, 664)

What was the outcome of the Federal attack at Secessionville?
The Union attack was repelled, with losses approaching 700 men. Confederate casualties were only 200. (Faust, 664)

What happened to Gen. Benham following the battle of Secessionville?
He was charged with disobedience of orders (he had been ordered not to initiate a battle). Confirmation of his general's commission was revoked by President Lincoln. Lincoln subsequently canceled the revocation and Benham returned to duty. (Faust, 664)

Stones River (Murfreesboro), December 31, 1862

Who were the army commanders at the battle of Stones River (Murfreesboro), Tennessee, December 31, 1862–January 2, 1863?
Union Army of the Cumberland: Maj. Gen. William S. Rosecrans. Confederate Army of Tennessee: Gen. Braxton Bragg. (Cozzens, 219, 227)

At Stones River, who commanded the Army of the Cumberland's three wings?

Center wing: Maj. Gen. George Thomas. Right wing: Maj. Gen. Alexander McD. McCook. Left wing: Maj. Gen. Thomas Leonidas Crittenden. (Spearman, 11)

The Army of the Cumberland contained how many men?

Almost 65,000, though 5,300 of that number were on extended garrison duty in Nashville. At the battle of Stones River, Rosecrans fielded about 47,000 men. (Cozzens, 21; Faust, 722)

Who led the two corps of the Army of Tennessee?

Polk's Corps: Lt. Gen. Leonidas Polk, Hardee's Corps: Lt. Gen. William J. Hardee. (Cozzens, 227, 228)

How many men did Gen. Bragg have in his Army of Tennessee?

Approximately 38,000. (Faust, 722)

For what action was Capt. Milton T. Russel awarded the Medal of Honor at Stones River?

Russel was the captain of Co. A, 51st Indiana Infantry. On the night of December 29, 1862, he was ordered to take his company across an unknown ford and determine the enemy's strength on the other side. Just as his company approached the enemy side of the river, Confederates delivered a "terrific volley" from behind a rail fence. Luckily for Russel and his men the Rebs fired high, and the volley hit the company's supports on the other side. Russel had to make a quick decision; retreat, or move forward. Thinking the enemy now had empty rifles Russel ordered his men to charge the Confederate position. The Yankees fired a volley, then fixed bayonets and ran forward, driving the Confederates back some 400 yards. For his quick thinking, Russel received his medal. (Spearman, 14)

What was the outcome of the first day of fighting at Stones River?

The Confederates had won the day by pushing Rosecrans's army back and into a line along the Old Nashville Pike whose left curved around toward Stones River. The day did end with the distinction of being the bloodiest single day of the war in Tennessee. (Spearman, 38, 39)

What was the fate of Brig. Gen. Joshua Woodrow Sill during the first day's fighting?
He was killed while trying to repulse a Confederate attack. Ft. Sill in Indian Territory was named for him. (Faust, 690)

Eli Lilly, who organized the 18th Battery, Indiana Artillery, in 1862, is better known for what business?
Lilly, despite having little military training, became an able leader, eventually reaching the rank of colonel. After the war he founded a small pharmaceutical company that today is one of the world's largest corporations, Eli Lilly and Company. (Mark Hughes, 15)

What happened in Munfordville, Kentucky, between September 14 and 17, 1862?
Near Munfordville, the Louisville & Nashville Railroad crossed the Green River. It was guarded by an earthen-bastioned Ft. Craig on the south side of the river and a blockhouse, garrisoned by three Indiana regiments and four cannon commanded by Col. John T. Wilder. Gen. Braxton Bragg, during his invasion of Kentucky, sent Brig. Gen. James R. Chalmers's Mississippi Brigade and Col. John S. Scott's First Louisiana Cavalry to Munfordville to destroy the bridge. When Wilder refused Chalmers's demand for surrender, the Confederate commander sent three of his regiments against Ft. Craig and two regiments against the blockhouse. The Confederates were repulsed, losing 228 men to the Federals' thirty-seven. That night the Confederates once again asked the Federals to surrender, and once again they were turned down. The situation became a siege for the rest of that day and the next. On September 15, Bragg arrived with his main force and prepared to attack but was talked out of it by one of his division commanders, Maj. Gen. Simon B. Buckner, who was a native of the area and worried for the safety of the local citizens. Finally, after meeting with Buckner, who showed him some of the Confederate lines, Wilder thought it best to surrender. The Federals surrendered on the morning of September 17, were disarmed and paroled, and sent back to Union lines. (Faust, 517–518)

EVENTS

On the first of January, Mason and Slidell were released and continued on to England on what ship?
The sloop-of-war HMS *Rinaldo*. (Denney, 107)

Which side enacted the first conscription law in American history?
The Confederate Congress, on April 16, 1862. (Catton, 141)

On what date was the preliminary Emancipation Proclamation issued?
September 22, 1862. The Emancipation Proclamation became "law" on January 1, 1863, and indicated that slaves in the rebellious sections of the country should be free. (Catton, 248; Faust, 242)

What Union ship was lost just after midnight on December 30, 1862?
The USS *Monitor*, which sank off the coast of Cape Hatteras, North Carolina. (Denney, 248)

When was the first Federal income tax signed into law?
Though a bill was signed levying a tax on personal and corporate incomes in 1861, it never went into operation. Rather, in early 1862, a bill was introduced to Congress that would impose a three percent tax on yearly incomes of between $600 and $10,000 and five percent on higher incomes. Passed by Congress, it was signed into law by President Lincoln on July 1, 1862. The tax was amended in 1864, placing a tax rate of five percent on incomes of $600 to $5,000. In 1872 the tax was repealed and ruled unconstitutional. (Faust, 380)

MISCELLANEOUS

What was the purpose of Lincoln's General War Order No. 1, dated January 27, 1862?
The order declared that on February 22, 1862, all land and sea forces would attack the Confederates. It was basically a desperation move to get McClellan to do something. (Denney, 118)

On January 31, 1862, Lincoln issued a supplement to his General War Order No. 1, directing George McClellan to take action against Manassas on or before February 22, 1862. What was McClellan's response?

He ignored it. (Denney, 118)

How did Pea Ridge Mountain, near the Pea Ridge, Arkansas, battlefield, get its name?

It was named for a variety of pea vines that once grew in the area. (Hughes, 8)

What did President Lincoln tell the King of Siam regarding the offer of war elephants to the Union Army?

"That the weather 'does not reach a latitude so low as to favor the multiplication of the elephant.'" (Denney, 121)

Where was "Willie" Lincoln buried and what eventually happened to him?

President Lincoln's son was buried in Oak Hill Cemetery in Washington, D.C. Following the president's assassination, Willie's body was taken to Springfield and buried with that of his father.

What Confederate commerce raider, after a short but successful career, was abandoned by Capt. Raphael Semmes and its crew in Gibraltar?

The CSS *Sumter*. Unfixable boiler problems were the cause. (Denney, 159)

What song did Lincoln think belonged to the Union by right of capture?

"Dixie." (Allen Guelzo, Gettysburg, PA)

What was the Dix-Hill Cartel?

A system set up to exchange prisoners. If Union troops captured twenty Confederates and the Confederates captured twenty Yankees, they would exchange the men of equal rank. It also set up a system of exchange for different ranks, such as one lieutenant for two privates or one general for sixty privates. If one side still had prisoners after the exchange, the extra men would sign paroles and agree not to fight until properly exchanged later. The system worked well for about a year until disputes began concerning troops going back into combat before they were properly exchanged and over fallout from the Emancipation Proclamation and black troops. (Davis, 443, 444)

What Federal prisoner-of-war camp had the highest mortality rate?
Some authorities indicate that it was Ft. Delaware on Pea Patch Island in the Delaware River south of Philadelphia. It was, however, Elmira in northwest New York State. (Davis, 451–452)

Following the evacuation of the Gosport Naval Yard, what happened to the CSS *Virginia*?
Having no home port and a draft too deep for the James River, on May 11 she was blown up by her crew off Craney Island in the Elizabeth River. (Denney, 168)

What was General Lee's favorite horse?
Traveller (spelled with two l's), pictured on page 111. Traveller, originally named "Jeff Davis," was raised in Greenbrier County in what is now West Virginia. Lee first became acquainted with the horse in the fall of 1861 and immediately took a liking to him. While serving in South Carolina in 1862 he again met the mount and borrowed him from the owner to see how the two suited each other. The owner of the horse offered to give Lee the mount but he refused and paid the owner $200 in February 1862. From that time until Lee's death, the two were constant companions. Traveller was iron-gray with black points, a long mane and flowing tail. He was sixteen hands tall, with a muscular figure, deep chest, short back, strong haunches, flat legs, a small head, quick eyes, broad forehead and small feet. The horse had a gait that many of Lee's aides found hard to keep up with. (Magner, 4–5)

What happened to the steamer *Planter*?
The steamer was in Charleston, South Carolina, and was manned by an all–African American crew. On the night of May 13, 1862, the

Robert E. Lee and Traveller. NA

ship's captain went ashore. The crew then sailed the ship out of the harbor and surrendered to the USS *Onward.* (Denney, 169)

What ship, launched on May 10, 1862, was considered to be one of the most powerful ships in the United States Navy?
The USS *New Ironsides.* She was built in Philadelphia, Pennsylvania, and was classified as a steam frigate. She carried sixteen 11-inch Dahlgrens. She first joined the South Atlantic Blockading Squadron, where she became the flagship of Rear Adm. Samuel F. Du Pont. In one engagement off of Charleston, South Carolina, the ship was struck fifty times but suffered no damage. In August 1864 she joined the North Atlantic Blockading Squadron, where she participated in the taking of Ft. Fisher. (Faust, 525; Fonvielle, 48)

What five Union ships made up the James River flotilla, and who commanded it?
The USS *Monitor, Galena, Aroostook, Port Royal* and *Naugatuck.* The flotilla was commanded by Commander John Rodgers. (Denney, 170, 171)

In May 1862, how close was the James River flotilla able to get to Richmond before being turned back by river obstructions and fire from Drewry's Bluff?
Eight miles. (Denney, 171)

What ship known as hull "290" was launched from the Laird Shipyards in Birkenhead, England, on May 15, 1862?
The *Enrica*, later to be recommissioned the CSS *Alabama.* (Faust, 3)

What was the Homestead Act, which President Lincoln signed into law on May 20, 1862?
It guaranteed 160 acres of public land to anyone who would settle on it and make improvements for five years. Many Civil War veterans took advantage of this to settle in the West. (Denney, 173)

Where did Stuart's men cross the Chickahominy on their ride around McClellan?
Jones or Forge Bridge just north of Charles City Court House. (Mewborn, 11)

On July 14, 1862, due to an act passed by Congress, what staple of the U.S. Navy was eliminated?
The daily ration of rum. Now they would get an extra five cents per day in their pay. (Denney, 193)

What were the CSS *Alabama*'s first five victims?
The *Ocumulgee, Starlight, Ocean Rover, Alert,* and *Weather Gauge.* (Denney, 209, 210)

What were "90-Day Gunboats?"
These were 507-ton steam-powered, shallow-draft craft used by the Federals for blockading southern ports. They were called 90-Day because from keel laying to commissioning took only three months. (Catton, 157)

What does the word Antietam mean, as in Antietam Creek?
It is a Native American word that translates into "the swift current." (Frye, 1)

What was the first monument dedicated at Antietam?
The "Private Soldier" in the Antietam National Cemetery was dedicated on September 17, 1880. (Frye, 168)

Where did Abraham Lincoln write most of the first draft of the Emancipation Proclamation?
In the military telegraph office where he waited for news from the war front. (Catton, 249)

How many slaves did the Emancipation Proclamation free?
Basically none, because it proclaimed the freedom of slaves in areas of the United States where the Washington government had no jurisdiction. (Catton, 248)

How did the Emancipation Proclamation change the face of the war?
By issuing the Proclamation, Lincoln changed the focus of the war from simply reuniting the Union to freeing the slaves.

Before the Civil War, what weapon did Ambrose Burnside invent?
The Burnside Carbine, a breech-loading carbine. The venture to produce the weapon for use by the military was a failure. (Warner, 57)

What was the name of the first cruiser constructed overseas for the Confederacy?
The CSS *Florida*. (Faust, 264)

Who initially commanded the CSS *Florida*?
Lt. John N. Maffitt. (Faust, 264)

What was the ultimate fate of the CSS *Florida*?
After capturing thirty-seven vessels she went into port in Bahia, Brazil, where she tied up near the USS *Wachusett*, where her crew thought her safe due to the rules of international warfare. Instead, the *Wachusett* rammed her and towed her to sea and eventually to Newport News, Virginia, where, under questionable circumstances, she was rammed and sunk. (Faust, 264)

Where was Ft. Darling?
The fort was located on Drewry's Bluff along the James River south of Richmond. Hastily constructed on May 12, 1862, it protected the Confederate capital from naval attack until the end of the war. (Boatner, 292)

Who was GATH?
George Alfred Townsend, who was to become the youngest war correspondent of the Civil War. He signed his reports with the pen name GATH. President Lincoln reportedly once commented regarding whether or not he should visit a battlefield, "No, it is not necessary for me to go there. George Alfred Townsend has been there." (Magner, 69)

Who was the first African American to become a military chaplain?
William Jackson, a Baptist minister attached to the 55th Massachusetts. (Henig, 62)

Which Union brigadier general shot and mortally wounded a major general on September 29, 1862?
Brig. Gen. Jefferson C. Davis had words with his commanding officer, Maj. Gen. William Nelson, in the Gault House in Louisville, Kentucky. Nelson slapped Davis and started to leave the hotel; meanwhile, Davis got a revolver and returned, then he shot Nelson. Davis was never punished for the murder and soon returned to duty. (Boatner, 226)

What was the Kearny Medal?

In November 1862, following the death of Maj. Gen. Philip Kearny, the officers of his former command adopted a gold medal in honor of the general. It was to be awarded to officers who had bravely served under Kearny. The medal was a Maltese Cross superimposed with a circle containing the words *Dulce et decorum est pro patria mori* and the name Kearny in the disk's center. There were about 317 of the medals awarded. (Boatner, 449)

What was the Kearny Cross?

David Bell Birney, who succeeded Kearny, determined that a "cross of valor" be given to any enlisted man who had distinguished himself in battle. The medal was a "bronze cross pattee with 'Kearny Cross' on the front and 'Birney's Division' on the back." Two of the first recipients of the Kearny Cross were vivandieres Ann Etheridge and Marie Tebe. (Boatner, 449)

Who were the Loudoun Rangers?

A Union force of Germans recruited northwest of Leesburg, Virginia, in June 1862. It was an independent command that subsequently was ordered to pursue Mosby's Partisan Rangers. Unfortunately they were no more successful in capturing Mosby than was the rest of the Federal Army. (Boatner, 493)

What is the "twenty Negro law" passed in October 1862 by the Confederate government?

A law whereby on any plantation owning twenty or more slaves, one overseer or owner would be exempt from military service. The law was eliminated in December 1863, but two months later was reviewed and changed from twenty to fifteen slaves in hopes of placating smaller plantation owners. (Henig, 41)

Who was the first rabbi to be commissioned a U.S. military chaplain?

Jacob Frankel of Philadelphia's Rodeph Shalom Congregation. Ultimately there were three rabbis who became military chaplains during the Civil War. (Henig, 61)

What bugle call did Brig. Gen. Daniel Butterfield compose while at Harrison's Landing?
Taps.

What was the name of the first bugler to play Taps?
Oliver W. Norton of the 83rd Pennsylvania. (Henig, 66)

What name did Lincoln give the Army of the Potomac following the battle of Antietam and McClellan's reluctance to move against Lee?
"Gen. McClellan's bodyguard." (Denney, 221)

What was Lincoln's reply to Horace Greeley's open letter to the president published in the August 20, 1862, issue of the New York Tribune?
Lincoln said, "My paramount object in this struggle is to save the Union, and is not either to save or to destroy slavery. If I could save the Union without freeing any slave I would do it, and if I could save it by freeing all the slaves I would do it; and if I could save it by freeing some and leaving others alone, I would also do that." (Catton, 477; Holzer and Shenk, 99)

What was the Second Confiscation Act of 1862?
This act, signed into law by President Lincoln on July 17, 1862, contained the first definite provisions for the emancipation of the slaves in the Confederacy. Any Confederate who did not surrender within sixty days would have his slaves freed. It also stated that any slaves who took refuge behind Union lines were to be freed. (Faust, 157)

What was a Corps Badge?
Corps badges were originally ordered by Maj. Gen. Philip Kearny when he mistakenly reprimanded officers who were not part of his command. To avoid the mistake again Kearny had his men sew two-inch-square red patches to the tops of their kepis. The patch became a mark of pride for the troops. After Maj. Gen. Joseph Hooker took over command of the Army of the Potomac in 1862, he had the badges assigned to the army

in order to boost sagging morale. Each division of a corps was assigned a color: red for the First Division; white for the Second; and blue for the Third. The badges came in different shapes for the different corps: a circle for the First Corps; trefoil for the Second Corps; and diamond for the Third Corps, for example. (Faust, 183, 184)

What was the "Ram Fleet"?
Following the destruction caused by the CSS *Virginia*, Secretary of War Edwin Stanton sent Charles Ellet Jr. (a civil engineer) west to create a "Ram Fleet" out of nine old steamboats. Ellet completed the task in fifty days. On June 6, 1862, two vessels of the ram fleet (*Queen of the West* and *Monarch*) engaged the Confederate Defense Fleet just above Memphis, Tennessee. Most of the Confederate fleet was either sunk or forced to flee or surrender, whereupon the city of Memphis surrendered to the ram fleet. During the fighting Ellet was hit in the leg by a pistol bullet and died two weeks later. (Magner, 15)

Who was Charles Rivers Ellet and for what act of bravery is he known?
Charles Rivers Ellet was the son of Charles Ellet Jr., builder of the Mississippi Ram Fleet. Following the surrender of Memphis, Tennessee, son Charles, at great personal risk, raised the Union flag over the city. A few months later he was promoted to colonel at only nineteen. He was reputed to be the youngest person to hold that rank in Federal service. (Magner, 16)

The Great Locomotive Chase

Who was the leader of the Union soldiers who stole a train in Big Shanty, Georgia, on April 12, 1862, and rode into history?
James J. Andrews, a little-known "spy," from what is now West Virginia. (Bogle, 11)

What was Andrews's goal in stealing the train?
His plan was to destroy the bridges along the Western & Atlantic Railroad, thus isolating Chattanooga from Atlanta. (Bogle, 11)

Who comprised Andrews's party?
Andrews and a civilian volunteer, William Campbell, plus twenty-two volunteers from Col. Joshua W. Sill's Ohio units. Nineteen men ultimately boarded the train, two having been forced to enlist in the Confederate army to avoid discovery and two others having missed their wakeup call. (Bogle, 11–13)

What was the name of the train locomotive stolen by Andrews and his men?
The *General*.

Who were the crew of the *General* when it left for its run on April 12, 1862?
Jeff Cain was the engineer, Andrew J. Anderson was the fireman, and the conductor was William A. Fuller. (Bogle, 12)

What was the name of the raider who became the *General*'s engineer?
William J. Knight. (Bogle, 14)

Once the *General* had left Big Shanty, who were the Confederates who chased it, and how?
Conductor William A. Fuller, engineer Jeff Cain, and Anthony Murphy, Superintendent of Motive Power, Western & Atlantic Railroad. They chased the engine first on foot, then they got a platform car, which was propelled by poles and kicking the railroad ties. (Bogle, 19)

What engines did the pursuers take at Etowah bridge?
First the *Yonah* and then at Kingston they commandeered the *William R. Smith*. They completed their chase using the *Texas*. (Bogle, 14, 22)

Where did the Great Locomotive Chase end?
About two miles north of Ringgold, Georgia. (Bogle, 47)

What was the fate of Andrews's raiders?
Eight were hanged: James J. Andrews, William H. Campbell, Samuel Robertson, Marion A. Ross, John N. Scott, Philip G. Shadrach,

Samuel Slavens, and George D. Wilson. Six were exchanged and eight escaped. (Bogle, 53)

Which six members of Andrews's raiding party were the first to receive the Medal of Honor?
William Pittenger, Jacob Parrott, William H. Reddick, Robert Buffum, William Bensinger, and Elihu H. Mason. All the raiders who were soldiers, except two, eventually received the medal. Andrews and Campbell were not given the award because they were civilians. (Bogle, 54)

Units

What regiment received its baptism by fire and was slaughtered after crossing and then seeking to recross the Potomac River at Boteler's Ford near Shepherdstown, Virginia, on September 20, 1862, following the battle of Antietam?
The 118th Pennsylvania—the Corn Exchange Regiment.

Who commanded the Irish Brigade on the Peninsula Campaign, Second Manassas Campaign, at Antietam and then Fredericksburg and Chancellorsville?
Brig. Gen Thomas Francis Meagher.

What regiments made up the Excelsior Brigade?
The 70th, 71st, 72nd, 73rd, 74th, and 120th New York. Although most soldiers enlisted in regiments that were later formed into brigades, the Excelsior Brigade was recruited as a brigade. The unit was raised by Daniel E. Sickles, who led it during the fighting at Seven Pines and the Seven Days' Battles. It was then led by various commanders until 1864, when it was disbanded because four of its regiments did not reenlist. (Faust, 250)

What was unique about the 15th Pennsylvania Cavalry at the battle of Stones River?
The 15th, known as the Anderson Troop, was made up of Pennsylvania "elite." They were formed expecting to serve as Gen. Don Carlos

120 THE CIVIL WAR QUIZ BOOK

Buell's personal escort. Unfortunately, when they got to Nashville, they found out that they were there to fight. When the regiment marched toward Murfreesboro, many of the green troops refused to go, so the unit's commander, Maj. Adolph G. Rosengarten, moved forward with only 200 men. In a skirmish with the 10th and 19th Consolidated South Carolina Infantry, the 15th was bloodied, losing Maj. Rosengarten (killed) and the second-in-command, Maj. Frank B. Ward (mortally wounded). Maj. Rosengarten is buried in Laurel Hill Cemetery in Philadelphia, Pennsylvania. (Spearman, 16; Magner, 78)

What regiment replaced the 29th Massachusetts in the Irish Brigade in November 1862?
The predominantly Irish 28th Massachusetts replaced the mostly Congregationalist/Yankee 29th.

What regiments made up the Stonewall Brigade?
The 2nd, 4th, 5th, 27th, and 33rd Virginia Infantry and the Rockbridge Artillery. By the end of the war, of the approximately 8,100 men who had served in the ranks, more than 1,000 had died. In total eight men commanded the brigade during the course of the war. (Wert, 32, 312–313)

Who were the commanders of the Stonewall Brigade?
Brig. Gen. Thomas J. Jackson (mortally wounded at Chancellorsville); Brig. Gen. Richard B. Garnett (killed at Gettysburg); Brig. Gen. Charles S. Winder (killed at Cedar Mountain); Col. William S. H. Baylor (killed at Second Manassas); Col. Andrew J. Grigsby; Brig. Gen. Elisha F. Paxton (killed at Chancellorsville); Brig. Gen. James A. Walker; and Brig. Gen. William Terry. (Wert, 321)

Who reputedly gave Gibbon's Western Brigade the nom de guerre "Iron Brigade"?
As early as September 14, 1862, General Gibbon was calling his men "my Iron Brigade." But the best evidence points to General McClellan conferring the name "Iron Brigade" on the unit. Brigade commander Gibbon, in his postwar writing, indicates he does not know where the name came from but it was in use after the battle of Antietam. (Wert, 188–189)

What was the fate of the 5th New York Infantry at the Second Battle of Manassas?
During Longstreet's attack on August 30, the 5th was hit by Hood's men. The regiment was pushed back and when they finally rallied on Henry Hill, only 60 of them found their colors. The regiment went into the battle with 490 men and suffered 297 casualties. The 5th New York sustained the highest number of casualties of any regiment during the battle. (Hennessy, 52; Fox, 191, 421)

At Antietam, what Federal regiment went the farthest on the Union left but was forced back with 64 percent casualties?
Hawkins Zouaves, the 9th New York. The men came closer to Sharpsburg and Lee's headquarters than any other regiment that day, being driven back by the arrival of A. P. Hill's troops. The regiment wore traditional Zouave dress, the uniforms having been tailored at Brooks Brothers. (Davis, 154–155)

What were two of the best-known Confederate Zouave regiments?
The First Louisiana Special Battalion, also known as Wheat's Tigers; and the First Battalion, Louisiana Zouaves or Coppens' Zouaves. Though their uniforms were not as gaudy as those of many Union regiments, the men who made up the units were just as undisciplined. (Davis, 156–158)

What unit was known as the "Graybeard" Regiment?
The 37th Iowa Volunteer Infantry. The regiment was raised by George W. Kincaid for three years and consisted of men over the age of 45. It ultimately boasted some of the oldest men in active service, including one 80-year-old. In December 1862, nine hundred and fourteen officers and men were mustered into service, and upon discharge in May 1865 there were still 460 names on the rolls. Their duty consisted of garrison, prison, and guard duties, and they served at Alton Prison in Illinois, Rock Island Prison in Mississippi, and Camp Morton, Ohio. They also rode guard on the Memphis & Charleston Railroad. (Faust, 321–322)

What regiment was made up of Danes, Swedes, and Norwegians?
The 15th Wisconsin, commanded by Hans Christian Heg. (Sifakis, 191)

Who sponsored the 40th New York Volunteers (the Mozart Regiment)?
Former New York City mayor Fernando Wood. (Livingston, 22)

What was the 51st New York Infantry also known as?
The "Shepard Rifles." Organized between July 27 and October 23, 1861, the regiment served on Burnside's Carolina Expedition, the Second Manassas Campaign, South Mountain, Antietam (where it participated in the capture of Rohrbach's Bridge), Vicksburg, The Wilderness, Spotsylvania, North Anna, Petersburg, and the Appomattox Campaign. (Dyer, 1591)

What regiment contained the tallest troops at the battle of Antietam?
The 27th Indiana. Fifty men who were six feet or taller were killed or wounded during the fighting of September 17. (Frye, 87)

At the battle of Antietam, what was the smallest brigade in the Army of the Potomac?
Stainrook's brigade, whose three regiments, the 3rd Maryland, 102nd New York, and 111th Pennsylvania, totaled only 523 men. (Frye, 90)

What was the 1st Tennessee known as?
The "Hogdrivers." (O'Reilly, 183)

∽ CHAPTER 4 ℃

1863

PERSONALITIES

In August 1863, whom did Jefferson Davis name as the second quartermaster general of the Confederacy?
Brig. Gen. Alexander R. Lawton, whose state troops had seized Ft. Pulaski on June 3, 1861. Though energetic and resourceful, he could not overcome the problems that plagued his department. (Faust, 427)

Who was Lt. Col. Charles Hale Morgan?
Beginning on January 1, 1863, he became Maj. Gen. Winfield Scott Hancock's chief of staff. He served with the general until the end of the war, including Hancock's time with the Veteran Reserve Corps and while Hancock was in the Middle Military Division. (Faust, 509)

What ship did the former USS *Monitor* captain command after he left the "cheesebox on a raft"?
The USS *Montauk*. (Denney, 258)

Ambrose Burnside was replaced by which Union general on January 26, 1863?
Maj. Gen. Joseph Hooker.

Name the two Union captains and one first lieutenant promoted to brigadier general on June 29, 1863?
Captains Elon J. Farnsworth and Wesley Merritt. First Lt. George Armstrong Custer was also promoted.

Who commanded the Iron Brigade before being wounded at Gettysburg?
Brig. Gen. Solomon "Long Sol" Meredith.

Following the battle of Gettysburg, whom did Gen. Meade make his chief of staff with the rank of major general?
Andrew Atkinson Humphreys. (Faust, 375)

Who was Charlie Hart?
The alias of William C. Quantrill. (Boatner, 381)

Who commanded the 54th Massachusetts, and what was his fate?
Col. Robert Gould Shaw. He was killed during the assault on Ft. Wagner near Charleston on July 18, 1863. Despised by the Confederates for leading African American troops, Shaw was buried on the beach with the other dead of his command. (Faust, 673)

Who commanded the CSS *Alabama*?
Capt. Raphael Semmes. Late in the war he was also given the rank of brigadier general, though this was never confirmed by the Confederate congress. His distant cousin, Paul Jones Semmes, was a brigade commander who was mortally wounded at Gettysburg on July 2, 1863. (Faust, 666–667)

Who commanded the Confederate troops at Vicksburg, and from what eastern city did he hail?
Lt. Gen. John C. Pemberton, who was born in and after the war lived near Philadelphia, Pennsylvania. He is interred in Laurel Hill Cemetery in that city. (Faust, 569; Magner, 43)

Who was the "Drummer Boy of Chickamauga"?
John Lincoln "Johnny" Clem. Johnny ran away from home in 1861 at the age of nine. After being turned down by one regiment he attached himself to the 22nd Michigan, acting as a drummer boy. At the battle of Shiloh his drum was smashed by an artillery round and the boy became known as "Johnny Shiloh." At the battle of Chickamauga he finally won national celebrity for his bravery and received his ultimate

sobriquet. Clem remained in the army, retiring in 1916 as a major general. (Faust, 145)

Who commanded the South Atlantic Blockading Squadron?
Rear Adm. John Adolph Bernard Dahlgren.

What was the name of Adm. Dahlgren's son, and what was his fate?
Ulric Dahlgren. Young Dahlgren served in many different capacities with the Army of the Potomac during the war. He lost his lower right leg on July 6, fighting in Hagerstown, Maryland, during Lee's retreat from Gettysburg. In February 1864 he accompanied Brig. Gen. Judson Kilpatrick on a raid on Richmond meant to free Union prisoners of war. Unfortunately, the raid was a fiasco, and Dahlgren was killed while leading his men in a retreat from the Confederate capital. On Dahlgren's body were found papers documenting that senior members of the Lincoln administration sanctioned burning Richmond and the assassination of President Davis and members of his cabinet. (Faust, 202)

What nephew of Confederate Jefferson Davis led a brigade of one North Carolina and three Mississippi regiments during the Gettysburg Campaign?
Brig. Gen. Joseph Robert Davis. He led his brigade in the attack on the Railroad Cut and then later supported the troops of Trimble and Pettigrew during the Pickett-Pettigrew-Trimble Assault on July 3, 1863.

What Union general was known as "Kil-cavalry" not only for his abuse of his horses but of his men?
Hugh Judson Kilpatrick.

What Gettysburg regimental commander's great-grandfather rode with Paul Revere and whose son was vice president of the United States and co-recipient of the Nobel Peace Prize?
Col. Rufus Dawes of the 6th Wisconsin Infantry. Dawes's great-grandfather was William Dawes who, unlike Paul Revere, escaped capture. His son, Charles Gates Dawes, was Calvin Coolidge's vice

president from 1925 to 1929. He, along with Frank B. Kellogg, would also receive the 1925 Nobel Peace Prize for their work to enable Germany to restore and establish its economy. (Graff, 719)

Who was the first of Lee's generals captured after his taking over command of the Army of Northern Virginia?
Brig. Gen. James J. Archer, on July 1, 1863, the first day of the battle of Gettysburg.

Who was Cornelia Hancock?
Miss Hancock performed duties as a nurse following the battle of Gettysburg. Though being young and pretty, traits that usually would have kept her from being a nurse, after Gettysburg she remained a nurse for the rest of the war. (Boatner, 372)

What Vermont general was captured by John Singleton Mosby at Fairfax Court House, Virginia, on March 8, 1863?
Edwin Henry Stoughton. Stoughton was captured along with 32 men and 58 horses. Upon his release the Senate did not confirm his generalship so he returned to civilian life as an attorney in New York City.

What was Abraham Lincoln's comment on the capture of Gen. Edwin Stoughton?
"I can make another general in five minutes but those horses cost $125 a piece."

What prominent Confederate officer was killed during the fighting at Kelly's Ford on March 17, 1863?
Maj. John Pelham. Also known as "The Gallant Pelham," the young man was a skilled artillery commander who fought in more than sixty engagements during his short career. (Faust, 568)

What Union major general was so disgusted with Joseph Hooker's performance at Chancellorsville that he requested a transfer?
Maj. Gen. Darius Nash Couch. He became the commander of the Department of the Susquehanna. (Faust, 187)

Who commanded the Federal cavalry during the Chancellorsville Campaign?
Maj. Gen. George Stoneman. (Faust, 721)

Whom did Hooker leave in Fredericksburg in command of the troops when he took the majority of his army to Chancellorsville?
Maj. Gen. John Sedgwick.

What became of Dr. Hunter McGuire following the death of Jackson?
He remained attached to the Army of Northern Virginia's Second Corps, serving as chief corps surgeon. He also organized the corps ambulance service, was the medical director of the Army of Northern Virginia, and finally served as medical director of Lt. Gen. Jubal Early's Valley Army. (Faust, 461)

Who led the first division to march into Vicksburg after its surrender?
Maj. Gen. John A. Logan. (Catton, 305)

Who was the best Confederate cavalry leader in the Western Theater and many say the entire Confederacy?
Lt. Gen. Nathan Bedford Forrest. (Catton, 352)

Where did George Thomas hail from and why did this cause him problems?
Thomas was born and reared in Southampton County, Virginia. When he chose to remain loyal to the Union, much of his family disowned him, while Federal authorities questioned his loyalty. (Catton, 387; Faust, 754)

Who wrote *Hospital Sketches*, a collection of letters written while a nurse in Georgetown?
Louisa May Alcott. (Boatner, 6)

Who was Maj. Gen. Napoleon Bonaparte Buford?
A Western Theater officer who was the half-brother of Brig. Gen. John Buford.

In May 1863 what Ohio politician did Abraham Lincoln banish to the South?
Clement Laird Vallandigham. He left the South and wound up in Canada where he ran an out-of-country campaign for the governorship of Ohio. He lost. Sneaking back into the United States in 1864, he delivered the keynote address at the Democratic National Convention. (Faust, 775; Boatner, 864)

What was Sherman's nom de guerre?
"Cump."

Who was William Tecumseh Sherman's younger brother?
Senator John Sherman (1823–1900). Sherman was chosen to succeed the former senator Salmon P. Chase in 1861. (Faust, 681)

Who raised William T. Sherman?
The Thomas Ewing family, after Sherman's father died in 1829. Sherman ultimately married Ellen Ewing, the daughter of his foster parents. (Faust, 681)

Which Confederate commander did Maj. Gen. Richard S. Ewell call "crack-brained"?
"Stonewall" Jackson. (Jeffry Wert, Centre Hall, PA)

Beginning on April 17, 1863, who led a Union cavalry raid that began in LaGrange, Tennessee, and ended in Baton Rouge, Louisiana, after covering 475 miles in 16 days?
Col. Benjamin H. Grierson. (Denney, 275)

Whose death brought mourning to the White House following the battle of Chickamauga?
Brig. Gen. Ben Hardin Helm, the husband of Mary Lincoln's half-sister Emily Todd. (Faust, 357)

What honor was given to Brig. Gen. John Buford on December 16, 1862?
He was promoted to major general just a few hours before his death from typhoid fever. (Denney, 353)

What happened to Maj. Gen. Earl Van Dorn on May 7, 1863?
He was murdered by an irate husband (Dr. George B. Peters) at his headquarters in Spring Hill, Tennessee. As an army commander he lost his two major battles but he was a competent cavalry leader. He was also known for being a ladies' man, which was his undoing. (Faust, 778; Roth, 15)

Why did Brig. Gen. William Smith get the nickname "Extra Billy"?
Before the war, he operated a mail coach service between Washington, D.C., and Milledgeville, Georgia. He frequently got extra payments from the Post Office Department for the mileage covered. (Faust, 698)

Who was Pauline Cushman?
A Federal spy working in the west. An actress, she used her talent to enhance her ability to find information on Confederate activities. At one point she was discovered, tried, and sentenced to hang; luckily for her, however, the Confederates abandoned her when Federal troops invaded the area. Now too well known as a spy, she lectured about her experiences and eventually wrote a book, *The Life of Pauline Cushman*. (Faust, 200)

What two Confederate generals attended Emory and Henry College as well as West Point, but during the war became bitter personal enemies?
William E. "Grumble" Jones and J. E. B. Stuart. (Jeffry Wert, Centre Hall, PA)

Who was Cpl. William Rihl?
William Rihl of Co. C, 1st New York "Lincoln" Cavalry, was the first Union soldier killed on Pennsylvania soil during the Gettysburg Campaign. He was killed during a skirmish at the Fleming Farm just north of Greencastle, Pennsylvania, on June 22, 1863. (Ted Alexander, Antietam National Battlefield)

What position did Frederick Law Olmsted, the famed landscape architect, hold during the Civil War?
He was the secretary general of the United States Sanitary Commission until forced to resign in 1863 due to ill health. (Sifakis, 294)

Who was Kate Chase Sprague?

Kate Chase was the daughter of the Secretary of the Treasury and was a belle of Washington. She married William Sprague, the former governor of Rhode Island and later senator, on November 12, 1863. By 1873 the marriage was falling apart as Sprague was drinking and Kate was being "intimate" with another Washington senator. In 1882 the couple divorced and she lived out her life by running a dairy and poultry farm. (Sifakis, 383)

Who was George Rallings?

Rallings was a New York City policeman. During the city's Draft Riots in 1863, Rallings found out the rioters were going to sack and burn the Negro Orphanage on Fifth Avenue. Rushing to the scene, he managed to evacuate and save about 260 children. (Sifakis, 325)

Who commanded Camp Letterman following the battle of Gettysburg?

Dr. Cyrus Chamberlain, a U.S. volunteer medical officer formally having served with the 10th Massachusetts Infantry. (Coco, 168)

Who was E. Porter Alexander?

A West Point graduate who served the Confederacy. He spent his military service with the Army of Northern Virginia, rising through the ranks from captain to brigadier general. He is perhaps best known for commanding the Confederate artillery that sent a 110-minute barrage at the Federal lines along Cemetery Ridge prior to the Pickett-Pettigrew-Trimble Assault on July 3, 1863. (Faust, 6)

Who was Maj. George Armistead?

Brig. Gen. Lewis A. Armistead's uncle. Maj. Armistead was in command of the garrison at Ft. McHenry in Baltimore, Maryland, when it was bombarded by the British fleet during the War of 1812. Of course the firing on the fort was the inspiration for Francis Scott Key to write the *Star Spangled Banner*. Before the firing started George sent his very pregnant wife, Louisa, out of the fort and north to safety. Soon after the end of the battle Louisa gave birth to a girl in the town of Gettysburg, Pennsylvania. Another Armistead would not visit the town until July 1863. (Motts, 8)

After being wounded in the Pickett-Pettigrew-Trimble Assault on July 3, what did Brig. Gen. Lewis Armistead die from?
He was wounded in the fleshy parts of the arm and the leg, injuries that normally would not be fatal. However, Armistead was suffering from shock, loss of blood, and pure exhaustion, the combination of which killed him. (Motts, 48–49)

Who was Antonia Ford?
A beautiful and intelligent young woman who threw her support behind the Confederacy. Among those who visited her were J. E. B. Stuart and John Mosby. She kept track of Federal movements and passed along the information to Confederate authorities. Perhaps the most famous incident involving her was the capture on March 8, 1863, of Union Brig. Gen. Edwin Stoughton. Stoughton had associated with Miss Ford, and John Mosby took advantage of this when he slipped into Fairfax Court House and gobbled up the general, some of his men, and quite a few horses. Miss Ford was arrested a few days after the incident and accused of espionage. Taken to the Old Capital Prison, she was held until the fall of 1863. A Union army officer, Willard, co-owner of the Willard Hotel, fell in love with her and helped to secure her release. The two were married the next spring on the agreement that he would quit the army and she would stop her spying. The marriage was short-lived, however, as Antonia Ford died in 1871, possibly due to complications of childbirth. (Heidler and Heidler, 716)

What happened to Lt. Stephen F. Brown of the 13th Vermont on the road to Gettysburg?
Though orders had been given to the brigade not to get out of the line of march, Brown took some canteens and filled them for his parched men. Caught and arrested, the lieutenant was relieved of his sword. Reaching the battlefield, on July 3 Brown armed himself with a camp hatchet and entered the fray during the Pickett-Pettigrew-Trimble

Assault. During the action he came upon a Confederate officer and, swinging the hatchet like a tomahawk, convinced the Rebel to surrender. Brown took his sword, pistol, and belt. Today they sit in the state capital in Montpelier, Vermont. (Benedict, 478)

Who was Sgt. James Scully?
Scully was a first sergeant in the 13th Vermont. When the order came to attack Kemper's right flank during the Pickett-Pettigrew-Trimble Assault, the 13th was guiding on Scully. It was later said of him that he was "the pivot man of the pivotal movement of the pivotal battle of the war." (Magner, 21)

MISCELLANEOUS

What was the Île à Vache venture?
An experiment whereby President Lincoln hoped to take freedmen and colonize them outside of the United States, in this case Haitian Île à Vache. In April 1863, 468 former slaves sailed for Haiti, only to find a jungle-covered island with none of the promised homes, school, or hospital. The venture was a failure, and within a year 368 survivors sailed back to America. (Faust, 378)

What was the Invalid Corps?
The Invalid Corps was formed in April 1863 and was made up of officers and men who had been disabled due to wounds, disease, and accidents. The corps was made up of two battalions. The first contained men who could bear arms and carry on garrison duty. The second battalion contained men who could only perform hospital service. The name eventually changed to the Veteran Reserve Corps and between 1863 and its disbanding in 1866, 60,000 men served in the organization. The Confederates formed a similar corps in 1864. (Faust, 383)

The explosion of what caused the deaths of forty-five women and children in Richmond on March 13, 1863?
The Confederate States Laboratory on Brown's Island in the James River. (Denney, 266)

What was the USS *Alligator*?
Designed by Brutus de Villeroi, the *Alligator* was a submarine. It was 47 feet long and from keel to deck it was 66 inches. In the original design the propulsion was by the use of folding oars. It eventually had the oars replaced by a hand-operated propeller. It was found that the *Alligator* was unable to perform its planned duties so it was never put into use. (Faust, 9)

What was the fate of the USS *Alligator*?
While being towed to Charleston, South Carolina, on April 2, 1863, it foundered in a gale and sank. (Faust, 9)

What legend surrounds the nickname given to prostitutes, many of whom hung around Joseph Hooker's headquarters?
That they were called hookers. This, however, is probably not true as there are sources that indicate the term "hooker" was used well before the Civil War.

What was the name of the relatively bloodless campaign in the Western Theater that took place at the same time as the Gettysburg Campaign?
The Tullahoma Campaign.

When did the Federal Signal Corps officially go into service?
On March 3, 1863, Congress passed a law making the position of Chief Signal Officer. During the course of the war some 300 officers and 2,500 enlisted men were members of the Signal Corps. (Henig, 92–93)

What negative comment did infantrymen usually use concerning the cavalry?
"Who ever saw a dead cavalryman?" Credit for the comment lies with Maj. Gen. Joseph "Fighting-Joe" Hooker. (Beattie, 26)

Where is Hickory Hill and what was its significance?
Hickory Hill, the Wickham family plantation, is located in Hanover County, Virginia. On June 26, 1863, Rooney Lee (Gen. Lee's son) was

captured at Hickory Hill where he was recuperating from the wound he received at Brandy Station. (Boatner, 399)

Who was "Sally the Dog"?
Sally was the mascot of the 11th Pennsylvania. At Gettysburg she got separated from the regiment but found her way back to where they had fought near Oak Ridge. She was found three days later, hungry, parched, but still guarding the men of her regiment. Sally was killed at the battle of Hatcher's Run on February 6, 1865. Some of the men stopped and buried her with military honors while still under fire. On the monument to the regiment at Gettysburg is a lifesize bronze of Sally. (Martin, 440)

When the two armies converged on Gettysburg, how many horses did they bring with them and how many became casualties of the fighting?
They brought approximately 72,243 horses and mules. Of these the number of injured horses is unknown but the number of killed ranges between 2,000 and 3,000. (Magner, 47)

How much horse manure was produced during the battle of Gettysburg?
Estimating that each horse or mule produces thirteen and one half pounds of manure per day, multiplied by 72,234 horses and mules, and considering that the majority of them were in the area from June 30 to July 4, the estimate would be 975,281 pounds per day. This totals 3,901,000 pounds (imagine the rose bush fertilizer). They would have also produced 578,000 gallons of urine, or basically enough to almost fill an Olympic-size swimming pool. (Magner, 47–48)

What was Forrest's underlying philosophy on warfare?
"War means fightin' and fightin' means killin'." (Faust, 269)

What was Forrest's greatest victory?
The battle of Brice's Cross Roads, June 10, 1864. (Faust, 270)

What does the word Chickamauga mean?
It is Cherokee for "river of death." (Catton, 393)

What was Camp Chase?
Camp Chase was initially a training camp but it soon became a Federal prisoner-of-war camp located on the outskirts of Columbus, Ohio. By 1865 it held close to 10,000 Confederates. (Boatner, 117; Faust, 110)

Who was Camp Chase named for?
Salmon P. Chase, former governor of Ohio and Lincoln's secretary of the treasury. (Faust, 109)

What was Point Lookout?
A Federal prison camp located in Maryland where the Potomac enters the Chesapeake Bay. It was established on August 1, 1863, and at one time held nearly 20,000 prisoners. The men were adequately sheltered, though they were forced to live in tents. (Boatner, 657)

What was the Swamp Angel?
It was a 200-pounder (8-inch) rifled Parrott gun on Morris Island manned by the Federals. It had a range of 7,900 yards and was used to shell Charleston. Though a few fires were started by the incendiary shells it fired, for the most part it was an ineffectual weapon. It blew up firing its thirty-sixth round. (Boatner, 822)

What was the "Enrollment Act" passed by the Federal Congress on March 3, 1863?
The Union's form of conscription. It indicated that all men between the ages of twenty and forty-five were eligible for three years of military service. (Henig, 41)

What was the significance of the 1st South Carolina Volunteers being mustered into Federal service on January 25, 1863?
It was the first time that African American soldiers officially became part of the United States Army. (Henig, 48)

What was the first officer candidate school in America?
The Free Military School for Applicants for Commands of Colored Troops. It opened on Chestnut Street in Philadelphia on December 26, 1863. The school offered noncommissioned officers and privates a course in the rudiments of military knowledge and tactics, thus allowing them, upon successful completion of the program, the chance to test for an officer's position in an African American unit. Before the school closed in September 1864 it turned out 484 graduates. (Henig, 54–55)

What was the training ship of the Confederate Naval Academy?
The CSS *Patrick Henry*. (Denney, 337)

Did Abraham Lincoln ever see John Wilkes Booth perform before April 14, 1865?
Yes, in a production of *The Marble Heart*, on November 9, 1863. (Denney, 399)

What was the Pomeroy Circular?
It was an anti-Lincoln letter that either was written by or was caused to be written by someone by Sen. Samuel C. Pomeroy of Kansas. Pomeroy was a supporter of Salmon P. Chase, who was quietly campaigning for the Republican presidential nomination. Privately circulated, it ended up being printed in several Washington newspapers. The circular mortified Chase. He offered Lincoln his resignation, which the president did not accept. Ohio Republicans came to Lincoln's defense and Chase ultimately ended his campaign. (Faust, 591)

When the Army of the Potomac needed horses, where did it get them?
By 1863 Giesboro Point in the District of Columbia (presently the site of the Anacostia Naval Air Station) was the supply depot for army horseflesh and mules. It was the largest facility for the Cavalry Bureau and had facilities for 30,000 horses. It could also treat 2,650 animals at a time. (Beattie, 25)

What were "horse leaves" and Company Q?

Because most Confederate cavalrymen supplied their own horses, it was necessary for them to find a replacement if the horse was injured or killed. In the case of a dead horse, the trooper was allowed to go home on "horse leave" in order to find a replacement mount. If a trooper's horse became disabled but could be nursed back to health, the cavalryman became a member of Company Q until either he got a new horse, captured a horse, or his own horse recuperated. (Beattie, 26)

What was the most famous Confederate prison for Union officers?

Libby Prison in Richmond. (Davis, 458)

What was the largest prison break of the Civil War?

From Libby Prison, on February 9, 1864. Under the eye of Col. Thomas E. Rose, twenty-five prisoners dug a tunnel from the prison's basement to the outside. It took them forty-five days. When completed, the tunnel was sixteen inches in diameter and almost sixty feet long. The twenty-five who dug the tunnel were the first to go, and after two hours the rest of the prisoners were told of the existence of the hole. In all, 109 men, including Col. Abel Streight, escaped; however, forty-eight of those were recaptured, including Rose. (Davis, 461–463)

What was the CSS *David*?

A fifty-foot-long, cigar-shaped steamer, an iron torpedo boat with a crew of four and a top speed of seven knots. Attached to a spar on the bow was a torpedo with 100 pounds of explosives. There were a number of these craft built in Charleston, but most remained unnamed. The *David* made three attacks; one on the USS *New Ironsides*, seriously damaging her though she stayed afloat; a second on the USS *Memphis*, though the torpedo did not explode; and a final attack on the USS *Wabash*, where the *David* was detected and forced to withdraw. What happened to the *David* is unknown, but speculation is that it was one of several David-type vessels that fell into Union hands after the capture of Charleston. (Faust, 205)

What two battles are regarded as Robert E. Lee's masterpieces of generalship?
Second Manassas and Chancellorsville. (Jeffry Wert, Centre Hall, PA)

Next to Gettysburg, what was the largest Civil War battle on Pennsylvania soil?
The battle of Monterey, July 4–5, 1863. Brig. Gen. Judson Kilpatrick's cavalry, numbering around 4,500, attacked a Confederate wagon train in the mountains east of Waynesboro, Pennsylvania. Confederate reinforcements numbering a few thousand joined in the fighting. The battle ended with forty Federal casualties and more than 1,000 Confederate (mostly prisoners). (Ted Alexander, Antietam National Battlefield)

What were the two breech-loading rifled cannon used at Gettysburg, and which side used them?
Whitworths. They were used by the Army of Northern Virginia and were located on Oak Hill. (Dale Beiver, Boyertown, PA)

On the march into Gettysburg, what was the rumor running through the 20th Maine?
On July 1 as the regiment trod its way toward the battlefield a rumor spread that at sunset the ghost of George Washington had been seen riding over the battlefield. Years later, even Col. Joshua Chamberlain admitted that he thought it might be true. (Magner, unpublished manuscript)

Who was the George Nixon who is buried in Row D #4 of the Ohio section of the Gettysburg Soldiers' National Cemetery?
Nixon was a member of Co. B, 73rd Ohio Infantry, who on July 2 was on the skirmish line along the Emmitsburg Road when he received a hip wound. As darkness fell, the regimental drummer boy, Richard Enderlin, crawled out to Nixon and got him back to the Union lines. Unfortunately, Nixon did not survive the wound, dying on July 14 and leaving a wife and large family. For his actions Enderlin was later awarded the Medal of Honor. George's chief claim to fame, however, is that he was the great-great-grandfather of the

thirty-seventh president of the United States, Richard M. Nixon. (Cole and Frampton, 38–39)

What was Mosby's "Ice Cream Raid"?

Toward the end of July 1863, Mosby and twenty-six of his men were planning to raid Fairfax Court House. Just west of town near Germantown (Jermantown), they captured a sutler's wagon. Leaving a few men with the wagon, Mosby continued on to the Court House, where they captured more sutler wagons. Returning to Germantown, they discovered in the wagons boots and other merchandise. In one they found ice cream, especially tasty on a hot July day. The men then termed the foray the "Ice Cream Raid." (Mewborn, 22)

Who was the only reputedly civilian killed at the battle of Gettysburg?

Mary Virginia "Jennie" Wade. As the battle raged north of town, the family moved to the house of her sister, Georgia Wade McClellan, on Baltimore Street. On the morning of July 3, as Jennie was in the kitchen kneading dough to make bread, a Confederate bullet passed through the outer door and hit her in the shoulder, killing her almost instantly. She was taken to the house's basement and was buried in the garden next to the house on July 4. In January 1864 her body was moved to the German Reformed Church's cemetery. Finally, in 1865, she was moved to her final resting place in Evergreen Cemetery. At the time of her death, she did not know that her fiancé, Jack Skelly, had died from wounds received in battle. The messenger bringing her the news was John Wesley Culp, who died fighting on family lands near Culp's Hill. Some sources say that the speaker's platform from which Lincoln gave the Gettysburg Address sat either atop or near where her grave is presently located. (Magner, unpublished manuscript)

What or who was "Historicus"?

The nom de plume was used by the author of two articles published in the *New York Herald*. The author identified himself as an eyewitness to the battle of Gettysburg and the articles were very partial to the importance that Maj. Gen. Dan Sickles played in the outcome of the battle. Though the exact identity of "Historicus" was never revealed many authorities suspect that it was either Sickles himself or one of his staffers, who wrote the articles with his blessing. (Magner, unpublished manuscript)

Which two Confederate generals had a duel in September 1863?
Brig. Gen. John Sappington Marmaduke and Brig. Gen. Lucius M. Walker. Marmaduke killed Walker, for which he was arrested; however, he was soon released. (Faust, 476)

What aide to Gen. John Gibbon wrote a letter to his brother that became one of the best first-person account books of the battle of Gettysburg?
Lt. Frank Haskell.

What was odd about Winfield Scott's Hancock's uniform whenever his men saw him?
He was always wearing a clean, pressed white shirt under his officer's frock. (Magner, 24)

BATTLES

Stones River (Murfreesboro), January 1–2, 1863

When did the fighting begin again at Stones River?
Although there was some minor skirmishing on January 1, the real action did not begin again until about 4:00 p.m. January 2. (Spearman, 38)

What was the outcome of the fighting of January 2, 1863, at Stones River?
An initially successful attack by troops under Maj. Gen. John C. Breckinridge was halted and turned back by the Federals. The repulse of the Rebels changed an initial victory into a stalemate and then, because Gen. Bragg opted to retreat on January 3, a disappointing loss. In total, the two days of fighting cost the Federals 12,906 casualties and the Confederates 11,739, but left the Federals in command of the field and Murfreesboro. (Spearman, 45)

What minor action took place in San Francisco on March 15, 1863?
The USS *Cyane* seized the schooner *J. M. Chapman*. The *Chapman* was suspected of being a Confederate commerce raider and, when boarded, was found to be carrying guns, ammunition, and other military stores. The cargo was offloaded and the twenty-one-man crew was sent to Alcatraz. (Denney, 267)

What happened near Kelly's Ford along the Rappahannock River on St. Patrick's Day 1863?
Around sunrise, about 2,100 Federal cavalry under Brig. Gen. William W. Averell attempted to cross from the east side of the river, planning to attack Confederate cavalry camped near Culpeper Court House. Knowing the Federals were coming, the Confederates put up a stubborn defense, delaying the crossing for some two hours. Once across the river Averell moved toward the Court House, halting about a mile from the ford. Meanwhile, Brig. Gen. Fitzhugh Lee had ridden up and, at about noon, attacked the Federals with only 800 troopers. The battle raged for about five hours, with each side pushing the other back and forth. After a final Confederate counterattack, which only led to more casualties, Averell withdrew. (Faust, 411)

What "challenge" was settled during the Kelly's Ford action on March 17, 1863?
A couple of weeks before the action at Kelly's Ford, on February 25, Brig. Gen. Fitzhugh Lee had routed some outposts of Brig. Gen. William Averell's Union forcers near Hartwood Church. Averell and Lee had been classmates at West Point, so Lee left Averell a note saying he should return the visit and bring some coffee. When Averell recrossed the river after the action, he left a sack of coffee and a note asking Lee how he liked the visit. (Faust, 411)

Grierson's Raid (April 17–May 2, 1863)

What did Benjamin H. Grierson do prior to the Civil War?
He was a music teacher and for a few years shared a partnership in a dry goods business in Jacksonville, Illinois (the business eventually

failed). At the outbreak of the war he became an aide to Col. Benjamin M. Prentiss of the 10th Illinois Infantry. He was later commissioned a major in the cavalry. Having almost died at the age of eight when a horse threw him and kicked him in the face, which left him scarred both physically and emotionally, Grierson wanted nothing to do with the cavalry. He unsuccessfully tried to get another assignment but to no avail, as even General Halleck indicated that Grierson looked like a good cavalryman. (Roth, 14–15)

What regiments made up Grierson's command?
Grierson commanded the 6th and 7th Illinois Cavalry, the 2nd Iowa Cavalry and a battery from the 1st Illinois Artillery, a total of 1,700 troopers. He turned out to be a good horse soldier and worked his way up through the ranks, first commanding a regiment and then as a colonel of his own brigade, known as Grierson's Cavalry. (Roth, 15)

What was the focus of Grierson's Raid?
He was to leave La Grange, Tennessee, and move down through northern Mississippi until he reached the east-west running Southern Railroad of Mississippi. General U. S. Grant figured that if the railroad could be cut, it would create problems getting supplies to Lt. Gen. John C. Pemberton, who had his headquarters in Jackson, Mississippi. He was also to destroy other railroads, including the Mississippi Central, the Mobile and Ohio, and the New Orleans, Jackson & Great Northern Railroad. (Roth, 13, 18)

What was the Quinine Brigade, formed on the third day of the raid?
On the morning of April 20, Grierson culled out 175 troopers and placed them under the command of Maj. Hiram Love of the 2nd Iowa. Grierson believed these men to be useless to the raid because they were either sick, exhausted, or had broken-down horses. Someone gave the group the name "Quinine Brigade." Love was to lead these men north over the same roads they had already passed over and back to La Grange. They also took with them one artillery piece, extra horses, captured property, and the prisoners who had been gathered up. They were to ride in such a fashion that if the Confederates came

across their tracks they would think the entire column had headed back north. The ruse was ultimately a failure. (Roth, 21, 23)

What were Grierson's plans for Col. Edward Hatch's 2nd Iowa on April 21st?

Grierson decided to split his command, sending Hatch and his regiment off toward Columbus, Mississippi. Passing through West Point, the Iowans were to destroy the railroad bridge across the Oktibbeha River, then, moving south toward Mason, they were to destroy the railroad and government stores. Once their mission was accomplished, they were to find their way back to La Grange. (Roth, 23–24)

As Grierson was moving south, what Confederates were chasing him?

Lt. Col. Clark R. Barteau and the 2nd Tennessee Cavalry, plus Mississippi state troops. Grierson had a pretty good lead on the Tennesseans but the hard-riding Confederates were able to slowly cut down on the time they were behind. (Roth, 23)

What happened at Palo Alto, Mississippi, that ended Hatch's raid?

Barteau's troops caught up with him and almost trapped the Union troopers. Unluckily, Barteau's Tennesseans had never been under fire, and they broke when charged by the 2nd Iowa. This enabled Hatch's men to escape and head north toward La Grange. He was shadowed by Barteau, who trailed him most of the way back to the Tennessee line. Hatch forgot about destroying the Mobile & Ohio Railroad; now his only aim was to save his regiment and reach Tennessee. (Roth, 24)

When did Grierson's men take Newton Station on the Vicksburg Railroad?

Grierson's scouts first rode into town early in the morning of April 24. These men were followed by two battalions of the 7th Illinois under Lt. Col. William Blackburn. Just as they entered the town, a freight train pulled into the station and shunted off onto a siding, where the crew was immediately captured. The train was filled with ordnance and commissary stores headed for Vicksburg. Soon a second train reached the station and was captured, this one consisting of one passenger car and twelve freight cars. Shortly after the second train was taken, Grierson and the main Union column rode into town. (Roth, 50–51)

Once taken, what did the Yankees do at Newton Station?
Both trains were burned. Grierson's troops went down the tracks and twisted rails and destroyed bridges and trestles. The telegraph wires were cut; the warehouse next to the station was torched. The rails were torn up, heated, and then twisted out of shape. Seventy-five patients in a nearby hospital were paroled and then the building burned. (Roth, 51)

What did Grierson do following the destruction at Newton Station?
He continued moving southwest through the Piney Woods country of south central Mississippi. Though his orders said to return north through Alabama, Grierson decided that he knew best how to get back to Union lines. (Roth, 52)

What stations and hamlets did Grierson's men destroy or capture as he continued his raid south?
Hazlehurst, Union Church, Bahala, Brookhaven, Bogue Chitto, Summit, and Greenwell Springs. (Roth, 58, 64)

How many casualties did Grierson suffer during his raid?
Three killed, seven wounded, and fourteen captured or missing. (Roth, 63–64)

Heros von Borcke, an aide to J. E. B. Stuart, was seriously wounded in a skirmish in what village?
Middleburg, Virginia, on June 19, 1863. Though the wound was at first thought to be mortal, the powerfully built Prussian rallied and survived, though he was never able to take the field again. (Faust, 791)

Chancellorsville

What is considered by many to be Robert E. Lee's greatest victory?
Chancellorsville.

When Jackson marched around to attack the Union right flank, how many men did he take with him?
Three divisions, totaling about 33,000 men, 108 cannon and three and a half regiments of cavalry, leaving Lee with 14,900 to face Hooker's 70,000. His divisions were led by Brig. Gen. Robert Rodes, Brig. Gen. Raleigh Colston, and Maj. Gen. A. P. Hill. In total they would march about fourteen miles. (Robertson, 714–715)

What harbinger of bad luck happened to Stonewall Jackson on the night of May 2?
His sword, which had been leaning against a tree, fell. Armistead Long of Lee's staff took it as an omen. Knights viewed a falling sword as a sign of bad luck. (Robertson, 713)

Who was Hubert Digler?
Digler was an artillery battery commander whom many consider to be the best battery officer of the Civil War. He commanded Battery I, 1st Ohio Light Artillery, and was attached to the Eleventh Corps. Perhaps his best battle was Chancellorsville, where on May 2 his battery engaged elements of Jackson's column as it attempted to reach the Union flank. Wounded and almost captured, Digler leapfrogged his battery back toward the Union main line while keeping up a continuous fire. At the battle of Gettysburg there is a story that Digler fired a round that went down the tube of a Confederate gun during the fight north of the borough. Digler never received promotion, remaining a captain throughout the war. Finally in 1893 he was awarded a Medal of Honor for his actions at Chancellorsville. (Heidler and Heidler, 597–598)

What happened to Joseph Hooker during the fighting?
A shell hit the pillar of the Chancellor House against which he was standing, splitting the column and knocking him senseless. Upon his recovery he had lost his ability to effectively lead the army.

What Confederate regiment fired the volley that hit Stonewall Jackson?
The 18th North Carolina, led by Lt. Col. Thomas J. Purdie. Purdie was killed on May 3. (Robertson, 728; Jordan, 305)

What were Gen. Jackson's wounds?
He was hit simultaneously by two .69-caliber bullets and one buck-shot from a smoothbore musket. One ball splintered bone and ten-dons three inches below the left shoulder before exiting the wound. A second ball entered the left forearm an inch below the elbow then exited above the wrist. The buckshot hit his right palm, broke two fingers, then lodged against the skin on the back of the general's hand. (Robertson, 729; Bearss)

Who else was wounded or killed when Gen. Jackson was hit?
The Hill and Jackson parties were not riding together. Riding with Jackson when he was shot were eight others; of these Pvt. William E. Cunliffe was killed and Joshua O. Johns wounded. Two horses were also killed. A. P. Hill had nine riding with him; of these Capt. Keith Boswell, James G. Forbes, Eugene Sanders, and W. T. Tucker were killed. Maj. William H. Palmer and Richard Muse were wounded. Taken prisoner were Conway, Howard, and G. W. Tucker. Of the nineteen men with Jackson and Hill, including the two generals, twelve became casualties. (Robertson, 726, 729; Krick, 236; Bearss)

Stonewall Jackson. USAMHI

Who amputated Stonewall Jackson's left arm following his wounding at Chancellorsville?
Dr. Hunter Holmes McGuire. (Faust, 461)

What three surgeons assisted McGuire in amputating Jackson's arm?
Dr. Harvey Black, who was the unofficial second in command under Dr. McGuire; Dr. J. William Walls, the surgeon of the 5th Virginia; and Dr. Robert T. Coleman, surgeon of the 21st Virginia. (Robertson, 735–736)

Where was Jackson's arm buried?
Ellwood Manor Cemetery, about a mile west of the Wilderness Tavern. The house was Maj. Gen. Gouverneur K. Warren's headquarters during the battle of The Wilderness. (Mertz, 55)

When did Jackson leave the battlefield in route to Guiney Station, and who accompanied him?
Around 6:00 a.m. on Monday, May 4, 1863. With Jackson in the ambulance was Col. Stapleton Crutchfield. McGuire rode alongside the ambulance driver and Jedediah Hotchkiss led the party. Also inside the ambulance were Chaplain Beverly T. Lacy and an aide, Lt. James Power Smith. The journey took about fourteen hours. (Robertson, 741–742)

Who owned the home at Guiney Station where Jackson was taken?
Thomas and Mary Chandler. The house was already a hospital, with wounded from the battle occupying the second floor. Chaplain Lacy arrived before the ambulance and indicated to Mrs. Chandler that Dr. McGuire would insist on quiet for his patient. Seeing a small building next to the house, which was actually an office, the chaplain asked if that could be used. Lacy then left to rejoin the ambulance and Mrs. Chandler and her two servants converted the office into a hospital. (Robertson, 742–743)

When did Jackson's ambulance reach Guiney Station?
About 8:00 p.m. Met by Thomas Chandler, Jackson was taken inside the building and placed in a double rope trellis bed with a headboard,

acorn posts on the corners, and pine runners. At the foot of the bed over the fireplace was a mantelpiece with a Gothic arched Ingraham clock. (Robertson, 743)

What was the sequence of events following Jackson's arrival at the Chandler House?

Monday—arrived and was placed in his room.

Tuesday—Appeared to be in good condition. His wife Anna was told of his injuries in Richmond.

Wednesday—Seemed to be doing well.

Thursday—Awoke at 1:00 a.m. complaining of nausea, fever, and pain in his left side. Believing it to be pneumonia, McGuire began treatment; he also sent for help from Samuel B. Morrison, Jackson's pre-war physician who was acting as chief surgeon of Early's Division. Anna, the baby, and a nurse arrived at noon.

Friday—Jackson seemed better but still had labored breathing. In the evening the delirium returned.

Saturday—Still suffering from fever and labored breathing, Jackson was told by Anna and by Dr. McGuire that he probably would not recover.

Sunday, May 10—Jackson awoke exhausted and with very bad symptoms. The nurse brought his baby daughter into the room so he could see her one last time. In the afternoon Jackson slipped into a deep coma. Then finally he said, "Let us cross over the river and rest under the shade of the trees." The gallant Stonewall Jackson had gone to meet his maker. (Robertson, 742–753)

What happened near Salem Church, Virginia, on May 3, 1863?
Elements of John Sedgwick's Federals, after storming the Confederate works on Marye's Heights and Willis' Hill in Fredericksburg, pushed west in an attempt to link up with Joseph Hooker and the Army of the Potomac fighting near Chancellorsville. As they approached Salem Church, about six miles west of Fredericksburg, they ran into a brigade of Alabamians commanded by Brig. Gen. Cadmus M. Wilcox.

Soon Maj. Gen. Lafayette McLaws arrived from Chancellorsville, sent by Gen. Lee with four brigades, two of which filed into position on Wilcox's right and two on his left. The Federals attacked the Confederates, who held the high ground and were pushed back with heavy casualties. The next day when the Rebs decided to renew the attack they discovered that Sedgwick had moved his men north and back across the Rappahannock River at Scott's Ford. Union casualties numbered around 4,700. (Faust, 652; Boatner, 717)

The Confederate Cavalry was considered to be far superior to its Union counterpart until what battle?
Brandy Station.

Brandy Station

What was the largest cavalry battle of the Civil War in which most of the participants fought mounted?
Brandy Station, June 9, 1863.

What was Jeb Stuart's headquarters at Brandy Station and who owned it?
Stuart made his headquarters at the home of a Mr. Miller, located on the southern end of a two-mile-long ridge about a mile northeast of Brandy Station. Miller had given his home the name "Fleetwood"; thus, this end of the ridge became known as Fleetwood Hill. (Beattie, 7)

What was the Federal strength at Brandy Station?
Brig. Gen. Alfred Pleasonton commanded 8,000 cavalry, 3,700 infantry, and artillerymen with thirty-four guns. Pleasonton's right wing was commanded by Brig. Gen. John Buford, with Col. Benjamin F. "Grimes" Davis and Col. Thomas C. Devin his brigade commanders; a reserve brigade led by Maj. Charles J. Whiting; and an infantry brigade under Brig. Gen. Adelbert Ames. His left wing was led by Brig. Gen. David McM. Gregg. Gregg's divisions were commanded by Col. Alfred N. Duffié and his own second division. An infantry brigade commanded by Brig. Gen. David A. Russell accompanied Gregg. Duffié's brigades were commanded by Col. Luigi P. di Cesnola, Col.

John Irvin Gregg, David McM. Gregg's by Col. H. Judson Kilpatrick and Col. Percy Wyndham. (Beattie, 29–30)

What was the Confederate strength at Brandy Station?
The cavalry division was led by Maj. Gen. J. E. B. Stuart. Stuart had 10,300 cavalry, 527 artillerymen, and twenty guns. His brigade commanders were Brig. Gen. William E. "Grumble" Jones, Brig. Gen. William H. F. "Rooney" Lee, Brig. Gen. Wade Hampton, Col. Thomas T. Munford, and Brig. Gen. Beverly Robertson. Maj. Robert F. Beckham led the horse artillery. (Beattie, 31)

At which two fords did the Federal forces cross on June 9, 1863?
At Beverly Ford, about five miles north of Rappahannock Station, and Kelly's Ford, about five miles south of the station.

What happened at Beverly Ford on the morning of June 9, 1863?
Brig. Gen. John Buford sent Col. "Grimes" Davis's men across the ford to clear out any Confederates who might be in the area. Following them would be the rest of Buford's men, including Davis's brigade, the Reserve Brigade, Devin's brigade, and Ames's infantry. Once across, they met the Confederate picket reserve made up of thirty men of the 6th Virginia cavalry of "Grumble" Jones's brigade. The ball had opened. (Beattie, 33–34)

What was the outcome of the meeting between Lt. R. O. Allen of the 6th Virginia cavalry and Col. "Grimes" Davis?
The lieutenant fired a bullet into Davis's brain and killed him. (Beattie, 41)

What did Gregg do after he crossed the river at Kelly's Ford?
He sent Duffié's Division to scout Stevensburg, where the Frenchman met Confederate cavalry. A sharp skirmish took place but the Confederates, being outnumbered by the Federals, fell back. Gregg took his other division and rode up the Fredericksburg Plank Road directly toward Brandy Station. He soon sent orders to Duffié that he should join him at the station. By the time Duffié joined Gregg, the fighting around the station had ended. (Beattie, 58, 64–65)

Who was Maj. Henry B. McClellan's (Stuart's chief clerk) famous relative?
Maj. Gen. George B. McClellan, former commander of the Army of the Potomac. (Beattie, 66)

Who led Brig. Gen. David McM. Gregg's second division toward Fleetwood Hill and the rear of the Confederate line at St. James Church?
Col. Percy Wyndham, a British soldier and gentleman who was dedicated to the Union cause. He was also a lucky man. Back in March 1863, the partisan ranger John S. Mosby had ridden into Fairfax Court House with plans to capture the Englishman. Fortunately, Wyndham was not at the courthouse that night. Instead Mosby got himself a brigadier general, Edwin Stoughton of the Second Vermont Brigade. (Beattie, 71)

What happened to Wyndham's movement?
With the 1st New Jersey in the lead, followed by the 1st Maryland and 1st Pennsylvania, the Federal cavalrymen managed to get close to the crest before being charged by the 12th Virginia cavalry and later the 35th Virginia cavalry battalion and 6th Virginia cavalry. After almost an hour of back-and-forth fighting, Wyndham's men were forced to retreat back down the western slope of the hill. About this time, Col. Judson Kilpatrick was bringing his brigade into the fray by attacking the southeast side of Fleetwood Hill. (Beattie, 75)

What happened to Kilpatrick's attack?
It ended the same way as Wyndham's; however, one regiment did shine before being repelled. The 1st Maine Cavalry (known as the Pilgrims) "launched one of the great saber charges of the war." A green regiment, they were hungry to show their mettle. They gained the crest of the hill but were eventually forced back. (Beattie, 77–78)

Who was watching the fighting as the 1st Maine rode by their position?
The Maine boys rode close to the Barbour House, known as "Beauregard." Possibly watching from the cupola of the house were Gens.

Robert E. Lee and Richard Ewell, who had earlier left Culpeper Court House to take a look at the fighting. (Beattie, 77–78)

Who won the battle of Brandy Station?
Over the years authorities have indicated that the battle was either a draw or a Union victory, but when all was said and done, the Stars and Bars still flew over the Brandy Station battlefield. The Union cavalry had done well, surprising Stuart and his cavalry twice in one day, both in the early-morning crossing at Beverly Ford and the later attack on Fleetwood Hill. In casualties Stuart lost 515 killed, wounded, and missing, while Pleasonton lost 868. (Beattie, 80–81)

The Road to Gettysburg: Aldie, Middleburg, Upperville and Winchester

What happened at Winchester, Virginia, on June 14–15, 1863?
The 6,900-man Union garrison was all but surrounded by elements of Lt. Gen. Richard Ewell's Second Confederate Corps. Under the command of Maj. Gen. Robert H. Milroy, the Federals put up a fight, but at dusk on June 14 their entrenchments were overrun. After holding a council of war Milroy decided upon a retreat, which began around 1:00 a.m. on June 15. The garrison headed north for Harpers Ferry but unfortunately ran into Maj. Gen. Edward Johnson's Division. Milroy suffered 450 in killed and wounded and nearly 4,000 captured. Confederate losses numbered around 266. Milroy himself, with 1,200 of his men, managed to reach the safety of Harpers Ferry. (Faust, 834–835; Coddington, 89)

What happened at Aldie, Virginia, on June 17, 1863?
There was a sharp engagement between Confederate cavalry under Col. Thomas T. Munford and Brig. Gen. Judson Kilpatrick's Federal cavalry. Though the Confederates were pushed out of town to the west the Federals were severely bloodied. Brig. Gen. Alfred Pleasonton did learn through the fighting that there were no Confederate infantry east of the Bull Run Mountains. (Faust, 5, 6; Coddington, 76–77)

What happened to Col. Alfred Duffié's 1st Rhode Island Cavalry at Middleburg on June 17, 1863?
Pushing into the town, he eventually found himself and the regiment virtually surrounded by Stuart's Confederate cavalry at a nearby farmstead south of the village. Of the 275 men in his command he was able to fight his way out of the situation with only thirty-one troopers, though sixty-five who had been left behind managed to later rejoin the regiment. (Heidler and Heidler, 28–29; Coddington, 78)

What happened on June 21 near Upperville?
Pleasonton sent Brig. Gen. David McM. Gregg against Brig. Gen. Wade Hampton and Brig. Gen. Beverly Robertson's cavalry, while further to the north John Buford's men threatened to turn Stuart's flank held by Grumble Jones's men. Stuart eventually pulled back to Ashby's Gap, through which Lt. Gen. James Longstreet's Corps had recently passed into the Shenandoah Valley. (Heidler and Heidler, 29)

At Goose Creek bridge, several miles east of Upperville, what Union infantry was brought up to support the Union cavalry?
Col. Strong Vincent's brigade, which included the 20th Maine. The brigade was to become famous less than two weeks later on Little Round Top at Gettysburg. (Coddington, 79)

What happened in Carlisle, Pennsylvania, late on July 1, 1863?
The town was visited by Jeb Stuart's cavalry during his much-debated ride around the Army of the Potomac. On the evening of July 1, Fitzhugh Lee's cavalry reached Carlisle and occupied the Barracks, which were later burned. The only Union troops present were several companies of the 37th New York Infantry. The Confederates shelled the town, and under a flag of truce, demanded its surrender. When town officials refused, the shelling resumed. Finally the Confederates ran out of ammunition. None of the town's civilians were injured, but two soldiers of the 37th were wounded, one mortally. On June 27, Rodes's Division of the Army of Northern Virginia had moved into Carlisle and remained until daybreak June 30. (Heidler and Heidler, 356–357)

Where did the majority of the Army of the Potomac cross the Potomac River?
Edwards' Ferry near Poolesville, Maryland.

What was the action in Hanover, Pennsylvania, on June 30, 1863?
J. E. B. Stuart headed his men toward Hanover on his ride around the Federal Army. Reaching town, he met up with elements of Judson Kilpatrick's Division and shots were fired. The fighting continued through the rest of the morning and much of the afternoon. Elon Farnsworth's men bore the brunt of the fighting on the Union side until midafternoon. George Custer's men were not seriously engaged but did contribute in the afternoon. The fighting finally stopped around sunset, with the Confederates suffering 75 casualties and the Federals 154. (Magner, unpublished manuscript)

Gettysburg

In June 1863, who traveled from Washington to Frederick, Maryland, to deliver secret orders to George Gordon Meade that placed him in command of the Army of the Potomac?
Lt. Col. James Allen Hardie. (Faust, 339)

What was Maj. Gen. George Gordon Meade's comment on being told that he was in command of the Army of the Potomac?
"Well, I have been tried and convicted without a hearing, I suppose I shall have to go to execution." (Catton, 313)

What did many of his men call Gen. Meade?
Some say, "A goggle-eyed old snapping turtle," while others state it was simply an "Old snapping turtle."

Who was the first reputed casualty of the battle of Gettysburg?
George Sandoe of the 21st Pennsylvania cavalry. Sandoe was killed on June 26 southeast of Gettysburg when he blundered upon the Confederates of Elijah White's Brigade. He had enlisted only six days prior to his death. (Magner, unpublished manuscript)

Who saved George Armstrong Custer's life at the battle of Hunters-town, Pennsylvania?
Norvel Churchill. When Custer became pinned under his mount during the first charge at Hunterstown on the afternoon of July 2, a Confederate took aim meaning to dispatch the general to meet his maker. Churchill killed the offending Rebel, pulled Custer from under his dead horse, and, riding double, took him back to the main Union line, whereupon Custer got another horse and rode back into the fighting.

Who replaced Maj. Gen. John Fulton Reynolds when he was killed on the first day of the battle of Gettysburg?
Maj. Gen. Abner Doubleday, though he only remained in command overnight. Doubleday was replaced as commander of the Federal First Corps on the early morning of July 2 by Maj. Gen. John Newton due to Meade's lack of confidence in Doubleday's abilities.

Where did Brig. Gen. John Buford make his headquarters when he entered Gettysburg on June 30, 1863?
The Eagle Hotel, on the corner of Washington and Chambersburg streets.

What cannon fired the first Union artillery round of the battle?
The piece was part of John Calef's Battery A, 2nd U.S. Artillery. The specific tube was No. 233 and today is part of the monument to Brig. Gen. John Buford located along the Chambersburg Pike on McPherson's Ridge. (Magner, unpublished manuscript)

What reputed veteran of the war of 1812 picked up his musket and went to fight with the Union troops along McPherson's Ridge?
John Burns, who initially tried to fight with the 150th Pennsylvania but ended up fighting with the Iron Brigade. He was wounded three times and left on the field when the Union line retreated.

Following Reynolds's death who was in overall command of the First and Eleventh Corps at Gettysburg?
Maj. Gen. Oliver O. Howard.

During the fighting what happened to Brig. Gen. Gabriel René Paul, who had commanded Ft. Union in the New Mexico Territory?
He was shot in the head and blinded. This was the most serious of the five wounds Paul received on July 1.

What regiment held the Union left flank on Little Round Top on July 2, 1863?
The 20th Maine. They were also accompanied by the other regiments of Vincent's brigade including, from left to right, the 83rd Pennsylvania, 44th New York, and 16th Michigan. Eventually, Col. Patrick O'Rorke's 140th New York, the 91st Pennsylvania, the 146th New York, and the 155th New York of Brig. Gen. Stephen H. Weed's brigade came in to hold the southwestern and western military crest of the hill. (Pfanz, 229, map, 449–450)

Who commanded the 20th Maine at Gettysburg?
Col. Joshua L. Chamberlain, who has been called the savior of Little Round Top. He was later awarded the Medal of Honor for his actions on July 2.

What did Lt. Charles E. Hazlett and Brig. Gen. Stephen Weed have in common?
They both died of wounds suffered on Little Round Top. Weed was hit and paralyzed and then asked to see Hazlett. As Hazlett leaned over Weed, he was hit in the head by a shot. The two were taken to hospitals behind the lines where they later died. (Pfanz, 240)

What was Weed's reply to his aide who commented, "General, I hope that you are not so very badly hurt"?
"I'm as dead a man as Julius Caesar." (Pfanz, 240)

What Eleventh Corps general hid in a pigsty at Gettysburg?
Brig. Gen. Alexander Schimmelfennig. The general did not actually hide in the sty; rather, he hid behind a wood pile in the backyard of the Henry Garlach home. He remained in his hiding place from the afternoon of July 1 to the morning of July 4.

Who was the oldest Union brigadier general at Gettysburg?
Brig. Gen. George S. "Old Pop" Greene, at the age of sixty-two.

What became known as the Gettysburg gun?
A 12-pounder Napoleon gun from Brown's Battery B, 1st Rhode Island Artillery. During the cannonade prior to the Pickett-Pettigrew-Trimble Assault the gun was hit by a Confederate shell. When the gunners tried to load the piece the cannonball got stuck in the opening and, try as they might using the rammer and an ax, they could not drive the load home. The gun was finally removed from the field. It had been hit by three shells and thirty-nine bullets. Today the gun sits, having been disarmed, in the Rhode Island State House, a relic of the battle. ("The Gettysburg Gun")

Who was Samuel Wilkeson and what tragedy met him at Gettysburg?
A reporter for the New York *Times* who was covering the fighting at Gettysburg. His son Bayard was an officer in the Battery G, 4th U.S. Artillery, fighting north of the town on July 1. During the fighting Bayard was hit in the leg by a cannonball. Using a pen knife, Wilkeson amputated his own leg and then was taken prisoner, dying in Confederate hands. Samuel managed to find his son's grave on July 4. (Davis, 220–221)

Who was Amos Humiston?
Sgt. Amos Humiston of the 154th New York was found dead on Stratton Street in Gettysburg following the battle (near today's Gettysburg firehouse). In his hand he was clutching a photograph of three children. With no other identification but the photograph, officials searched for the dead man's family. The photograph was published in newspapers, and a poem was written about it. Eventually Humiston's wife and children were located in New York. Mrs. Humiston went on to become the first matron of an orphanage opened in Gettysburg using proceeds from the sale of the image. (Sifakis, 205)

Who was the youngest casualty of the battle of Gettysburg?
Edward McPherson Woods. Though it happened after the battle, Woods, at the age of three, became a fatality of the battle. Woods

and his older brother were wandering the field after the battle and the older child picked up a musket. Still loaded, the musket fired and hit young Woods, killing him. (Sifakis, 464)

Who gave general absolution to the members of the Irish Brigade before they went into action on July 2?
Father William Corby.

What did Father Corby say in his absolution of the Irish Brigade?
"Dominus noster Jesus Christus vos absolvat, et ego, auctoritate ipsius, vos absolvo ab omni vinculo, excommonunicationis interdicti, in quantum possum et vos indigetis dendie ego absolvo vos, a peccatis vestris, in nomini Patris, et Filii, et Spiritus Sancti. Amen!"
    Basically, in English; "*May our Lord Jesus Christ absolve you, and I by his authority absolve you from every bond of excommunication and interdict as far as I am able, and you have need. Moreover, I absolve you of your sins, in the name of the Father, and of the Son, and of the Holy Ghost. Amen.*" Some stories say that after he gave this absolution he said that anyone who turned his back on the enemy and ran would be denied a Christian burial and would go to hell. (Corby, 183)

As Daniel Sickles watched the action of his men during the fighting at the Peach Orchard salient, what happened to him?
He was struck in the lower right leg by an artillery round. Able to dismount his horse, he was attended to with makeshift dressings. He was eventually removed from the field and taken somewhere where his leg was amputated. There are numerous places where the act was supposed to have happened, but some experts believe it was at the Daniel Sheaffer Farm on the Baltimore Pike. (Pfanz, 333; Coco, 80)

What was the name of the doctor who amputated Daniel Sickles's leg?
Dr. Thomas Sim. (Pfanz, 334)

What was the name of the stretcher bearer who made a tourniquet from a saddle strop that stopped Daniel Sickles's bleeding and perhaps saved his life?
Pvt. William H. Bullard. (Pfanz, 333)

What was the council of war held on the night of July 2 and who was there?

Meade called a council of war to discuss with his generals plans for the rest of the battle. Held at the Widow Leister house, Meade's headquarters, the officers attending included Meade, Butterfield, Warren, Slocum, Hancock, Gibbon, Williams, Birney, Sykes, Howard, Sedgwick, and Newton. The meetings lasted until nearly midnight, and the only officer who did not take active part was Warren, who, slightly wounded and exhausted, sat down and slept in a corner. The final decision was that the army should stay in place, remain on the defensive, and wait perhaps a day before deciding on another plan. (Coddington, 449, 451)

Who hosted the famed Federal "lunch" just prior to the Pickett-Pettigrew-Trimble Assault on July 3rd?

Brig. Gen. John Gibbon and his staff. One of the staff had "picked up" an old tough rooster, which went into the pot. The meal was eventually joined by Generals Meade, Hancock, Newton, and Pleasonton. Gibbon's aide commented, "I think an unprejudiced person would have said of the bread that it was good; also of the potatoes before they were boiled. Of the chickens he would have questioned their age, but they were large and [in] good *running* order." (Magner, 23)

Who was General Meade's favorite horse?

Old Baldy. Baldy was raised on the western frontier and at the battle of First Manassas was owned by Col. (later Gen.) David Hunter. Meade purchased the animal in September 1861 for $150 and gave him the name Baldy due to his white face. At first Meade did not like the horse but eventually became very attached to him. During the course of the war Old Baldy was wounded as many as fourteen times; one of the most serious was at Gettysburg where a ball passed though Baldy's side and entered his stomach, just missing Meade's leg. Meade thought that Baldy had seen his last, but the horse recovered to be ridden again. When Baldy was hit again by a shell at Weldon Railroad in 1864, Meade finally retired him. (Magner, 6–7)

Old Baldy. CWLM

Who came to Lewis Armistead's aid as he lay wounded inside the Union lines on July 3?
Capt. Henry H. Bingham, who took a number of the general's personal effects to deliver to Gen. Hancock. Following Gettysburg, Bingham went on to receive the Medal of Honor for his actions during the battle of The Wilderness, and to be promoted to brevet brigadier general. After the war he was elected to Congress, where he served until his death in 1912. (Magner, 1)

What was the final major action of the Gettysburg Campaign?
The fight between Union and Confederate soldiers near Falling Waters, Maryland. When Lee reached the Williamsport and Falling Waters area late on July 6, he found the Potomac River over its banks due to heavy rains. Setting up a defensive position, he managed to stave off a Federal attack at Falling Waters until the river fell and he was able to lay down pontoon bridges. This, along with a drop in the

water level at Williamsport which made the ford at that point passable, enabled the Army of Northern Virginia to escape back into friendly territory. However, at Falling Waters, there were still two divisions on the wrong side of the river on July 14, and they were attacked by elements of Brig. Gen. John Buford's and Brig. Gen. Judson Kilpatrick's cavalry. During the fighting, the Confederates lost more than 1,000 soldiers but were able to make it back across the river. (Faust, 253)

Who was the last major Confederate casualty of the fighting at Falling Waters?
Brig. Gen. James J. Pettigrew. The general was wounded while, possibly, chasing a Federal cavalryman. Shot in the left side of his abdomen, the round passed through his body and came out his back. Pettigrew was taken across the Potomac, where he lingered for several days before dying. (Faust, 253; Tagg, 346)

Following the battle of Gettysburg what was the largest hospital established in the area?
Two weeks after the battle there were some sixty different hospitals containing 20,000 Union and Confederate wounded. Camp Letterman was established on July 20 on land about a mile east of the center of town on the York Pike adjoining the railroad. Many of the wounded were transferred elsewhere, but approximately 4,200 remained. At its peak, the hospital had some 400 tents, and every medical officer was in charge of between forty and seventy patients. Over the course of the summer the number lessened, until by November 10, only one hundred remained. The hospital closed on November 20, the day after Lincoln's speech. The hospital was named for Dr. Jonathan Letterman, medical director of the Army of the Potomac. (Coco, 167, 172)

Vicksburg

Where did Grant cross the Mississippi River, beginning his campaign toward Vicksburg?
Bruinsburg, Mississippi. (Bearss, 6)

Gen. John A. McClernand established his headquarters at the plantation of Alfred and Elizabeth Ingraham near Willow Springs, Mississippi. Who was Elizabeth's famous brother?
Maj. Gen. George Gordon Meade, commander of the Army of the Potomac. (Bearss, 7)

Who was accompanying Grant during the Vicksburg Campaign?
His twelve-year-old son Fred. (Bearss, 10)

Where was Lt. Gen. John C. Pemberton born and why was he fighting for the Confederacy?
Pemberton was born in Philadelphia, Pennsylvania; however, in 1848 he married Martha "Pattie" Thompson of Norfolk, Virginia, which probably played a part in his deciding to join the Confederacy. After the war, he lived in Penlyn, Pennsylvania, and upon his death was buried in Laurel Hill Cemetery in Philadelphia. (Magner, 43)

Who commanded the two forces at the battle of Raymond, Mississippi?
The Union force was comprised of the Seventeenth Corps, Army of the Tennessee, under Maj. Gen. James B. McPherson and included Maj. Gen. John A. Logan's Third Division, Brig. Gen. Marcellus M. Crocker's Seventh Division and a cavalry battalion under Capt. J. S. Foster. The Confederate forces were under the command of Brig. Gen. John Gregg. (Bearss, 17)

As the Federals approached Jackson, Mississippi, where did Gov. John J. Pettus move the capital?
Enterprise, Mississippi. (Bearss, 47)

Why was the Federal victory at Jackson, Mississippi, so easy?
Gen. Joseph E. Johnston had ordered the evacuation of all the Confederate troops in the city.

What did Grant do with his army once he took Jackson?
Turned it to the west and headed for Vicksburg.

What two major battles occurred once Grant began moving toward Vicksburg?
Champion Hill and Big Black Bridge.

Where was perhaps one of the shortest charges of the Civil War?
At the battle of Big Black Bridge. Brig. Gen. Michael K. Lawler lined his Federals up like a battering ram, sending them forward on a narrow two-regiment front. As the Union troops began their charge very close to the Rebel line, it did not take long to reach the Confederates. The Confederates broke, some heading for the river, while others surrendered. In all, the charge lasted three minutes. (Bearss, 49)

What was the first Union attack on Vicksburg?
May 19, 1863, when Maj. Gen. Frank Blair's Division led the Fifteenth Corps in an attack on the Stockade Redan area to the northeast of the city. The assault was repulsed. (Winschel, 10, 12)

How many men were awarded the Medal of Honor for their actions at Vicksburg, and who was the youngest?
A total of 122 men received the medal, the youngest being fourteen-year-old Orion P. Howe, who was the only survivor of four men sent back from the front line. Howe was a member of the 55th Illinois and delivered a message directly to Gen. Sherman, saying the regiment was out of ammunition. (Winschel, 10, 12)

During the assault of May 22, 1863, Capt. David Todd was one of the Confederates defending the Great Redoubt. Who was his brother-in-law?
President Abraham Lincoln. (Winschel, 14)

When did the siege of Vicksburg begin?
May 25, 1863. (Winschel, 16)

What was "Coonskin's Tower"?
Lt. Henry C. Foster of the 23rd Indiana was considered one of the better shots in the army. Known as "Coonskin" for the coonskin cap

he wore, he and some of his comrades built a tower out of railroad ties. Climbing atop their creation, they were able to pick off Confederates within their nearby works, the 3rd Louisiana Redan. The tower stood throughout the siege and became a popular "tourist" attraction for the soldiers. So many asked Foster if they could climb it that he started charging twenty-five cents. Thus he not only increased his reputation as a marksman but also added to his army pay. (Winschel, 20)

What happened when Gen. Grant visited "Coonskin's Tower"?
He was very lucky. Wearing his usual enlisted men's uniform with just his shoulder boards on, he climbed the tower and observed the goings-on in the Confederate line. A Rebel soldier saw him and yelled at him to get down. A Rebel captain admonished the soldier for using obscenities, then looked across the lines and recognized Grant. Luckily for Grant, the officer only admonished the soldier rather than telling him to shoot the Yankee commander. Grant, realizing he was in a precarious position, soon climbed down from his perch. (Winschel, 20)

The most famous story about mining under enemy lines is that of the Crater at Petersburg, but where else did Union troops cause a crater?
Vicksburg. Sappers dug entrenchments closer and closer to the 3rd Louisiana Redan, eventually getting so close that miners were called in to dig a tunnel under the redan. Completed on June 25, 2,200 pounds of black power were set in place. At 3:28 p.m. an explosion caused a crater fifteen feet deep and thirty feet wide, into which the Union infantry poured. The Confederates were ready, and a twenty-hour fight ensued. As at Petersburg, the Union assault failed; the Federal forces suffered 243 casualties while the Confederates only suffered 94. (Winschel, 21–22)

Who was Abraham and why did he become a celebrity at Vicksburg?
After the mine explosion of June 25 the Federals once again dug another mine. The Confederates sank a counter-mine, using eight African Americans to do the digging overseen by a white sapper. This

gallery was packed with 1,800 pounds of explosive and, when detonated, seven of the diggers were killed, as was the white sapper. One African American named Abraham was blown sky-high and thrown 150 feet into the Union lines. When he landed he was barely hurt and thus became famous. He was placed in a tent and an admission charge was paid for those interested in seeing "the man who was blown to freedom." (Winschel, 22)

What did Gen. Joseph E. Johnston do to help the beleaguered Vicksburg?
Nothing. His reply to Pemberton's request for aid was met with an answer that he was too weak to assist. Even when sent a message from Confederate Secretary of War James A. Sheldon pleading with him to assist the city, Johnston did not move until time was running out. (Winschel, 24)

Which two generals of Pemberton's staff rode out of Vicksburg under a flag of truce to deliver a letter to Grant asking for an armistice to discuss the city's surrender?
Brig. Gen. John S. Bowen and Lt. Col. Louis Montgomery. (Winschel, 47; Faust, 73)

What were Grant's initial terms?
Same as at Ft. Donelson; unconditional surrender. (Winschel, 47)

What happened in New York City between Monday, July 13, and Friday, July 17, 1863?
The New York City Draft Riots. On Monday morning, thousands of laborers failed to show up for work. They began roaming the streets in groups that continued to grow, eventually becoming a mob. The crowds threw rocks and then started setting buildings ablaze. The draft office on Third Avenue and the Colored Orphan Asylum on Fifth Avenue were burned. Blacks were hung from trees and lampposts. The mobs soon grew into thousands of people and went after anyone who was wealthy, black, or connected with conscription. (Livingston, 62, 64)

The majority of the rioters where made up of what ethnic group?
Irish, though many different ethnic groups participated. (Livingston, 64)

How was the rioting finally stopped?
The army was called out. Three days after it began, troops fresh from the Army of the Potomac and the Gettysburg battle reached the city. The troops moved street by street and tenement by tenement with bayonets, clearing out the rioters. There were often clashes between the soldiers and the crowds. In one such fight between the cavalry and the mob a howitzer was used. Twenty-eight rioters and seven soldiers were killed. (Livingston, 65)

What was the ultimate cost of the damage of the riots?
It has been estimated that more than a million dollars in damage was done, 105 people were killed, and many hundreds more were injured. (Livingston, 65)

Who were some notables wandering the streets of New York during the riots?
Col. Arthur Fremantle of the Coldstream Guards, who was in the city to catch a ship back to England. Henry J. Raymond, editor of the *New York Times*, got two Gatling guns and set them up in the windows to protect his newspaper; Raymond stayed with one of the guns while Leonard Jerome, a *Times* stockholder, manned the other one. In the end they did not have to use them. Jerome, eleven years later, would become Winston Churchill's grandfather. Brig. Gen. Judson Kilpatrick commanded the few cavalry in the city. Finally, taking time to check on his brother Edwin's house near Gramercy Park, John Wilkes Booth was in town. (Livingston, 64–65)

On July 16, 1863, what happened in Shimonoseki, Japan?
A battle was fought between American forces and those of the prince of the Choshiu clan. The prince fortified the Straits of Shimonoseki and then purchased and armed three ships. On June 26, 1863, the American ship *Pembroke* sailed near the fortifications and ships, where she was fired upon. A couple of weeks later, after Cmdr. David S. McDonald

heard of the altercation, he sailed the USS *Wyoming* into the area. Once again fired upon, McDonald took his ship and engaged the Japanese, sinking two of the ships and severely damaging the third. (Faust, 685)

What honor did William H. Carney, a former slave and sergeant in the 54th Massachusetts receive for his actions at Ft. Wagner, South Carolina, on July 18, 1863?
He became the first African American to receive the Medal of Honor. (Hughes, 12)

What did Robert E. Lee say to A. P. Hill on October 15, 1863, following the debacle at Bristoe Station?
"Well, well, General, bury these poor dead men and let us say no more about it." (Miller, 49)

Which Confederate brigadier general was hit in the leg during the fighting at Bristoe Station and later died of his wounds?
Brig. Gen. Carnot Posey, who led a Mississippi brigade in the battle. (Miller, 49)

What saved Warren's Second Corps at the battle of Bristoe Station?
Darkness. When night fell, Warren was able to get his corps across Broad Run and reunite with the rest of the army the next day. (Miller, 49)

On August 21, 1863, what Kansas town was all but destroyed by William Clark Quantrill?
Lawrence. Quantrill's men entered the town and killed about 150 men and boys and destroyed $1.5 million in property, leaving much of the town a smoldering ruin. (Faust, 427)

Chickamauga

What two armies clashed at Chickamauga, and who commanded them?
The Army of Tennessee, commanded by Gen. Braxton Bragg; and The Army of the Cumberland, led by Maj. Gen. William S. Rosecrans. (Robertson, 6)

What was the opening action of the battle of Chickamauga?
At 2:00 a.m. on the morning of September 19, 1863, the 69th Ohio, under Lt. Col. Joseph Brigham, recovered Reed's Bridge over West Chickamauga Creek, capturing several Confederate pickets. The Ohioans then set fire to the bridge and returned to their lines. (Robertson, 7)

The opening shots of the battle were between what two units?
Brig. Gen. H. B. Davidson's Confederate cavalry of Forrest's Corps and Col. Daniel McCook's brigade of the Federal Reserve Corps. (Robertson, 7–8)

Where were the initial shots of the battle fired?
In the area of Jay's Mill on the northern portion of the battlefield. (Robertson, 8)

What is the significance of the death of Pvt. John Ingraham of Co. K, 2nd Battalion, 1st Confederate (Georgia) Infantry?
His is the only officially marked grave on today's Chickamauga battlefield. (Robertson, 25)

On September 20, what Union general, in moving his troops to fill a supposed gap in the line, actually created one?
Brig. Gen Thomas J. Wood. Rosecrans had been told of a gap in his line so he ordered Wood to take his men and plug it. Wood protested, saying there was no gap, but then followed his orders. A gap now existed where Wood had been, which was soon filled with Confederate troops under Lt. Gen. James Longstreet. Rosecrans and half his army were routed and driven off the field. (Faust, 137)

Where did Maj. Gen. George Thomas make his stand at Chickamauga, thus saving Rosecrans's army?
Snodgrass Hill. Thomas's men were able to hold their line until dusk, when Thomas ordered them back, eventually setting up a rear guard at Rossville Gap. The Confederates retained possession of the battlefield. (Faust, 137)

For this stand what nom de guerre did Thomas receive?
"Rock of Chickamauga."

Chattanooga (Missionary Ridge/Lookout Mountain)

By the end of October 1863, what was the alignment of the two armies around Chattanooga?
Rosecrans and his Army of the Cumberland were cooped up within the city. To the southwest and southeast were Bragg's Army of Tennessee. On Bragg's left near Lookout Mountain was Longstreet's Corps. To his right along the crest of Missionary Ridge were the Corps' of Breckinridge and Cheatham. (Sword, 10)

With his inability to retake Lookout Mountain and the increasing misery of his troops due to lack of supplies, what happened to Rosecrans on October 19?
He was replaced by Maj. Gen. George H. Thomas. Four days later, Maj. Gen. Ulysses S. Grant arrived in Chattanooga, having been made the overall commander of the vast area. (Sword, 12)

What was the "Cracker Line"?
When Gen. Grant took command of the Federal troops in Chattanooga on October 23, 1863, the garrison was on reduced rations because the closest supply depot was in Bridgeport, Alabama, some sixty miles away. The few rations that did come through traveled over bad roads through the Sequatchie Valley, across Walden's Ridge and crossing the Tennessee River. The trains often came under attack, and arrival in Chattanooga was questionable. Grant's chief engineer, Maj. Gen. William F. Smith, suggested opening a water route down the Tennessee River from Bridgeport. On October 27, Brig. Gen. William B. Hazen took his brigade by pontoon to Moccasin Point, a dry spit of land opposite Raccoon Mountain. At the same time, Brig. Gen. John B. Turchin marched his brigade overland to Moccasin Point. While these two brigades bested the small Confederate detachment at Brown's Ferry, Maj. Gen. Joseph Hooker's men pushed the Confederates off Raccoon Mountain. The river was

now clear, and on November 1 the first steamboat arrived at Brown's Ferry, ending the siege. (Faust, 189)

Who commanded the Union troops that assaulted and captured Lookout Mountain?
Maj. Gen. Joseph Hooker.

What is another name for the battle of Lookout Mountain?
The "Battle above the Clouds."

What happened in the action around Wauhatchie during the night fighting of October 28–29, 1863?
Two brigades under Brig. Gen. John W. Geary were camped near Wauhatchie (near the western foot of Lookout Mountain near Lookout Creek). About 12:30 a.m. on October 29, a single Confederate brigade under Col. John S. Bratton stumbled onto the camp and a sharp fight broke out that lasted almost two hours. Finally Bratton was told by Brig. Gen. Micah Jenkins to break off the engagement because elements of Hooker's command were pushing south out of Brown's Ferry. During the fighting, Lt. Edward R. Geary, the general's son, was killed, and Brig. Gen. George Greene of Gettysburg fame was severely wounded in the face. (Sword, 16, 19; Heidler and Heidler, 818; Tagg, 164)

What were the first two vessels to open the cracker line?
The *Paint Rock*, towing two barges, and the *Chattanooga*, a converted scow. (Sword, 19)

Following the opening of the cracker line, what did Braxton Bragg do to James Longstreet?
Longstreet, like many of Bragg's subordinates, was a thorn in his side. Bragg decided to get rid of him by sending him off on a campaign to Knoxville aimed at driving out Maj. Gen. Ambrose E. Burnside. Thus on November 5, 1863, Longstreet and his men boarded trains and headed to East Tennessee. (Sword, 19–20)

How did Lookout Mountain finally fall?
On November 24, troops under Gen. Geary attacked the mountain from the west, moving north along a plateau and driving before them

the Confederates who retreated farther up the mountain. As Geary's men approached the northern end of the mountain, Federal troops under Gen. Peter Osterhaus attacked from the north. Confederate leadership failed, and finally Gen. Bragg, thinking his Missionary Ridge line more important, decided to abandon Lookout Mountain. (Sword, 48–54)

Who were the first Union troops to reach the summit of Lookout Mountain?

On the morning of November 25, Union troops looked up at the mountain expecting to see Rebel soldiers; instead, they saw a Yankee waving the Stars and Stripes. Before daylight, rumors that the Rebs had left began circulating, so Capt. John Wilson took a six-man squad from the 8th Kentucky Infantry and scaled the heights. Reaching the summit and finding no enemy troops they unfurled the colors and planted them at today's Point Park. The sun soon burned away the clouds, illuminating the flag, which caused a cheer to go up from the Federals in Chattanooga Valley. (Sword, 55)

Who commanded the Army of the Tennessee during the fighting around Chattanooga?

Maj. Gen. William Tecumseh Sherman, who arrived in Chattanooga on November 19. (Sword, 20)

Following the Confederate defeat at Chattanooga, what was the fate of Braxton Bragg?

Bragg, at his request, was relieved of command and replaced temporarily by Lt. Gen. Joseph E. Johnston, who relieved William J. Hardee as commander of the Army of Tennessee on December 27, 1863. Bragg was transferred to Richmond, where he became the chief military advisor to Davis. (Catton, 407)

Who was Arthur MacArthur of the 24th Wisconsin and why was he important in the attack on Missionary Ridge?

MacArthur was awarded the Medal of Honor for planting his regiment's colors on the crest of Missionary Ridge during the Federal attack. He was also the father of Douglas MacArthur of World War One and Two fame. (Dickson, 234)

What happened at Baxter Springs, Kansas, on October 6, 1863?
Another massacre perpetuated by William Clark Quantrill. Baxter
Springs held a small garrison of Union troops, two companies of the
3rd Wisconsin Cavalry, and one company of the 2nd Kansas Colored
regiment, commanded by Lt. James B. Pond. The site had a small fort,
but many of the soldiers were away from the structure getting their
midday meal when Quantrill's men rode up, causing the Federals to
run. Many of the fleeing soldiers were gunned down in cold blood.
Pond unlimbered a howitzer and fired on the guerrillas, stopping the
carnage. Meanwhile, a wagon train guarded by 100 cavalry troopers
and containing the personal property of Maj. Gen. James G. Blunt
blundered into the fighting. Blunt was in the process of transferring
the headquarters of the Army of the Frontier from Ft. Scott to Ft.
Smith. When Quantrill attacked, Blunt realized he had a problem,
so he and some of his men escaped. Unfortunately, the men in one
of the wagons and a military band could not escape and were killed
and mutilated. Ninety-eight Federals were killed, with three guerrillas killed and four wounded. When Blunt and the survivors reached
Ft. Scott he was relieved of command for not properly protecting his
column. (Faust, 47)

Where and what was Ft. Sanders?
Ft. Sanders (known to the Confederates as Ft. Loudon) was located
on the northwest corner of Knoxville's entrenchments. The fort was
protected by a twelve-foot-wide ditch that was eight feet deep. The
walls were almost vertical, rising fifteen feet to the top of the parapet.
On November 29, 1863, the fort was manned by elements of the
29th Massachusetts, 2nd Michigan, 20th Michigan, and 79th New
York, along with twelve guns. At the time of the Confederate attack,
the fort had approximately 440 defenders. When the Confederates
attacked they managed to make it to the ditch, but without scaling
ladders, the steep slope of the parapet, along with frozen ground and
sleet, brought the attackers to a halt. The Confederates finally withdrew with a loss of 813; Federal losses inside the fort were eight killed
and five wounded. (Boatner, 297–298)

What was the result of the action at Rappahannock Station on November 7, 1863?
Following the action at Bristoe Station on October 14, 1863, Lee decided to move his army south of the Rappahannock River and wait for any new offensive by Maj. Gen. George G. Meade. It was Meade's plan to retake the ground between the Rappahannock and Rapidan rivers. Lee fortified the river crossings at Rappahannock Station and Kelly's Ford, hoping that Meade would cross at Kelly's Ford. Once the Federals were across the river, Lee would attack them. On November 7, Maj. Gen. William French crossed at Kelly's Ford, and Maj. Gen. John Sedgwick assailed the Rappahannock Station bridgehead. In an unusual dusk attack, Sedgwick's men captured the Confederate brigade defending the bridgehead, taking 1,675 prisoners east of the river, thus taking control of the crossing. In all, Lee lost that day at Kelly's Ford and Rappahannock Bridge about 2,044 men, and the Federals 461. Lee then ordered a general withdrawal, and by November 10 was south of the Rapidan. (Faust, 615)

EVENTS

The Gettysburg Address

When was Gettysburg's Evergreen Cemetery established and in 1863 who was president of the board?
The cemetery was established in 1854 and the president of the board was David McConaughy, a Gettysburg attorney. (Magner, 103)

Who was the superintendent of Evergreen Cemetery in 1863?
Peter Thorn. During 1863, Thorn was serving with the 138th Pennsylvania, so his pregnant wife Elizabeth was taking care of his duties. (Magner, 104)

Who were the two individuals who came up with the idea for the Soldiers' National Cemetery in Gettysburg?
Local attorney David Wills and Dr. Theodore Dimon. Wills was a resident of Gettysburg and acted as Governor Curtin's on-site agent

to assist various soldiers and their families. Dr. Dimon was a surgeon who was in Gettysburg attending to the New York wounded and was acting as the New York state agent for reburials. (Magner, 103–104)

Where was the original site for the planned cemetery?
Raffensperger's Hill (today's East Cemetery Hill) across the Baltimore Pike from Evergreen Cemetery. Unfortunately, McConaughy had already arranged a deal with the owners of the property, so when Wills approached with his idea, an argument erupted. Finally, Wills gave up, and striking a deal with McConaughy, acquired properties to the west of the Evergreen Cemetery, where the National Cemetery sits today. The only stipulation was that only an open iron railing fence separate the two cemeteries. (Magner, 104, 109)

What is unique about the iron fence that today is sited between Evergreen Cemetery and the National Cemetery?
Part of the fence immediately behind the Soldiers' National Monument originally bounded Lafayette Square in Washington, D.C., and it was against one of these sections that Philip Barton Key fell when he was shot by Daniel Sickles. When the fence was removed from Lafayette Square in 1905, Sickles, then chairman of the New York Civil War Monuments Commission, arranged for the fence's transfer and relocation at Gettysburg. (Magner, 109)

Who designed the National Cemetery?
William Saunders. Saunders was a landscape gardener who had been trained at the University of Edinburgh in Scotland. He arrived in Gettysburg six weeks after the battle and began his work. (Magner, 106)

Who was hired to dig up and re-inter the Union soldiers buried on the battlefield?
Frederick W. Biesecker. Biesecker came in with the low bid of $1.59 per body. Basil Biggs was in charge of a crew of eight to ten African Americans whose job it was to dig up the bodies, place the remains into coffins, and transfer them to the cemetery. (Magner, 106–107)

Who was the superintendent of exhumation?
Samuel Weaver. Free blacks were doing the work and every grave that
was opened was done so with Weaver watching. (Magner, 106)

**Who was the first soldier to be buried in the new Soldiers' National
Cemetery?**
Pvt. Enoch M. Detty of Co. G, 73rd Ohio, on October 27, 1863.
(Magner, 106)

When were all the bodies finally transferred to the cemetery?
The work in 1863 went on until the ground became too frozen to
dig. It was continued in the spring, and finally, on March 19, 1864,
Weaver reported to Wills that the job was complete. In all, 3,512 bodies had been moved. There are also 158 Union soldiers' remains buried
in Evergreen Cemetery. (Magner, 108–109)

**What was the original date set for the dedication of the National
Cemetery?**
October 23, 1863. Unfortunately, the featured speaker, Edward Ever-
ett, could not be in Gettysburg until November 19. (Magner, 106)

**Besides Edward Everett, whom did David Wills invite to the cem-
etery dedication?**
Vice President Hannibal Hamlin, various cabinet members, foreign
ministers, and a large number of generals. He also contacted the poet
Longfellow, the chaplain of the House of Representatives, and the
president of the nearby Lutheran Seminary. And, as an afterthought,
the president. General George Meade declined the invitation due to
his duties with the Army of the Potomac, and General Winfield Scott
declined because of his infirmities. Both Salmon P. Chase and Longfellow also declined to attend. (Klement, 9)

Where did President Lincoln stay while he was in Gettysburg?
The home of David Wills, along with Edward Everett and Governor
Curtin. The house was located on the east side of the Diamond in the
center of the town. Next door was the home of Robert G. Harper,
which was where Secretary of State Seward stayed. (Klement, 11–12)

Where was the platform from which Lincoln gave his speech?
It was not, as many old sources indicate, on the site of the Soldiers' National Monument. Rather, it was located behind the Soldiers' Monument, near a mausoleum in the Evergreen Cemetery. (Magner, 112; Guelzo; Magner, unpublished manuscript)

What was the seating arrangement on the speaker's platform?
President Lincoln sat in the middle of the front row, with Edward Everett to his right. Secretary of State Seward sat to the president's left, with Governor Curtin sitting next to him. (Klement, 16)

Who gave the invocation at the Gettysburg ceremonies?
Rev. Thomas H. Stockton. (Klement, 17)

How many words were in the Gettysburg Address and how long did it take Lincoln to deliver it?
The address contained 272 words and was delivered in a little over two minutes.

How many copies are there of the Gettysburg Address in Lincoln's handwriting?
Six: the first draft (known as the Nicolay Copy); the second draft (the Hay Copy); the third or "lost" draft (the Wills Copy); the fourth draft (the Everett Copy); the fifth draft (the Bancroft Copy); and the sixth draft (the Bliss Copy). (Klement, 139, 147, 152, 166, 170, 174)

How many bands participated in the National Cemetery dedication?
Four bands marched in the procession and two bands played during the ceremonies, including the Marine Band directed by Francis Scala. (Klement, 192, 198)

Where and with whom did President Lincoln attend church on the afternoon of November 19, 1862?
He went to the Presbyterian Church with William Seward and the local town hero John Burns. (Klement, 18)

Who was Lincoln's parade marshal at the Gettysburg cemetery dedication?

Ward Hill Lamon. He was also the master of ceremonies. (Allen Guelzo, Gettysburg, PA; Klement, 27)

UNITS

What unit was known as the Second Yager Regiment?

The 41st New York. It was also known as the "De Kalb Regiment." Mustered in on June 9, 1861, it was commanded by Lt. Col Heinrich Detleo Von Einsiedel. The regiment was at Ball's Bluff before seeing action in the Shenandoah Valley. It participated in the Seven Days' Battles, Maryland Campaign, Fredericksburg, Chancellorsville, Gettysburg, the Overland Campaign, and the Siege of Petersburg. (Davis, 183; Fox, 1419–1420; Raus, 59)

What regiments made up George Custer's Cavalry Brigade?

The 1st, 5th, 6th, and 7th Michigan Cavalry. Named by Custer his "Wolverines," he led them until October 1, 1864, when he replaced Brig. Gen. James H. "Harry" Wilson as a division commander. During the war, the brigade lost 524 troopers, the highest percentage of men killed in any Federal cavalry brigade. (Faust, 200–201)

The men of Mosby's Raiders were part of what unit?

The 43rd Battalion Virginia Partisan Rangers. For twenty-seven months they wreaked havoc on Federal units. When the regiment disbanded on April 21, 1865, around 1,900 men had ridden with the unit.

The Philadelphia Brigade, which fought at the Angle during the Pickett-Pettigrew-Trimble Assault, was made up of what regiments?

The 69th Pennsylvania, 71st Pennsylvania, 72nd Pennsylvania, and 106th Pennsylvania. They were the Second Brigade of John Gibbon's Second Division, commanded by Brig. Gen. Alexander S. Webb. (Magner, 10)

What four regiments of the Philadelphia Brigade were also known as California Regiments?

71st Pennsylvania (First California Regiment), 69th Pennsylvania (Second California), 72nd Pennsylvania (Third California), and 106th Pennsylvania (Fifth California). The 72nd was also known as "Baxter's Philadelphia Fire Zouaves." In 1861, these regiments were part of Col. Edward Baker's "California Brigade," which fought at Ball's Bluff; however, only the First California participated in the battle. (Raus, 120, 121, 129)

What regiment was known as "Biff Sticks"?

The 3rd United States Infantry. Originally organized in 1815, during the Civil War they participated in actions at First Manassas, the Peninsula Campaign, Second Manassas, Antietam, Fredericksburg, Chancellorsville, and Gettysburg. (Raus, 150; Dyer, 1710–1711)

CHAPTER 5

1864

PERSONALITIES

Who was inaugurated governor of Virginia in January 1864?
Maj. Gen. William "Extra Billy" Smith. (Faust, 698)

What future famous Philadelphia architect was awarded the Medal of Honor for his actions at the battle of Trevilian Station?
Frank Furness. A member of the 6th Pennsylvania Cavalry, he carried a box of ammunition across an open space swept by Confederate fire. During his career he designed some of Philadelphia's most prominent buildings and is the only American of note to have received the Medal of Honor. Today he is considered to be the first real "All-American" architect. (Magner, 72)

What fate befell the talented Brig. Gen. Micah Jenkins?
On May 6, 1864, as Lt. Gen. James Longstreet and Gen. Jenkins were entering the action on the second day of the battle of The Wilderness, both generals were mistaken for Federals and shot by their own troops, probably members of the 12th Virginia. Longstreet was seriously wounded, but Jenkins took a bullet in the brain and soon died. (Faust, 394–395)

Who took command of the Federal forces in the Western Theater when Ulysses S. Grant became general in chief and was transferred to the Eastern Theater?
Maj. Gen. William T. Sherman.

Name the two Federal generals who hid in a bomb-proof behind the lines getting drunk during the battle of the Crater near Petersburg?
Brig. Gen. James Hewett Ledlie and Brig. Gen. Edward Ferrero. Ferrero, in his early years, including his time at West Point, taught dance.

Who was Abraham Lincoln's running mate in the presidential election of 1864 and from what state did he come?
Gov. Andrew Johnson of Tennessee.

Who was Joseph Holt?
Holt first served as postmaster general in President Buchanan's administration and succeeded John B. Floyd as secretary of war on the latter's December 29, 1860, resignation. Holt first came to prominence when Abraham Lincoln appointed him judge advocate general of the army in September 1862. In 1864 he became the first head of the Bureau of Military Justice with the rank of brigadier general. Finally, in 1865, when President Johnson appointed a military commission to try those charged in the Lincoln assassination, Holt was one of the trio who conducted the government's case. Later he was accused of not showing the recommendation of the commission requesting the president commute the death penalty of Mary Surratt to life in prison. Holt remained judge advocate general until 1875 and spent the rest of his life insisting that Johnson had seen the clemency recommendation. (Faust, 367)

Whom did Abraham Lincoln choose to replace Chief Justice Taney upon his death on October 12, 1864?
Former Secretary of the Treasury Salmon P. Chase. (Faust, 742)

Who was U. S. Grant's military secretary?
Col. Ely Samuel Parker, a Seneca Indian. (Faust, 556)

What Union officer led a daring tunnel escape from Libby Prison in Richmond?
Col. Thomas E. Rose led 109 men through the tunnel. Forty-eight were recaptured, two drowned, and the rest managed to make it back to Union lines. (Denney, 373)

What was Navy Lt. Commander Thomas O. Selfridge's problem with the letter "C"?

It seems that every ship he was stationed on that began with the letter "C" sank. First was the USS *Cumberland*, which went down on March 8, 1862, when rammed by the CSS *Virginia*. Then it was the USS *Cairo*, which sank on December 12, 1862, when it hit two torpedoes. This was followed by the USS *Conestoga*, which was rammed by the USS *General Price* and sank in four minutes on March 8, 1864. Admiral David Dixon Porter decided to place Selfridge on a ship further down in the alphabet, which he did by assigning him to the USS *Osage*, which saw action on the ill-fated Red River Campaign. Selfridge's next ship was the *Vindicator*. (Denney, 383)

On Wednesday March 9, 1864, what honor was bestowed on Ulysses S. Grant?

President Lincoln handed him his commission as lieutenant general. (Denney, 384)

What did Grant do after he got his new commission?

He began by having private conversations with the president, then he left for the front, arriving the next day and conferring with Maj. Gen. Meade. (Denney, 384)

Who was William Barker Cushing?

Cushing was a naval officer who led a daring attack on the Confederate ram *Albemarle* at Plymouth, North Carolina, on October 27, 1864. With fifteen men Cushing rammed a spar torpedo into the *Albemarle*, sinking her. Only Cushing and one other man managed to avoid capture after the sinking. Following the incident he was promoted and given the thanks of Congress. His brother Alonzo Cushing commanded an artillery battery and was killed at Gettysburg. (Faust, 199–200)

Who was Stephen Dodson Ramseur?

On June 1, 1864, Ramseur, at the age of twenty-seven, became the youngest West Pointer to attain the rank of major general in the Confederate Army. Ramseur, a North Carolinian, had served the

Confederacy well, fighting in most of the battles of the Army of Northern Virginia. For a furious counterattack at Spotsylvania he received the personal thanks of Robert E. Lee; a high honor indeed. He was wounded at Malvern Hill and Chancellorsville, and mortally wounded at Cedar Creek, dying on October 20, 1864. (Faust, 613)

What event, which took place on November 29, 1864, led to the resignation of Col. John M. Chivington, who was instrumental in the Union victory at Glorieta Pass?
He led a regiment that attacked a Cheyenne village. Known as the Sand Creek Massacre, the soldiers butchered Black Kettle's men, women, and children. Chivington resigned rather than face a court-martial. (Faust, 140; Kliger, 59)

What was the fate of Col. William R. "Dirty Shirt" Scurry?
Following his adventures in New Mexico Territory, he was promoted to brigadier general. He led a brigade in the Red River Campaign and was mortally wounded at Jenkins' Ferry on April 30, 1864, during the Camden Expedition. (Kliger, 59)

Who was John A. Huff?
A member of the Michigan Cavalry, who, it has been said, mortally wounded Gen. Jeb Stuart at the battle of Yellow Tavern on May 11, 1864. Huff himself was mortally wounded a little over two weeks later at Haw's Shop. (Boatner, 416)

Who was the supreme commander of the Sons of Liberty?
Formerly known as the Knights of the Golden Circle, the organization was run by Clement Laird Vallandingham. (Boatner, 466)

What happened to Maj. Gen. John Sedgwick on May 9, 1864, at the battle of Spotsylvania Court House after he said, "Why, what are you dodging for? They could not hit an elephant at that distance"?
He was hit by a shot from a Confederate sharpshooter and killed. (Catton, 422)

What was Robert E. Lee's mournful comment on hearing of the death of J. E. B. Stuart?
"He never brought me a piece of false information." (Catton, 426)

What Confederate lieutenant general was killed at Pine Mountain, Georgia, on June 14, 1864?
Lt. Gen. Leonidas Polk, who was struck in the chest by a Federal artillery shot. (Denney, 425)

Following the Union Army Group's almost unopposed July 8 crossing of the Chattahoochie River, who replaced Joe Johnston on July 17 as the Army of Tennessee commander?
Lt. Gen. John Bell Hood. (Faust 368)

What two serious wounds had John Bell Hood suffered earlier in the war?
At the battle of Gettysburg he was shot in the left arm, leaving it partially disabled. At the battle of Chickamauga he was again wounded when shot in his right hip, which necessitated a disarticulated amputation. (Faust, 369)

Whom did Grant place in command of the Army of the Shenandoah on August 7, 1864, and what were his orders?
Maj. Gen. Phil Sheridan. He was to rid the Shenandoah Valley of Jubal Early and his army. (Denney, 442)

What woman editor/poet was instrumental in convincing Lincoln that he should create the Thanksgiving holiday?
Sarah Josepha Buell Hale. She was an editor for *Godey's Ladies Book* and is also given credit for writing the well-known poem *Mary Had a Little Lamb*. (Magner, 64)

Who was John Rodgers Meigs and what was his fate?
The son of quartermaster general Montgomery Meigs. On October 3, 1864, while returning from a surveying assignment, he was shot and killed (supposedly in cold blood) by three Confederate cavalrymen. His

grave, near his father's in Arlington National Cemetery, has a bronze casting of Meigs as he looked after he was killed, sprawled in a muddy road with his pistol lying beside him. (Faust, 485)

When Maj. Gen. Winfield Scott Hancock was forced to step down because his Gettysburg wound failed to heal, who replaced him as commander of the Second Corps?
Maj. Gen. A. A. Humphries, who remained in command of the corps until the surrender at Appomattox Court House. (Faust, 375)

Who commanded the Confederate troops in Savannah, Georgia, upon Sherman's arrival?
Lt. Gen. William J. Hardee. (Faust, 338)

What was William J. Hardee's nom de guerre?
"Old Reliable." (Faust, 338)

Who became the first vice admiral in U.S. History?
David G. Farragut. (Denney, 507)

Who started a dump-Lincoln movement from within Lincoln's own cabinet?
Salmon P. Chase. (Allen Guelzo, Gettysburg, PA)

What was Lincoln's eldest son Robert nicknamed?
"The Prince of Rails." (Allen Guelzo, Gettysburg, PA)

Who was George N. Barnard?
A photographer who, after a short stint with Mathew Brady, went west to Tennessee. He followed Sherman's army during the Atlanta Campaign and was eventually contracted by the U.S. government to photograph the Confederate defenses and fortifications of Atlanta. Following the war he produced *Photographic Views of Sherman's Campaign*, a book of sixty-one full-sized prints. (Faust, 39, 40)

Who was the leader of the "raiders" at Andersonville Prison?
William "Mosby" Collins of the 88th Pennsylvania. (Davis, 457–458)

Who was Henry Watkins Allen?
A former Confederate senior officer, who at one time was colonel of the 4th Louisiana Infantry. He was badly wounded at Shiloh's Hornet's Nest, later to become a brigadier general who was elected governor of Louisiana in January 1864. (Faust, 7)

Who was William Wirt Allen?
The last major general appointed by Jefferson Davis, on March 4, 1865. Unfortunately, the Confederate government was in such disarray that the promotion was never confirmed by the Senate. (Faust, 8)

Who was Senator John Conness?
A Senator from the state of California instrumental in getting a bill passed to protect the Yosemite Valley from exploitation and to save the area's natural wonders. On June 30, 1864, President Lincoln signed the bill giving Yosemite Valley and the Mariposa grove of giant sequoias to California as an "inalienable public trust." This was the first time that the Federal government set aside scenic lands for the people. It eventually helped pave the way to making Yellowstone the first national park in 1872. (NPS, Yosemite National Park, 1)

Who was Thomas Ryan?
Reputed to be one of the top bounty jumpers during the war, Ryan was credited with having enlisted thirty times. He was eventually caught in 1864, court-martialed, and sentenced to be executed by firing squad. Lincoln, known for commuting death sentences, did not do so in this case, and Ryan met his fate late in the year. (Sifakis, 349)

What happened to Maj. Gen. Robert Rodes at the battle of Opequon Creek (Third Winchester) on September 19, 1864?
While leading a counterattack against two Union commands, he was mortally wounded when struck in the head by fragments from a bursting shell. His actions, however, allowed Early's defeated army to retreat. (Faust, 640, 835)

What Gettysburg hero was wounded during the assault at Petersburg on June 18, 1864?
Col. Joshua Chamberlain. While leading a brigade against the Confederate line, Chamberlain was hit in the right hip by a minié ball that passed through his body, coming to rest in his left hip just below the skin. Placing his sword tip on the ground he remained standing so as not to demoralize his men. Eventually, due to loss of blood, he finally went down to one knee, then slumped over. Lieutenants West Funk and Benjamin Walters pulled him back from his exposed position. He spent almost an hour lying in the dirt before he was removed from the field and taken to a field hospital, where the surgeon pronounced the wound mortal. Chamberlain didn't die, however; he was present at the surrender at Appomattox Court House before going home to become a professor and eventually governor of Maine. Following Chamberlain's wounding, General Grant promoted him on the spot to brigadier general. (Trulock, 209, 210, 212)

EVENTS

When did the first Union prisoners enter Andersonville Prison?
February 25, 1864. By July, the prisoner population had risen to around 32,000. (Faust, 16)

MISCELLANEOUS

Who was the first commandant of Andersonville?
Col. Alexander W. Persons. (Davis, 454)

What was the name of the contaminated creek that ran through the center of the Andersonville camp?
Stockade Branch of Sweet Water Creek. (Davis, 454)

Who were "the raiders" at Andersonville?
A band of prisoners who were thieves and killers. They preyed on the weak prisoners, stealing food, clothing, or whatever they could. (Davis, 457)

What happened to Andersonville's "raiders"?
With the permission of commandant Henry Wirz the prisoners took matters into their own hands and arrested the men. After a trial, six of the raiders were hanged on July 11 while three others died of beatings. The men were buried in a separate part of the prison cemetery, where they still remain today, segregated from those whom they had mistreated. (Davis, 457, 458)

Under Grant's planning, what three Union armies in Virginia would go after the Army of Northern Virginia and the Confederate capital, and who commanded them?
The Army of the James under Maj. Gen. Benjamin Butler, the Army of the Potomac led by Maj. Gen. George Meade, and an army in the Shenandoah commanded by Maj. Gen. Franz Sigel. (Catton, 411)

What were "bounty jumpers"?
Men who enlisted to collect a bounty, then at the first opportunity deserted. Often these men would then go to another district where they would perform the process again. One bounty jumper who was caught admitted having gone through the routine some thirty times. Men who were caught were imprisoned, and in some cases, executed. (Henig, 44)

What was the other name for the third battle of Winchester on September 19, 1864?
The battle of Opequon Creek. (Faust, 547)

What led to the demise of Confederate spy Rose O'Neal Greenhow?
She was returning from Europe in 1864 on the blockade runner *Condor* on October 1, 1864, when the ship got stuck on a sandbar off the coast of Wilmington, North Carolina. The captain sent Greenhow and two companions to shore in a lifeboat but the vessel capsized. Greenhow drowned when the $2,000 in gold she was carrying dragged her down. Her body was later recovered and buried in Wilmington. (Faust, 324)

What were "bummers"?
Union foragers who were part of Sherman's March to the Sea and the Carolina Campaign. The men had been authorized to live off the land; they did so by plundering and pillaging in an attempt to live in such a way that, in Sherman's opinion, "made Georgia howl."

Who wrote the poem "Sheridan's Ride," praising Phil Sheridan's ride from Winchester to Cedar Creek?
Thomas Buchanan Read. Living in Rome, he returned to the United States and served on the staffs of generals Lew Wallace and William Rosecrans. Read wrote his eight-stanza poem in only a few hours after seeing Thomas Nast's drawing "Sheridan's Ride to the Front." (Magner, 66)

What was Belle Plain, Virginia, used for?
During the Overland Campaign it was used as a supply depot and holding area for Confederate prisoners before they were shipped north to prisoner of war camps. (Catton, 425)

By 1864 what financial problem was rampant in the North?
Almost half of the paper money in circulation was counterfeit. (Craughwell, 41)

Whom did Salmon P. Chase and Edwin Stanton employ to work for the Treasury Department with the of job tracking down counterfeiters?
William P. Wood, who at the time was the superintendent of the Old Capital Prison. Chase and Stanton technically overstepped their bounds in making what was technically a new government bureau, not having asked for the approval of Congress or the support of Lincoln. Wood was an unsavory character who hired out-and-out crooks to work for him, but he successfully rounded up more than 200 counterfeiters within his first year of operation. (Craughwell, 43, 44)

What was Grant's campaign order to Meade at the beginning of the Overland Campaign?
"Wherever Lee goes, there you will go also." (Denney, 390)

What tragedy struck the Confederate White House on April 30, 1864?
President and Varina Davis's five-year-old son, Joe Davis, fell from the veranda of the Confederate White House and was killed. (Denney, 398)

What national holiday did Lincoln proclaim as being on the last Thursday of November on October 20, 1864?
Thanksgiving Day. (Denney, 477)

What three boats did Nathan Bedford Forrest's cavalry capture on October 30, 1864?
The gunboat *Undine*, and two transports, *Venus* and *Cheesemen*. (Denney, 482)

On November 8, Abraham Lincoln was reelected president by what percentage of the popular vote?
More than 55 percent, and he received 212 electoral votes to McClellan's 21. (Denney, 484)

How much of the soldier vote did Lincoln receive?
Seventy-eight percent. (Catton, 512)

What was the Sand Creek Massacre?
Near Ft. Lyon in the Colorado Territory there was a camp of some 500 peaceful Arapaho and Cheyenne. Because of raids around the Denver area by local Indians, the inhabitants thought that these Indians might be involved. Col. John M. Chivington took his 3rd Colorado into the Indian camp on November 29 and slaughtered many men, as well as a significant number of women and children. (Faust, 140)

Who was Roman Nose?
Roman Nose, a Northern Cheyenne warrior, led a group of his braves against the whites in retaliation for the Sand Creek Massacre. On January 7, 1865, in an attack on Julesburg, located on the South Platte River in northeast Colorado, they killed eighteen men who had been members of the 1st Colorado Cavalry; and then on January 14–15,

near today's Marino, Colorado, the Lakota and Cheyenne warriors killed some ranchers who had been members of the 3rd Colorado Cavalry. (Sifakis, 339)

What was Col. John Chivington's fate after the Sand Creek Massacre?

He was investigated by Congress and found to be "a frightening, pathological racist," whereupon he resigned his commission to avoid a court-martial. After the war he wandered the West until his death in 1894. (Faust, 140)

What was the strangeness of Sherman's garb on the road to Savannah, Georgia, and Goldsboro, North Carolina?

It was said that Sherman didn't get much sleep and that he could be seen around the campfire in very early hours. He was said to be in bare feet and slippers, red flannel drawers, a woolen shirt, and an old dressing gown with blue cloth (half cloak) cape. On the line of march he often lay next to the road and never wore boots, simply a pair of low-cut shoes with only one spur. (Denney, 498)

Where was Saltville, Virginia, and what was it known for?

Saltville was located in the mountains of southwestern Virginia and, as the name indicates, was known for the salt produced in the area. Union raiding parties operating out of southeast Kentucky on two occasions (October 2 and December 20, 1864) raided Saltville. (Faust, 654)

Who became inspector general and was assigned to the war department in Richmond in the spring of 1864?

Lee's former chief of staff, Robert Hall Chilton. (Faust, 139)

What was the CSS *Albemarle*?

She was an ironclad gunboat built at Edwards' Ferry, North Carolina. The boat was 152 feet long with a 34-foot beam. She had a 9-foot draft and carried two 6.4-inch Brooke guns. Her first commander was Cmdr. James W. Cooke. She was commissioned on April 17, 1864. (Faust, 5)

What was the Dutch Gap Canal?
Maj. Gen. Ben Butler, in his attempt to get out of being bottled up in the Bermuda Hundred, decided to dig a canal across a 174-yard neck of land created by a sharp turn in the James River. This was in the attempt to avoid both Confederate defenses that had been placed in the river and artillery fire from Trent's Reach. Construction began in August 1864. On January 1, 1865, dissatisfied with the time consumed in digging the canal, Butler had a 12,000-pound charge set off that, rather than fixing the problem, collapsed some of the channel. The canal was not completed until April 1865. (Faust, 231–232)

What was the CSS *Stonewall* and what was her fate?
The CSS *Stonewall* was one of two rams built for the Confederacy in Bordeaux, France. In December 1864 she became the only European-built ram to reach the Southern States. The *Stonewall* was 172 feet long with a 33-foot beam. First sold to Denmark, she was returned to the builders due to her poor performance at the end of the Schleswig-Holstein War. When bought by the Confederacy it was hoped that she could raise the blockade of Wilmington, North Carolina, intercept California gold ships, and attack Northern ports and fishing fleets. Delays due to performance eventually forced the captain to return to Spain for repairs. By the time the *Stonewall* sailed to Nassau and then continued on to Havana, the war was over, so the ship was surrendered to Spanish authorities. The *Stonewall* never engaged a Northern ship, so its performance in battle was never tested. The crew said the ship was unreliable and unseaworthy and that it leaked badly. After the war she was sold to the Japanese and renamed the HIJMS *Azuma*. She served until 1908, when she was scrapped. (Faust, 723–724)

What happened to Pvt. William H. Howe of the 116th Pennsylvania Infantry on August 26, 1864?
He was hanged. Howe, who was wounded at Fredericksburg, helped rescue wounded Union soldiers following the battle. After partially recovering, he returned home to Pennsylvania. He was hunted down for desertion in 1863 and, during his initial arrest, shot and killed a man. Finally arrested in Reading, Pennsylvania, he was put on trial for desertion and murder. At the trial he was eventually found guilty

and sentenced to hang. He was held at Ft. Mifflin in Casemate Number 11 for a while, then transferred to the Eastern State Penitentiary in Philadelphia. He sent two letters to President Lincoln asking for clemency that were not answered. On August 26, 1864, he was taken back to Ft. Mifflin, where he was hanged. His was the only U.S. Army execution for which tickets were sold to the public. President Johnson did commute his sentence to time served, but by that time Howe was already dead. It is said that his ghost can still be heard and seen at the fort. (Cavanaugh, *Civil War News*)

BATTLES

The Kilpatrick-Dahlgren Raid

What was to be the purpose of the Kilpatrick-Dahlgren Raid in February 1864?
The raid, led by Kilpatrick, was to distribute a Lincoln amnesty proclamation in the raided area, destroy enemy communications, destroy rail lines, and ultimately free Union prisoners in Richmond. (B. Venter, 8)

What did Kilpatrick use as a feint to cover his movements?
He sent George Custer, supported by elements from Gen. John Sedgwick's Sixth Corps, on a raid toward the Confederate left. The raid was successful in that Jeb Stuart chased him but unsuccessful in that he was unable to destroy a railroad bridge near Charlottesville. During his raid he lost no men but wore out his mounts. (B. Venter, 10)

What happened to Kilpatrick's column when it reached Mt. Pleasant, south of Spotsylvania Court House?
It split. Kilpatrick, with most of the column, headed toward Beaver Dam Station on the Virginia Central while Dahlgren led his men toward Frederick's Hall Station. (B. Venter, 12)

When Dahlgren's men reached Frederick's Hall Station, what did they miss?
An hour before they reached the station, a train carrying Gen. Robert E. Lee had passed through. (B. Venter, 13)

As they rode toward Richmond, what happened to Dahlgren's African American guide?

When the guide could not find a James River crossing, Dahlgren became infuriated with the guide and had him hanged leaving the body for the passing troopers and civilians to see as they rode by the river. (B. Venter, 16)

What happened to Dahlgren's command as it neared King and Queen Courthouse on the night of March 2–3, 1864?

What was left of Dahlgren's column came upon a hastily organized group of Confederates that was led by Lt. James Pollard of the 9th Virginia Cavalry, part of the 42nd Virginia Cavalry Battalion, and old men and boys of the King and Queen County home guards. In a brief skirmish, Dahlgren went down with five bullets in him. Regrouping, the rest of the command, with the exception of forty men who escaped, surrendered. (B. Venter, 47)

What happened to Dahlgren's body?

It was stripped of valuables, including a gold ring, which necessitated cutting off his finger. His body was then buried beside the road, only to be dug up the next day and taken to Richmond, where it was put on display. On the orders of President Davis, the body was then interred in Oakwood Cemetery. Secretly dug up again by agents of master spy Elizabeth Van Lew, the body was taken to a farm north of Richmond and buried again. Following the surrender at Appomattox Court House, the body was dug up yet again and taken to Philadelphia, where it was placed in Laurel Hill Cemetery. Today the grave is marked by a small stone that reads, "Ulric Dahlgren U.S. Army Killed March 2, 1864 21 Years 11 Mo." (B. Venter, 48; Magner, 13)

Who has been credited with finding the now-infamous "Dahlgren Papers"?

Thirteen-year-old William Littlepage. The boy came across the body and went through the colonel's personal effects, in which he found a watch, a cigar case, some papers, and a memorandum book. The boy then gave them to his teacher, Capt. Edward Halbach, who realized their importance and sent the items up the chain of command. (B. Venter, 48)

What did the Dahlgren Papers reveal?

That there was more to the raid than just freeing prisoners. The papers revealed that the raiders were to burn the city of Richmond and capture President Davis and his cabinet. Should the president attempt to escape he was to be killed. (B. Venter, 48)

The Wilderness

What were the sizes of the two armies that converged on The Wilderness in early May 1864?

The Army of the Potomac numbered 105,000 men, including 12,000 cavalry and 274 cannon. The Army of Northern Virginia mustered only 52,000 infantry, with 8,000 cavalry and 224 pieces of artillery. (Mertz, 10)

What units made up the Union Army approaching The Wilderness in May 1864?

The Army of the Potomac under Maj. Gen. George Gordon Meade was comprised of the Second Corps commanded by Maj. Gen. Winfield Scott Hancock; the Fifth Corps commanded by Maj. Gen. Gouverneur K. Warren; the Sixth Corps of Maj. Gen. John Sedgwick; the Cavalry Corps under Maj. Gen. Philip H. Sheridan; and the Artillery commanded by Brig. Gen. Henry J. Hunt. An independent unit comprised of Maj. Gen. Ambrose E. Burnside's Ninth Corps was also attached to the army, but reported to General-in-Chief Grant. (Mertz, 19)

What did Grant do to change the strategy of the Army of the Potomac?

Up until Grant took over, the focus of the army had been the capture of Richmond. Grant changed this to destroying Lee's Army of Northern Virginia.

What were the only two changes Grant made to the officer corps of the Army of the Potomac when he took command of the armies?

He replaced Alfred Pleasonton with Maj. Gen. Philip H. Sheridan as commander of the army's Cavalry Corps. He also placed Brig. Gen. James H. "Harry" Wilson, a former member of his staff and a protégé, in command of the Third Division of the Cavalry Corps. (Mertz, 11)

When Grant started his Overland Campaign on the night of May 3–4, 1864, where did his army cross the Rapidan River?
Warren's Fifth Corps and Sedgwick's Sixth Corps crossed the river at Germanna Ford. About five miles downriver, Hancock's Second Corps crossed at Ely's Ford. (Mertz, 12)

Where was Grant's and Meade's headquarters during the battle of The Wilderness?
On a knoll near the intersection of the Germanna Plank Road and the Orange Turnpike.

Via what three roads did the Army of Northern Virginia approach The Wilderness battlefield?
Ewell's Second Corps used the Orange Turnpike, while Hill's Third Corps came up the Orange Plank Road. Finally, Longstreet's First Corps would march over the Catharpin Road. (Mertz, 14)

Fighting between what two units opened the battle of The Wilderness?
Warren's Fifth Corps and Ewell's Second Corps. The action began about 1:00 p.m. along the Orange Turnpike across Saunder's Field. (Mertz, 20–21)

What Federal brigade suffered the most casualties on the first day of fighting in The Wilderness?
Hays's Second Corps' brigade took 1,390 casualties, including its commander, Brig. Gen. Alexander Hays. (Mertz, 51)

What Confederate general was killed during the fighting in Saunders' Field on May 5, 1864?
Brig. Gen. John M. "Rum" Jones, who commanded a Virginia brigade. (Mertz, 62)

What action started the fighting on the second day of the battle of The Wilderness, May 6, 1864?
Hancock's reinforced Second Corps line attacked Hill's Corps along the Orange Plank Road east of the Widow Tapp farm. (Mertz, 11)

What Federal general officer was mortally wounded during the fighting late in the morning of May 6?
Brig. Gen. James S. Wadsworth. Wadsworth had just led the 20th Massachusetts in an attack when his horse became unmanageable and bolted. When the general finally got the animal under control he was just yards from the Confederate line. Turning in an attempt to escape, he was shot in the head and mortally wounded. After initially lying beside the road, Wadsworth was eventually taken to the Pulliam farm near Parker's Store, where he died two days later. He was posthumously promoted to major general to date from his wounding at The Wilderness. (Mertz, 60)

What Confederate general was seriously wounded during the fighting of May 6?
Lt. Gen. James Longstreet. Longstreet and a number of officers were riding east via the Orange Plank Road when the 12th Virginia, mistaking some of the infantry with the general for Yankees, fired a volley. A ball hit Longstreet in the neck and exited though his right shoulder. At the same time, Brig. Gen. Micah Jenkins was shot in the head and killed. It is interesting to note that Longstreet's wounding happened just a few miles from and almost exactly a year after Stonewall Jackson was mortally wounded by friendly fire at Chancellorsville. (Mertz, 18)

What happened in The Wilderness that brought fear to wounded and healthy alike?
Fire. It had been a dry spring in the area and the woods were a tinderbox. The heavy fighting started numerous fires which the healthy could avoid but often killed the already suffering wounded.

What was the final casualty list for the battle of The Wilderness?
Grant's army suffered 17,666 casualties, while Lee only had 11,000. Unfortunately for the Confederates, Grant could easily replace his losses, while the Confederate manpower shortage made the losses more problematic. (Mertz, 49)

Following the fighting in The Wilderness, what did Grant do with his army that was different from every other commander up to this point in the war?
Rather than go back, he went forward. Instead of retreating back across the Rapidan or Rappahannock rivers to lick his wounds, Grant took the Army of the Potomac and swung around Lee's right flank in an attempt to reach Spotsylvania Court House before him.

What was the outcome of the fighting at Spotsylvania Court House?
Lee won the race to the Court House, where the Confederates began entrenching. Between May 8 and May 19 Grant launched numerous assaults against the Confederate works, some gaining success but none scoring a decisive breakthrough. On May 10, Col. Emory Upton massed twelve regiments on a narrow front and managed to breach the Confederate line, but could not follow up with a victory. On May 12, Gen. Hancock's entire Second Corps struck the apex of the Confederate line where, for twenty hours in a blinding rainstorm, the men in blue and butternut fought some of the most vicious actions of the war. When Lee withdrew to a new line Grant assailed those, only to be thrown back. Finally, on May 21, Grant pulled his men out and once again sidestepped Lee in his attempt to get to Richmond. (Faust, 709)

What was the name of the salient attacked by Hancock on May 12?
The Mule Shoe.

Besides Brandy Station, what was one of the largest cavalry actions of the Civil War?
The fighting at Haw's Shop, on May 28, 1864. Confederate Wade Hampton and Federal David Gregg fought a battle during which most of the horse soldiers fought dismounted for several hours. It has been estimated that approximately 10,000 cavalry participated in the fighting, with the Federals taking 350 casualties and the Confederates approximately the same number. At the end of the fighting, one of the Yankee dead was John Huff, who had mortally wounded Jeb Stuart several weeks before. (Richmond, 14)

What was the objective of Grant's orders to Brig. Gen. George Crook that led to the battle of Cloyd's Mountain on May 9, 1864?
Destroy the Virginia & Tennessee Railroad. (Faust, 146)

Who commanded the Confederate forces at the battle of Cloyd's Mountain?
Brig. Gen. Albert G. Jenkins. Jenkins had been seriously wounded during the engagement. A surgeon amputated his arm; however, the general failed to rally, and died on May 21, 1864. (Faust, 146, 394)

What was the outcome of the battle of Cloyd's Mountain?
After a vicious fight, it was a Union victory. The Confederates lost 23 percent of their men while the Federal casualties were about 10 percent of those engaged. Crook and his men burned the New River Bridge at Dublin, Virginia, on May 10, shutting down the Virginia & Tennessee Railroad. (Faust, 146)

What future president of the United States commanded a brigade of the Union forces at Cloyd's Mountain?
Rutherford B. Hayes. (Faust, 146)

During the campaign from the North Anna River to Cold Harbor, who replaced Richard Ewell as commander of the Army of Northern Virginia's Second Corps?
Jubal Early, on May 29. Ewell had collapsed during the fighting near Spotsylvania Court House, first on May 10 and then on May 19. Lee ordered him onto sick leave and replaced him. (Richmond, 16)

As the two armies stared at each other across Totopotomoy Creek, where did Gen. Hancock make his headquarters?
In the Col. Edwin Shelton house. In 1754 orator, statesman, and patriot Patrick Henry married Sarah Shelton in the home. The house stands today nestled in a relatively pristine area overlooking Totopotomoy Creek. (Richmond, 17, 60)

What is the meaning of Cold Harbor?
The name is of British origin, meaning a shelter without sustenance. (Richmond, 21)

The battlefield at Cold Harbor shares its real estate with what 1862 battle?
The battle of Gaines' Mill.

What is the 8th New York Heavies' claim to fame?
The 8th was one of the heavy artillery units converted into infantry during the 1864 Overland Campaign. During the fighting at Cold Harbor on June 3, 1864, the unit suffered 505 casualties, more than any other regiment. (Richmond, 55)

For what action did Sgt. LeRoy Williams receive the Medal of Honor?
For recovering the body of Col. Peter A. Porter of the 8th New York Heavies. After the fighting ended, Williams and a group of men searched for Porter's body. After finding it they returned to the Federal lines but were sent out again to retrieve the corpse. Returning to Porter's body, which was only yards from the Confederate entrenchments, they tried to get him back but failed. Williams sent back for a rope that was brought forward and tied around Porter's feet, enabling them to drag off the body. For this Williams received the medal. (Richmond, 55)

What happened to Frank Haskell, Gibbon's former aide and Gettysburg letter-writer, at the battle of Cold Harbor?
In early 1864, Haskell was named colonel of the 36th Wisconsin Infantry. During the attack at Cold Harbor on June 3, 1864, Haskell's brigade commander was killed, and he took over command of the unit. Ordering his men to lie down, Haskell stood over his line to make sure the men were complying. While doing so he was hit by a Confederate bullet and killed. (Catton, xii)

Following Cold Harbor, where did Grant go?
He moved his army south once again, crossing the Chickahominy River at Jones' Bridge and Long Bridge. Grant then crossed the James River at Wilcox's Landing on boats and at Weyanoke on a pontoon bridge. (Richmond, 57–58)

Later in life, what was Grant's comment on the fighting at Cold Harbor on June 3, 1864?
"I have always regretted that the last assault at Cold Harbor was ever made." (Richmond, 58)

The Atlanta Campaign

Who led the Union forces during the Atlanta Campaign and what did those forces consist of?
Maj. Gen. William Tecumseh Sherman. Sherman commanded an Army Group of three armies. The first and largest was the Army of the Cumberland, led by Maj. Gen. George H. Thomas. The army included a cavalry corps (Brig. Gen. Washington L. Elliott), the 4th Corps (Maj. Gen. Oliver O. Howard), the 14th Corps (Maj. Gen. John M. Palmer), and the 20th Corps (Maj. Gen. Joseph Hooker). The second, the Army of the Tennessee, was commanded by Maj. Gen. James B. McPherson, and included the 17th Corps (Maj. Gen. Francis P. Blair Jr.), which did not take part in the opening phase of the campaign because it was on veteran furlough, part of the 16th Corps (Brig. Gen. Grenville M. Dodge), and the 15th Corps (Maj. Gen. John A. Logan). The third unit, Army of the Ohio, was commanded by Maj. Gen. John M. Schofield and consisted of one corps, (the 23rd, led by Schofield himself) and a cavalry division (led by Maj. Gen. George Stoneman). (McMurry, 11)

Who commanded the Confederate forces and what did that force consist of?
General Joseph E. Johnston commanded the Army of Tennessee, which contained two infantry corps, one led by Lt. Gen. William J. Hardee and the other by Lt. Gen. John Bell Hood. The army also contained a cavalry corps commanded by Maj. Gen. Joseph Wheeler. When the campaign began Johnston received troops led by Lt. Gen. Leonidas Polk, which consisted of a cavalry division and three infantry divisions. (McMurry, 12)

How did Sherman get most of his supplies during the Atlanta Campaign?

By railroad. There were no rivers close enough to use as supply routes, so Sherman depended on the railroads. Between Chattanooga and Dalton he had two, the Western & Atlantic Railroad and the Tennessee and Georgia Railroad. From Dalton, Georgia, south he had to depend only on the Western & Atlantic. (McMurry, 14, 16)

What three gaps crossed Rocky Face Ridge that separated Sherman's Yankees in Chattanooga from Johnston's Confederates in Dalton?

Mill Creek Gap (or Buzzard's Roost), Dug Gap, and Snake Creek Gap. (McMurry, 17)

What aide to Maj. Gen. Daniel Sickles at Gettysburg received the Medal of Honor for his actions at the battle of Resaca, Georgia?

Maj. Henry E. Tremain. Sickles was on a fact-finding tour of the South during the Atlanta Campaign, and Tremain was still part of his inner circle. Maj. Gen. Daniel Butterfield (also a close confidant of Sickles) commanded a division in Hooker's Twentieth Corps. Tremain volunteered for duty with Butterfield's command and during the fighting, as noted in the medal's citation, "Voluntarily rode between the lines while two brigades of Union troops were firing into each other and stopped the firing." It is interesting to note that Medals of Honor were received by Tremain for Resaca, Butterfield for Gaines' Mill, and Sickles for Gettysburg. (McMurry, 49)

What future president's troops became the recipients of a "friendly fire" incident at the battle of Resaca?

Col. Benjamin Harrison's 70th Indiana. (McMurry, 49, 53)

Following the war, what distillery did Maj. Gen. Benjamin Franklin Cheatham endorse?

Jack Daniels. (Kelly, 46)

For what gallant act was Confederate Col. William H. Martin rewarded by Union officers during the days June 10–July 3, where the blue and gray confronted each other along the Kennesaw Mountain Line?
When the Federals were repulsed on June 27, they fell back, leaving their dead and wounded behind. The debris on the floor of the woods caught fire and threatened to burn the wounded to death. Martin, who commanded the 1st and 15th Consolidated Arkansas Regiment, ordered his men to stop firing, then called for the Yankees to come and get their men. For a short time Union and Confederates worked together to rescue the wounded. The next day, during a truce, Union officers gave the colonel a brace of Colt's six-shooters as thanks. (Kelly, 48)

What happened in Roswell, Georgia, on July 5, 1864?
Federal cavalry under Brig. Gen. Kenner Garrard rode in and captured the town, which was an important textile manufacturing area that produced cloth for the Confederacy. The mill's supervisors approached Garrard, saying that they were French and British subjects, even going so far as to fly a French flag over the factory offices. Inspecting the factory, Garrard found bolts of cotton cloth with C.S.A. woven into them. He immediately shut the mills down, evacuated the workers, who were mostly women, and then burned fifteen buildings. He then charged everyone with treason and marched them off to Marietta; from there they were shipped north, where they were to spend the rest of the war. Stories abounded about how they all disappeared; in reality, however, after the war many families were reunited and returned to Roswell, which once again became an important textile producer. (Kelly, 57)

Who were the first Union troops to cross the Chattahoochee River on July 8, 1864?
Maj. Gen. John M. Schofield's Army of the Ohio. A similar crossing was made the next day by Kenner Garrard's cavalry. (Kelly, 57)

What happened to Gen. Joseph E. Johnston on July 17, 1864?
He was relieved of command of the Army of Tennessee by officials in Richmond and replaced by Gen. John Bell Hood. The exchange of command happened on July 18. (S. Davis, 10)

What were the sizes of the opposing armies when Hood took over?
Hood indicated that he had 48,750 effectives, while Sherman led three
Army Groups that totaled 106,070 men. (S. Davis, 10)

**What Federal unit fired the first artillery shell into the city of
Atlanta on July 20?**
A 20-pounder Parrott from Capt. Frances DeGress's Battery H, 1st
Illinois Artillery, of John A. Logan's Fifteenth Corps. Fired from two
and one half miles away, the shell landed on the corner of Ivy and East
Ellis streets, killing a little girl. (S. Davis, 12, 15)

**After crossing the Chattahoochee River, what was the first major
action in the quest to capture Atlanta?**
The battle of Peachtree Creek, where Thomas's Federal Army of the
Cumberland fought the corps of Lt. Gen. Alexander P. Stewart and
Lt. Gen. William J. Hardee. The fighting went badly for the Con-
federates for a number of reasons, including bad terrain, Federal for-
tifications, disoriented attacks, timing, and a lack of coordination.
(S. Davis, 12, 17)

**Who was the only Union army commander to be killed during the
war?**
Maj. Gen. James Birdseye McPherson, leader of the Army of the Tennessee. During the battle of Atlanta, McPherson and his staff were riding down a wagon road when they blundered into elements of Patrick
Cleburne's command. Capt. Richard Beard of the 5th Confederate
(Tennessee) called for the general to surrender, whereupon the general raised his hat in a salute, turned, and galloped for the rear. Beard
ordered Cpl. Robert F. Coleman to fire, and it was Coleman's shot that
hit McPherson in the back near the heart, killing him. Later, one of
the general's staff officers took an ambulance back to the scene, recovered the body, and took it to Sherman's headquarters. (S. Davis, 20)

**Whom did Sherman appoint as Army of the Tennessee commander
following the death of McPherson?**
Initially, "Black Jack" Logan, but he was soon replaced with a permanent commander, Maj. Gen. Oliver O. Howard. (S. Davis, 25)

What three of Sherman's commanders had a fistfight on July 25 over the actions of their men?
Sixteenth Corps commander Maj. Gen. Grenville Dodge and division commanders Brig. Gen. Thomas W. Sweeny and Brig. Gen. John W. Fuller. The men were talking when Sweeny accused Fuller's men of being cowards. Dodge defended Fuller, to which Sweeny replied, "You are a God-damned liar, sir!" followed by "You are cowardly son of a bitch, sir!" and "You are a God-damned *inefficient* son of a bitch, sir!" (Sweeny was, after all, addressing a senior officer, thus the "sir.") Dodge smacked Sweeny, and then all three went at it. Sweeny was arrested and sent to Nashville for court-martial. (S. Davis, 26)

What was the outcome of Stoneman's Raid in late July 1864?
Sherman sent Maj. Gen. George Stoneman on a raid to the east and south of Atlanta. Stoneman was to connect with Brig. Gen. Edward McCook near Lovejoy's Station, destroy the Macon & Western Railroad, then free prisoners at Macon and Andersonville. Unfortunately, near Sunshine Church on July 31, Stoneman and his men found themselves virtually surrounded and were forced to surrender. Stoneman and 700 of his men were taken prisoner. The officers were taken to Camp Oglethorpe at Macon and the enlisted men to Andersonville. (S. Davis, 28, 29; Faust, 721)

What was the outcome of the battle of Ezra Church on July 28, 1864?
In a series of uncoordinated attacks, Stephen D. Lee's and A. P. Stewart's Corps' fought Logan's Corps of Howard's Army of the Tennessee. Unable to overcome the strong Union line, the Confederates pulled back, then withdrew under cover of darkness. During the fighting, Union casualties totaled 562 while Confederate casualties were at least 3,000, some estimate as high as 5,000. (S. Davis, 30, 33; Faust, 250–251)

What did Sherman learn from the fighting at Utoy Creek between August 5 and 7?
That assaulting well-entrenched Confederates was futile (he probably already knew this). The two days of fighting had cost him around

1,000 casualties, while Hood suffered only a few hundred. He also learned that Hood had extended his line far enough to protect the railroad from Atlanta to East Point. (S. Davis, 36–39)

After Utoy Creek, where did Sherman send his army?

He began sending some of his corps farther to the southwest beyond the left of the Confederate line, hoping ultimately to destroy the Atlanta & West Point Railroad. Finally on August 31, Howard's Army of the Tennessee was across the Flint River and within a mile or two of Jonesboro. Facing him were the troops under S. D. Lee and Patrick Cleburne under the overall command of William J. Hardee. (S. Davis, 49–52)

What happened during the fighting at Jonesboro on August 31 and September 1?

As were his orders, Hardee sent his troops forward in a headlong attack on the Federal defenses on August 31. The Union soldiers had, in a short amount of time, thrown up entrenchments and sent a galling fire against the attackers. The Confederates had spent quite some time in trenches of their own and the long march to Jonesboro, on top of being out of shape, took a toll on their energy and morale. They also knew that attacking an entrenched enemy was foolhardy and dangerous. By the end of the fighting on August 31, the Confederates had been repulsed, with casualties numbering around 1,700, to only 179 for the Federals. The next day it was the Federals' turn to attack, which they did in force. Hardee, however, was able to keep his line intact, suffering around 1,400 casualties to the Federals' 1,400. Around midnight the Confederates began withdrawing south to Lovejoy's Station. (S. Davis, 52–60)

Once the railroad was cut, what did Hood do?

He issued orders for his army to evacuate the city. He threw open warehouses and distributed food to the civilians, then blew up an ammunition train that had been unable to get out of the city. He then marched his army south to Lovejoy's Station. (S. Davis, 61)

Who surrendered the city of Atlanta?

Mayor James M. Calhoun, on September 2, 1864. (S. Davis, 61)

After the capture of the city, what message did Gen. Sherman send to Washington on September 3?
"Atlanta is ours, and fairly won." (S. Davis, 61)

Monocacy

When Grant finally decided to send troops to Baltimore due to Jubal Early's movements near Frederick, Maryland, whom did he send?
Initially, Brig. Gen. James Ricketts's Sixth Corps division. (Cooling, 13)

Who were the two future literary figures who fought at the battle of Monocacy?
Gen. Lew Wallace (*Ben Hur*) and Col. Theodore O'Hara (*The Bivouac of the Dead*). (Cooling, 49)

What was the outcome of the battle of Monocacy?
It was a Confederate victory, with Gen. Lew Wallace and Ricketts's people retreating from the field. The casualties were given as 1,294 for the Federals and between 700 and 900 for the Confederates. (Cooling, 56)

What did Early do with his army following the fighting at Monocacy?
He kept moving his worn-out men toward Washington. Early's raid ended, however, at Ft. Stevens, within sight of the city, on July 12. Fresh Federal reinforcements from the Sixth and Nineteenth Corps, along with the jaded condition of his men, prompted Early to head back to Virginia. He may have failed in his attempt to capture Washington, but he did recross the Potomac River with 2,000 head of cattle, 1,000 horses, and $200,000 in greenbacks. (Cooling, 56)

Who was the most prominent visitor to Ft. Stevens during the fighting there?
President Abraham Lincoln, the only president to come under enemy fire during a war. He visited twice, once on July 11 and a second time

on July 12. Mary Todd Lincoln accompanied him once, and Seward and Welles also visited with him there. At one point, a surgeon who was standing near him was hit by a sharpshooter's bullet. Though he stood behind the parapet, his height still made him a target. At one point a young captain shouted to him, "Get down, you damned fool, before you get shot!" The young officer was Oliver Wendell Holmes Jr., who would go on to become a respected associate justice of the United States Supreme Court. Though this story is doubted by most authorities, evidence compiled in the 1940s includes a conversation with Justice Holmes in which he mentions the incident. Holmes's story must be taken with a grain of salt, however, as he only mentioned yelling at the president a few times during his life, and the last time in 1940 when he was ninety years old, with almost seventy years of hindsight. The most probable scenario is that when Lincoln came under fire, Maj. Gen. Horatio G. Wright stepped up to the president, placed his hand on his shoulder, and escorted him off the parapet to a safer place. (Goodwin, 643; Cramer, 101–124)

Mobile Bay

What three Confederate forts protected the entrance to Mobile Bay?
Ft. Morgan guarded the main shipping channel into the bay. The second was Ft. Gaines, located on the eastern end of Dauphin Island, which protected several little-used shallow channels and was of no support to Ft. Morgan, which was three miles away. The last was Ft. Powell, on the banks of Grant's Pass, a fairly shallow channel that had been a major channel between Mobile and New Orleans prior to the war. (Bergeron, Jr., 6)

Who commanded the Confederate naval forces in Mobile Bay?
Adm. Franklin Buchanan, whose flagship was the ironclad *Tennessee*. (Bergeron, Jr., 7)

Who commanded the Union naval forces in the Gulf of Mexico?
Rear Adm. David Glasgow Farragut. (Bergeron, Jr., 8)

How many Confederates manned the forts on the entrance to Mobile Bay?
In total for all three forts, approximately 1,040 men. (Bergeron, Jr., 10)

What Union monitor was sunk during the initial attack on Mobile Bay?
The *Tecumseh*, commanded by Cmdr. Tunis A. M. Craven. Just off of Ft. Morgan, the ship struck a torpedo and sank immediately. Ninety-four of her crew went down with her, including her commanding officer. (Bergeron, Jr., 10–13)

What did Adm. Farragut do during the attack?
The smoke was so thick that he could not see what was going on from the deck of his flagship, the *Hartford*, so he grabbed his telescope and climbed into the riggings, taking up a position just under the main-top platform. The *Hartford's* captain, Percival Drayton, ordered one of his men to tie the admiral to the shrouds so that he would not fall. (Bergeron, Jr., 14)

What did Farragut reputedly say during the attack?
When the *Brooklyn's* captain saw what he thought were torpedoes, and knowing what happened to the *Tecumseh*, rather than continuing forward he reversed and sent word to the *Hartford* warning of the explosives. Farragut then said, "Damn the torpedoes! Full speed ahead!" While he probably did not say those exact words, it is almost certain that the air around him turned blue with foul language. (Bergeron, Jr., 14)

What mischief did the *Tennessee* cause after the Union breakthrough into Mobil Bay?
Buchanan decided to continue the battle and try to inflict as much damage as he could on the Union fleet. Buchanan's target was the *Hartford*, but two other ships stood in the way, the *Monongahela* and the *Lackawanna*. These two vessels rammed the *Tennessee* but caused no damage. Finally reaching the *Hartford*, the *Tennessee* scraped sides with her and the two traded cannon fire. During this exchange, Farragut once again climbed into the rigging and had to be tied in. The

Hartford managed to get out of the way but was accidentally rammed amidships by the *Lackawanna* as she attempted to get at the Confederate craft. Finally, the *Tennessee*'s steering chains were cut, then her rudder chains fouled, and finally her smokestack was shot away, filling the vessel with smoke. Buchanan, already seriously wounded, ordered the ironclad's captain to surrender her. (Bergeron, Jr., 20, 46)

When did Ft. Morgan surrender?
At 2:00 p.m. on August 23, 1864, after a continual bombardment by naval and land-based infantry units. With the surrender, around 600 men and forty-six pieces of artillery were taken by the Federals. (Bergeron, Jr., 51–52)

The March to the Sea

Who was in charge of the destruction of Atlanta?
Capt. Orlando M. Poe, Sherman's chief of engineers. Beginning on November 14, he destroyed the railroad depot, machine shops, roundhouse, foundry, oil refinery, and freight warehouse. Then, all sorts of debris such as tents, bedding, wagons, and equipment were piled on the ruins and set afire. The fire eventually spread into the heart of the city, destroying theaters, slave markets, the jail, and fire stations. The only structures in central-city Atlanta to survive the fire were the city hall, churches, the medical college, and about 400 homes. (Scaife, 18)

When Sherman set off on his march, what was his army made up of?
61,602 men and sixty-eight cannon organized into four corps. (Scaife, 18)

How was Sherman's army organized?
The left wing, commanded by Henry W. Slocum, consisted of Jefferson C. Davis's Fourteenth Corps and Alpheus S. Williams's Twentieth Corps. The right wing was commanded by Oliver O. Howard and included the Seventeenth Corps of Frank. P. Blair and the Fifteenth Corps under Peter J. Osterhaus. Judson Kilpatrick commanded the cavalry. (Scaife, 20)

On what date did Sherman's March to the Sea begin?
November 15, 1864. (Scaife, 21)

What was the largest battle of the March to the Sea?
Griswoldville, on November 22. Georgia militia attacked a Union brigade posted behind fence-rail barricades in an unauthorized and useless attack. At its end, the Confederates had suffered 474 casualties to the Federals' 94. (Scaife, 22–24)

What Confederate cavalry genius met and defeated a superior Federal force at the battle of Brice's Cross Roads on June 10, 1864?
Maj. Gen. Nathan Bedford Forrest.

Who was Forrest's adversary at Brice's Cross Roads?
Brig. Gen. Samuel D. Sturgis. The cost of the loss was high for the Union troops, as they lost their artillery and 170 wagons full of supplies, and suffered more than 2,600 casualties. (Denney, 422)

Who was Archibald Gracie Jr.?
He was a graduate of the Military Academy Class of 1854 and a brigadier general in the Confederate Army. He fought at Chickamauga, Knoxville, and was wounded at Bean's Station, Tennessee, in December 1863. After recuperating he served under Gen. P. T. G. Beauregard and in the trenches of Petersburg. On December 2, 1864, while observing enemy movements, he was killed by Union artillery. His grandfather built the Gracie Mansion on the Upper East Side of Manhattan that, since 1942, has been the residence of the mayor of New York City. (Faust, 316–317; Livingston, 16)

Petersburg

What regiment of coal miners from Schuylkill County, Pennsylvania, dug the tunnel under Elliott's Salient at Petersburg, and who commanded it?
The 48th Pennsylvania, which was commanded by Lt. Col. Henry Pleasants. They began digging on June 25 and completed it on July 23.

The shaft was 510 feet long, five feet high, four and a half feet wide at the bottom, and two feet wide at the top. At the end there were two lateral galleries into which the Pennsylvanians placed 320 kegs of gunpowder; in all, 8,000 pounds (Faust, 190; Cavanaugh and Marvel, 10)

When the fuses were lit to explode the black powder, what happened?

There was ninety feet of fuse in three lines when Pleasants touched them off at 3:00 a.m. It was estimated that it would take about thirty minutes to burn. Thirty minutes came and went—nothing. Then, around 4:00 a.m., Sgt. Henry Reese and Lt. Jacob Douty volunteered to go into the shaft to see what happened. Pleasants refused until 4:15 a.m., when he told Reese to go in. About halfway to the split between the galleries Reese found that the fuses had gone out. He went to cut them in order to resplice the line but found he had no knife. Heading back out, he ran into Lt. Douty, who had a jackknife. The two went back, fixed the fuse, and headed for the exit. Finally, at 4:44 a.m., the charges went off, creating a hole 170 feet long, sixty to eighty feet wide, and thirty feet deep. (Cavanaugh and Marvel, 37–40)

What happened on July 30, 1864, in Petersburg?

After the mine blew, the African American troops of Brig. Gen. Edward Ferrero were to spearhead the Federal assault. However, the day before, Grant and Meade decided they did not want to use black soldiers as cannon fodder, so they changed their orders, substituting white troops. The task was given to the white division of Brig. Gen. James Ledlie. The attack went as planned, with the Union troops pouring into the Crater soon supported by two other divisions. By this time, however, the Confederates had regrouped and were pouring a murderous fire into the Federals. Finally, Maj. Gen. Ambrose Burnside ordered in Ferrero's black troops, but it was too little, too late. The Confederates slaughtered the black men, killing many after they had surrendered. By 1:00 p.m., the Federals had been pushed back to their lines. The day ended with 3,800 Federal casualties and 1,500 Confederate. The ultimate blame for the failure eventually fell on Burnside, Ledlie, and Ferrero. (Faust, 190)

What were the major Confederate units that fought off the Federal attack at the Crater?

Col. David Weisiger (Mahone's Brigade), Lt. Col. Matthew R. Hall (Wright's Brigade), and Col. John C. C. Sanders (Wilcox Brigade), all of Anderson's Division commanded by Brig. Gen. William Mahone. Brig. Gen. Stephen Elliott (Elliott's Brigade) and Col. J. Thomas Goode (Wise's Brigade) of Maj. Gen. Bushrod Johnson's Division. (Cavanaugh and Marvel, 101, 125–127)

What was the outcome of the fighting at Jerusalem Plank Road, June 21–23, 1864?

Grant sent the Second Corps, now led by Maj. Gen. David Birney, and Maj. Gen. Horatio G. Wright's Sixth Corps on a mission to destroy the Weldon Railroad. While moving on the railroad the two corps became separated and Brig. Gen. William Mahone broke through the gap and began rolling up the flank of the Second Corps. Meanwhile, Brig. Gen. Cadmus Wilcox attacked the Sixth Corps head on. The Federals suffered 2,500 casualties while the Confederates only took 570. The next day part of the Vermont Brigade reached the railroad and did some damage, but all were eventually captured. (C. Calkins, 8)

What happened during the fighting at Globe Tavern (the Weldon Railroad) on August 18 and 19, 1864?

Maj. Gen. Gouverneur K. Warren's Fifth Corps managed to reach the Weldon Railroad near the tavern and began destroying it. Leaving one division near the tavern, Warren moved Ayres's and Crawford's commands north. These divisions soon met two brigades of Confederates sent out of the Confederate defenses by Gen. P. G. T. Beauregard. Heavy fighting broke out and continued the rest of the day. Toward evening elements from the Ninth Corps came up to support Warren. On the 19th the fighting went badly for the Federals. At the end of the day, however, despite being pushed back, they did manage to gain back much of the ground lost and still kept a hold on the railroad. The Federals took a beating, with around 550 killed and wounded and almost 2,600 missing (mostly prisoners). Confederate losses are unknown but thought to be light. (C. Calkins, 8–20)

What was the ultimate outcome of the fighting at Globe Tavern following the actions on August 20 and 21?
The fighting continued on August 20, but it was mostly skirmishing as the Federals concentrated on strengthening their defensive line. On August 21 the Confederates attacked once again, with William Mahone hitting the Federal left and Gen. Henry Heth assailing the northern portion of the line. Despite the heavy fighting during the day, the Confederates were unable to dislodge the Federals, whose earthworks now became a permanent part of the Union line. The Weldon railroad line was cut, forcing supplies to be brought into Petersburg on a thirty-mile roundabout route. (C. Calkins, 20–23)

What happened at City Point, Virginia, on August 9, 1864?
An ammunition barge blew up, destroying 700 boxes of artillery ammunition, about 2,000 boxes of small arms, between 600 and 700 blank cartridges, and one keg of mortar powder; all in all around $2 million in damage. The explosion threw debris into the air, falling even into army headquarters and barely missing Gen. Grant. Forty-three were killed in the explosion and 126 wounded. (Rayburn, 28, 32)

What was the cause of the City Point explosion?
A "horological torpedo" (basically a time bomb) was placed aboard the barge by the Confederate Secret Service agent John Maxwell, with the assistance of R. K. Dillard. (Rayburn, 32)

What was the tactical outcome of the battle of Reams' Station, August 25, 1864?
It was a Confederate victory and a great embarrassment to the Union's famed Second Corps. The blame for the loss is given to many, but perhaps the major offender was Second Corps commander Maj. Gen. Winfield Scott Hancock. First he led his men into entrenchments that were faulty; he also left a four-mile gap between his corps and that of Gen. Warren at Globe Tavern. Gen. Meade also deserves some of the blame for sending reinforcements via a circuitous twelve-mile route rather than from Warren's Corps a scant four miles away. The Union losses were 2,742 and the Confederates' 814. (Venter, 42–50)

Following the fighting at Reams' Station, what took place between Gen. Hancock and his most trusted division commander, Maj. Gen. John Gibbon?

During the Overland Campaign, personal relations between corps commander Hancock and Gibbon had soured and reached the breaking point. The two officers became involved in an acerbic argument about how Gibbon had handled his troops during the battle. A number of terse notes were exchanged, and they parted ways. Following the battle of the Boydton Plank Road (October 27–28), Hancock went on extended sick leave, returned to Washington, and sought to recruit a Veterans Reserve Corps. Gibbon soon left his command and by January 1865 was leading the Twenty-Fourth Corps. (Venter, 50; Faust, 309)

What did the "Hicksford Expedition" become known as?

The "Apple Jack Raid." Between December 7 and 12, Warren's Fifth Corps plus a portion of the Second Corps was sent south to destroy more of the Weldon Railroad. The men reached Jarratt's Station and then headed south toward the Meherrin River, ultimately destroying sixteen miles of track. The raid turned into a fiasco when the soldiers found in many homes applejack that had been made for the upcoming Christmas season. Drunken soldiers destroyed buildings and raped a number of women. Locals in response turned into bushwhackers and murdered a number of Union soldiers. One soldier later wrote that the raid was "the most vindictive that the army had ever engaged in." (C. Calkins, 18–24)

What was the Dictator?

The Dictator was a 13-inch mortar that was mounted on a reinforced railroad car. It weighed 17,000 pounds, and its twenty-pound charge could throw a 200-pound mortar-round 4,325 yards. During the siege of Petersburg it was served by Co. G, 1st Connecticut Heavy Artillery, commanded by H. L. Abbott. It fired some forty-five rounds, nineteen of which were fired during the battle of the Crater. (Boatner, 240)

What action took place at Peebles's Farm from September 30 to October 2, 1864?

On September 30, while major units of Maj. Gen. Benjamin Butler's Army of the James attacked north of the James River, Grant sent part of the Army of the Potomac against the Confederate lines four miles southwest of Petersburg. In a midmorning assault, Brig. Gen. Charles Griffin's Fifth Corps Division attacked across Peebles's Farm and captured Ft. Archer, a line of trenches, and one hundred prisoners. Later in the day, Brig. Gen. Robert Potter's Ninth Corps Division moved past Griffin, hitting the enemy infantry of Maj. Gens. Henry Heth and Cadmus Wilcox. Though initially repulsed, with the help of another Ninth Corps Division and finally Griffin, Potter held his position. The next day was spent in a long-range fight between the two sides. October 2 found the Federal cavalry attacking on the infantry's flank. Eventually, Brig. Gen. Gershom Mott's Second Corps Division came up and probed the Confederate works before retiring. The Federals lost about 2,880 men; the Confederate casualties were about 1,500. (Faust, 567–568)

Ft. Fisher–Wilmington, North Carolina, 1864

What was the most important Confederate seaport by 1864?
Wilmington, North Carolina. Despite three years of U.S. Naval blockading and the fact that all other southern ports had been captured or closed, goods continued to flow into the city. Sitting on the east bank of the Cape Fear River, about twenty-five miles north from where the river flows into the Atlantic, Wilmington in 1860 sported a population of around 10,000. It had two shipbuilding yards, an iron works, five banks, and three railroads. (Fonvielle, 11)

Who was Ft. Fisher named for?
Col. Charles F. Fisher, the popular commander of the 6th North Carolina who was killed at the first battle of Manassas on July 21, 1861. (Fonvielle, 12)

What was the biggest gun in Ft. Fisher's arsenal?
A 150-pounder Armstrong gun. The Armstrong gun was designed by Sir W. G. Armstrong & Co. in England. It was a breech- or muzzle-loading weapon, and the one at Ft. Fisher had an 8-inch bore. The weapon was a gift from the manufacturer to President Jefferson Davis. (Fonvielle, 14; Faust, 24–25)

Who commanded the Confederate forces at Wilmington?
Gen. Braxton Bragg. (Fonvielle, 18)

Who were the Union commanders assigned to capture Ft. Fisher?
The naval commander was Rear Adm. David Dixon Porter. The land forces were commanded by Maj. Gen. Godfrey Weitzel, with Maj. Gen. Ben Butler in overall command of the expedition (at least that is what Butler wanted Weitzel to believe). (Fonvielle, 19–21)

What was the first unsuccessful attempt by the Federals to capture Ft. Fisher?
Wetzel was to land his infantry, which did not happen. Porter then took possession of an old steamer, *Louisiana*, with 215 tons of gunpowder packed aboard. The ship was then to be taken and run aground near Ft. Fisher and exploded. The resulting explosion, it was hoped, would destroy the fort and associated works. The ship was grounded close to the fort, fuses were set, and to insure an explosion, a fire was set in the forecastle. The explosion went off at 1:40 a.m. on Christmas Eve, and was a failure. The fire had ignited the gunpowder before the fuses detonated it. In addition, the strong undertow had pulled the ship away from the beach, so when it did explode, it was about a half-mile north of the fort. (Fonvielle, 21)

What was the largest naval bombardment of the Civil War?
The one on Christmas Eve afternoon against Ft. Fisher. Fifty-nine ships with 601 cannons over the course of five hours fired around 10,000 rounds at the fort. Unfortunately, as with the *Louisiana* fiasco, the results were disappointing. Though Ft. Fisher's commander's headquarters was knocked down and some of the garrison's quarters set on fire, there were few Confederate casualties. (Fonvielle, 21)

When did the Union infantry assault Ft. Fisher?
Christmas Day, when Weitzel put some 2,200 of his 6,500 men ashore about three miles north of the fort. Moving south, they managed to get near Shepherd's Battery, a salient at the west end of the fort's land face. Col. N. Martin Curtis was leading the Federal advance and thought that he could capture the fort. Unfortunately, Gen. Weitzel

seems to have lost his nerve. It was clear that two days of pounding the fort by the navy had done little damage. He reported back to Butler, who ordered the men taken off the beach, and re-embarked. While getting the men into the boats for the return trip, the seas became so rough the operation was halted. Curtis was stranded, along with 600 or 700 men and the Confederate prisoners. A cold nor'easter raged for two days and it wasn't until December 27 that the men were rescued. (Fonvielle, 48–49)

What happened to Gen. Butler following the failed attack?
He was eventually relieved of duty by the War Department, at Grant's request, and sent home to Massachusetts to await orders. Those orders never came. (Fonvielle, 50)

Who replaced Butler?
Brig. Gen. Alfred H. Terry. Terry was one of the few non–West Point officers to become a major general of volunteers. (Fonvielle, 52; Faust, 748)

What Federal ship did the *H. L. Hunley* sink on February 17, 1864?
The USS *Housatonic*. The *Hunley* rammed a torpedo into the side of the Union ship, which exploded, sinking the vessel. The *Hunley* backed off and then disappeared. (Boatner, 412)

Who commanded the *H. L. Hunley* and what were the names of her crew?
Lt. George E. Dixon commanded the vessel. The crew consisted of C. Simpkins, James Wicks, Joseph Ridgeway, Arnold Becker, C. R. Carlson, Fred Collins, and C. Lumpkin. (Hicks and Kropf, xvi)

When researchers were removing Lt. Dixon's body from the submarine, what did they find that was so exciting?
A twenty-dollar gold coin that was Dixon's good-luck piece (though on his last trip it did not work). The coin had been given to him by Queenie Bennett, his Mobile sweetheart. Dixon had carried it off to war and, at the battle of Shiloh, a bullet had hit it rather than his

thigh. Following that he carried the coin with him constantly. (Hicks and Kropf, 236)

What was the name of Admiral David G. Farragut's flagship at the battle of Mobile Bay, and who commanded her?
The USS *Hartford*, commanded by Captain Percival Drayton. (Faust, 347; Magner, 14)

What was the Red River Campaign?
An ill-fated plan to send a combined army-navy force up the Red River to capture Shreveport, Louisiana, the temporary capital of Confederate Louisiana, a major supply depot, and the gateway to Texas. The naval force was to be under the command of Adm. David D. Porter and the army contingent was commanded by Maj. Gen. Nathaniel P. Banks. The expedition began in early March 1864 and met with initial success, with the capture of Ft. De Russy on March 14, 1864. Detachments from the Sixteenth and Seventeenth Corps coming from Sherman's Army Group soon put the campaign behind schedule. On April 8, Banks was defeated at the battle of Mansfield, which was the closest the Federals got to Shreveport. Beginning a retreat, conditions grew more serious with the falling water level in the Red River. By the time Porter's squadron reached Alexandria, the water over the rapids had fallen to three feet, with seven feet needed for crossing. One of the army's engineers, Col. Joseph Bailey, devised a plan to build a pair of dams to back up the water. On May 9, after eight days of work and when it was almost completed, it collapsed, though four boats were able to cross. Beginning again, the dam was finally successfully completed by May 13, and the rest of the boats made it downriver. When the campaign was over on June 19, 1864, it had accomplished nothing. (Faust, 619–620)

What ship sank the CSS *Alabama* in a naval battle off the coast of Cherbourg, France, and who commanded the ship?
The USS *Kearsarge*, which was commanded by Capt. John A. Winslow. (Faust, 409)

What was the northernmost Confederate raid of the Civil War?
The October 19, 1864, raid on St. Albans, Vermont.

How many men made up the St. Albans raiding party, and who commanded it?
There were twenty raiders, commanded by Bennett H. Young.

How much money did the St. Albans raiders get and where did they go when they left town?
They robbed three banks, getting about $200,000. Once they had the cash, they crossed the border into Canada.

What was the fate of the St. Albans raiders?
They were arrested by Canadian authorities. The Federal government asked for extradition, but the Canadian courts ruled that the raiders were soldiers under orders, and released them on bond. (Faust, 651)

What happened at Allatoona, Georgia, on October 5, 1864?
In late September, Hood marched north, his mission to wreck the Western & Atlantic Railroad, which was Sherman's supply line. Hood hoped to get the Union general to chase him and that they would engage on ground favorable to the Confederates. Allatoona Pass, just south of the Etowah River, was a Union supply base and was where the railroad passed through the hills and a deep cut. Sherman, knowing of the movement, notified Brig. Gen. John M. Corse that he should send reinforcements to the pass. Corse arrived early on October 5 as Maj. Gen. Samuel G. French prepared to attack the garrison. Though the Confederates came close to breaking through several times, by early afternoon French decided the position could not be taken and withdrew from the field. The Federals suffered a reported 706 casualties while the Confederate loss was about 900. (Faust, 7)

Name the six Confederate generals killed at the battle of Franklin, Tennessee, on November 30, 1864.
Brig. Gen. Patrick R. Cleburne, Brig. Gen. Hiram B. Granbury, Brig. Gen. Otho F. Strahl, Brig. Gen. John Adams, Brig. Gen. John C. Carter (died on December 10, 1864), and Brig. Gen. States Rights Gist. (McDonough and Connelly, 161–166)

Where were the bodies of four of the dead Confederate generals laid out before being removed for burial?

"Carnton," the home of Col. Randall McGavock. During the fighting, the mansion and outbuildings were pressed into hospital service.

Who commanded the Union and Confederate armies at the battle of Franklin, Tennessee?

Union: Maj. Gen. John M. Schofield. Confederate: Lt. Gen. John Bell Hood. (Faust, 284)

What engagement preceded the battle of Franklin?

Spring Hill, Tennessee, on November 29, 1864.

What was the outcome of the fighting at Spring Hill?

Confederate commander Gen. John Bell Hood planned to get around the Federal troops under Maj. Gen. John M. Schofield and take Spring Hill so that he could block the road to Nashville. Hood sent three of his divisions toward the town in an uncoordinated attack while he himself retired to his headquarters some three miles from the battlefield. During the night Schofield pushed his men north through the town, ultimately reaching Franklin. (Faust, 710)

What was Hood's condition during the action at Spring Hill?

Apparently he simply did not know what he was doing. He was confused, exhausted, and in pain from his previous wounds; he may also have been under the influence of painkillers. (Faust, 710)

What began on May 4, 1864?

Grant's Overland Campaign against the Army of Northern Virginia. (Denney, 399)

Where did Sheridan (now in command of the Union cavalry) and Jeb Stuart first mix it up in battle?

Todd's Tavern at the intersection of the Brock and Catharpin roads, south of The Wilderness battlefield. (Denney, 400)

After the fighting ended in The Wilderness, what did the Army of the Potomac do?
Rather than falling back as in almost every other battle it had participated in the army moved around Gen. Lee's right flank and headed southeast toward Spotsylvania Court House and ultimately Richmond.

In what battle did students from the Virginia Military Academy take part?
The battle of New Market, Virginia, May 15, 1864. Two hundred forty-seven students took part in the Confederate victory, losing ten killed and forty-seven wounded. (Denney, 408)

Who commanded the Federal troops at the battle of Olustee, Florida, on February 20, 1864?
Brig. Gen. Truman Seymour. (Faust, 545)

What is another name for the battle of Olustee?
The battle of Ocean Pond. (Faust, 545)

Who was in command of the Confederate troops at the battle of Olustee?
Brig. Gen. Joseph Finegan. (Faust, 545)

Who commanded the Federal and Confederate forces at the battle of Monocacy, Maryland, on July 9, 1864?
The Union forces were led by Maj. Gen. Lew Wallace and the Confederates by Lt. Gen. Jubal Early. (Weeks, 348)

Why is the battle of Monocacy referred to as the battle that saved Washington?
Although the battle was a Union defeat, sustaining 1,294 casualties, it did delay Early's movement on Washington, allowing Sixth Corps troops from Grant's army more time to reach the city. (Weeks, 350)

Who commanded the Confederate raid on July 30, 1864, that led to the burning of Chambersburg, Pennsylvania?
Brig. Gen. John McCausland. When the Confederate troops demanded $500,000 in greenbacks from the citizens of the town in retribution for the destruction of private homes in the Shenandoah Valley, the people refused to pay, whereupon McCausland evacuated the town and burned the business district. When the Confederates left town, more than 550 buildings were in ashes or gutted, with the damages running into the millions of dollars, and more than 2,000 people were left homeless. (Faust, 125, 456)

What happened to Andrew J. McElwain as the Confederates left Chambersburg in July 1864 following McCausland's raid?
McElwain was the county school superintendent. The Confederates asked him if he had ever taught black students. After he replied that he had, a squad of Rebels burned his home. (Chambersburg, 127)

What did some of the men of the 1st Michigan Sharpshooters do at the battle of the Crater on July 30, 1864?
Some members of Co. K, 1st Michigan, were Ojibway Indians. During the action many of them pulled their blouses over their heads and sang their death song. (Ted Alexander, Antietam National Battlefield)

What was Maj. Gen. Sterling Price's plan when he led the Army of Missouri north in the fall of 1864?
His plan was to capture St. Louis and then move to Jefferson City, where he would install a new Confederate government and renew the war in the West. (Weeks, 21)

What was the first action of Price's Missouri Raid?
Pilot Knob, on September 27, 1864, which turned into a Confederate defeat. Because of the repulse and heavy casualties at Pilot Knob, Price was forced to change his plan, abandoning the idea of taking St. Louis and Jefferson City. Instead, he set his sights on Kansas City. (Boatner, 654; Weeks 21)

The pincer-type movement of Maj. Gen. William S. Rosecrans at what battle ended Price's Missouri Raid?
"At the battle of Westport on October 23, 1864, Maj. Gen. James Blunt pushed Maj. Gen. Samuel R. Curtis along Brush Creek which flows from west to east. Confronting them were two of Maj. Gen. Sterling Price's divisions (Fagan's and Shelly's) and Brig. Gen. John S. Marmaduke's division. Maj. Gen. Alfred Pleasonton's Union cavalry was placed along a north-south line. The Confederate cavalry, as well as Pleasonton's, fought dismounted. The combat along and south of the Brush Creek line was bitter and initially ebbed and flowed. In the end numbers prevailed and Blunt's troops gained the upper hand in the fighting south of Brush Creek as Pleasonton gained ground at Marmaduke's expense. Price pulled his troops back and headed south. Only a stout rear guard action fought on the grounds of today's Forest Hill Cemetery enabled the Confederates to disengage and retreat down the State Line Road. Estimated casualties on each side were about 1,500." (Bearss)

Where and when was the battle of Marais des Cygnes?
Marais des Cygnes was a delaying action fought by Brig. Gen. John Marmaduke against Federal troops, chasing what was left of Sterling Price's Army of Missouri after its defeat at Westport. Marmaduke and his men blocked a crossing on the Marais des Cygnes River for about four hours on the morning of October 25, 1864, before retreating to rejoin Price. The site is near Pleasanton, Kansas. (Weeks, 25)

What battle effectively destroyed Sterling Price's army?
The battle of Mine Creek, about ten miles south of Marais des Cygnes. While the Confederates were trying to get their wagons and men across a narrow ford on the Post Scott Road, Price sent some 7,000 of his men to delay the Federals. When the Federals attacked, the Confederates were routed, suffering 1,200 casualties, including the capture of two of their generals, Brig. Gen. John S. Marmaduke and Brig. Gen. William L. Cabell. (Weeks, 25–27)

Savannah

Where was Ft. McAllister located?
This earthenwork fort sat on the Ogeechee River, about fifteen miles west of Savannah, Georgia. For much of the war it served as a full-scale military laboratory, and, during the autumn of 1862 and winter of 1863, Union monitors tested their big Dahlgren guns in duels with the fort's guns. In December 1864 it became a target for Maj. Gen. Sherman's army. (Weeks, 195)

What was the first U.S. monitor to steam up the Ogeechee River and fire on Ft. McAllister?
The USS *Montauk*, on January 27, 1863. Over the course of the next week, Rear Adm. Samuel Du Pont sent two more missions up the river. In each case the monitors fired on the fort for extended periods, but it suffered little damage. (Weeks, 196–197)

Who commanded Ft. McAllister during Du Pont's raids on it?
Maj. John Gallie, who was killed when the *Montauk*, on February 1, made her second assault on the fort. As the ships that attacked it, the fort, built of sand and sod, also held up fairly well. (Weeks, 197)

When Sherman approached Ft. McAllister in December 1864, who commanded the fort and how many men garrisoned it?
Maj. George Anderson had 230 men inside the fort with him. For the most part Anderson was unprepared and undermanned for what was coming at him. (Weeks, 197)

What happened to Ft. McAllister when Sherman attacked it on December 13, 1864?
Thirty-five hundred troops under Brig. Gen. William Hazen attacked the fort just before sundown. Union sharpshooters picked off the artillerymen, followed by the Union assault. The fort fell within fifteen minutes. (Weeks, 197–198)

What three commanders led the forces defending Savannah's line under Lt. Gen. William Hardee?

The right of the line was commanded by Maj. Gen. Gustavus W. Smith, with Maj. Gen. Lafayette McLaws in the center and Maj. Gen. Ambrose R. Wright on the left. In all, Hardee had less than 10,000 men. (Durham, 14)

What was the alignment of Sherman's men around Savannah?

The Left Wing, commanded by Maj. Gen. Henry W. Slocum, had Brig. Gen. Alpheus S. Williams's Twentieth Corps on the left and Brig. Gen. Jefferson C. Davis's Fourteenth Corps on the right. The Right Wing, under Maj. Gen. O. O. Howard, had the Seventeenth Corps of Maj. Gen. Frank P. Blair on Davis's right, and then Maj. Gen. Peter J. Osterhaus's Fifteenth Corps. Brig. Gen. Judson Kilpatrick's cavalry operated south of the Ogeechee River. (Durham, 16–17)

When did Sherman first contact Hardee demanding the surrender of Savannah?

On December 17. Sherman got Hardee's reply on December 18, a refusal saying he intended to defend the city. All the while, however, bridges were being built across the Savannah River to be used in an evacuation which was to take place on December 19. (Durham, 46–47)

When did the Confederates abandon Savannah?

Though the evacuation was scheduled for December 19, the bridges were not completed until the evening, so Hardee postponed the departure until the next day. Early on December 20, Hardee moved the supply wagons and those wounded who could be moved across the river. These were soon followed by the civilians. Finally, at 8:00 p.m., Wright's Division moved out of their position and began the march north. They were followed by McLaws at 10:00 p.m. and Smith at 11:00 p.m. By 1:00 a.m. December 21, the Confederate defenses of Savannah had been abandoned. In all, Hardee managed to get 9,089 soldiers out of the city, as well as forty-nine cannon. (Durham, 47, 48)

How and when did Hardee leave Savannah?
He departed aboard the *Swan* at 9:00 p.m. He left behind a Lt. Col. Paul, who was to keep order in the city, gather up stragglers, and then destroy the bridges across the river. (Durham, 48)

Who surrendered the city of Savannah at 4:00 a.m., December 21, to the Federals?
Mayor Richard Arnold and two aldermen, Mr. O'Byrne and Mr. Lachlison. The three men walked out the Louisville Road until they came to its junction with the Augusta Road. Here they were met by Union pickets and taken to Brig. Gen. John Geary. Geary accepted the surrender of the city and made arrangements for the protection of the citizens and their private property. (Durham, 48)

What was the first Federal unit to march into Savannah?
Col. Henry A. Barnum's brigade of General Geary's Division of the Twentieth Corps. They reached the City Exchange around 6:00 a.m. and raised the U.S. flag over the city. (Durham, 48)

Where was General Sherman when Savannah surrendered?
At Hilton Head Island, meeting with Adm. Dahlgren. In the evening he boarded the *Harvest Moon* and began the trip back to Savannah, but heavy weather caused the ship to take the inland waterway behind the barrier islands, where the going was easier. Unfortunately there was a low tide and the ship grounded on a mud bank, so Sherman spent much of December 21 stuck in the mud. He was finally taken aboard a tug that had come to give him the news of the surrender, and was taken back to his headquarters. He finally reached the city on December 22. (Durham, 48)

While in Savannah, where did Sherman have his headquarters?
In the residence of Charles Green on Madison Square. The author has visited this house and readers who go to Savannah should be sure to take the house tour. (Durham, 42, 43)

What did Sherman's men capture when they entered the city?
More than 200 heavy cannon and 30,000 bales of cotton. (Durham, 48)

What did Sherman say in his December 22, 1864, telegram to President Lincoln?

"I beg to present you as a Christmas gift, the city of Savannah, with one hundred and fifty heavy guns and plenty of ammunition, also about twenty-five thousand bales of cotton." (Durham, 48)

What was the fate of the *Rebecca Hertz*?

The *Rebecca Hertz* had probably been the last blockade runner to slip out of Savannah before the arrival of Federal troops. After trading her cargo of cotton for tea, sugar, coffee, salt, and pepper in Nassau, she headed back to Savannah. On January 2, 1865, after slipping past Ft. Pulaski in the dark, the ship dropped anchor in front of the city. It was a happy crew, thinking they would make a nice profit from their trip. When the captain went to the Customs House he noticed some things had changed; for instance, the U.S. flag flying over the City Exchange. Much to the captain and crew's dismay, the ship was confiscated and the supplies aboard her were used to feed the Union army. (Durham, 51)

Who commanded the Union and Confederate troops at the battle of Saltville, Virginia?

Federal: Brig. Gen. Stephen G. Burbridge. Confederate: Brig. Gen. Felix H. Robertson, including a company of bushwhackers under Capt. Champ Ferguson. (Faust, 654)

What was the outcome of the Federal attack at Saltville?

The Federal attack failed, leaving about 350 casualties. The Confederates reported 108 casualties. (Faust, 654)

Why has the battle of Saltville become infamous?

A number of the attacking Federals were members of the 5th U.S. Colored Cavalry. The morning after the battle, Confederates moved among the casualties, where they began shooting and killing helpless blacks. Probably more than one hundred were massacred. (Faust, 654)

What happened to the Confederate commanders at Saltville because of the massacre of African Americans?

Nothing happened to Robertson, but Ferguson, the commander of the bushwhackers, was captured, tried, and hanged. (Faust, 654)

What happened to the CSS *Albemarle* on October 28, 1864?
She was sunk while moored at Plymouth, North Carolina, using a spar torpedo, by fourteen men led by Lt. William B. Cushing (brother of Alonzo Cushing of Gettysburg fame). The boat was later raised, stripped of its armor and guns, and towed to the Norfolk Navy Yard as a war prize. The hulk was finally sold for scrap in 1867. (Faust, 5)

Shenandoah Valley 1864

What were the major battles of Gen. Philip Sheridan's Shenandoah Valley Campaign in late 1864 and early 1865?
Opequon Creck or Third Winchester (September 19), Fisher's Hill (September 22 and October 9), Tom's Brook (October 9), Hull's Hill (October 14), Cedar Creek (October 19) and Waynesboro (March 2). (Heidler and Heidler, 1757)

What happened in Lexington, Virginia, on June 11, 1864?
Maj. Gen. David Hunter's Union troops entered the town, and burned the Virginia Military Institute and the home of former Virginia governor John Letcher. (Patchan, 6)

What was the outcome of the battle of Cool Spring on July 18, 1864?
Federal units under the command of Col. Joseph Thoburn crossed the Shenandoah River at Island Ford near Berryville, Virginia. Once across they ran into elements of Lt. Gen. Jubal Early's Army of the Valley District, led by Maj. Gen. John B. Gordon and Brig. Gen. Gabriel C. Wharton. Later in the day these Confederates were reinforced by elements of Maj. Gen. Robert E. Rodes. Though Brig. Gen. James B. Ricketts's troops were brought up they were not thrown across the river, leaving Thoburn to fend for himself. Eventually the Federals were forced back across the river, at a cost of 422 casualties. The Confederates reported 397 casualties. The outcome of the battle was a successful rear-guard action for Early, but did nothing to change the overall campaign. (Patchan, 8–15)

What happened at the battle of Rutherford's Farm on July 20, 1864?
A small Union force under Brig. Gen. William W. Averell went up against Maj. Gen. Stephen Dodson Ramseur's Confederate division. Unlike the results at Cool Spring two days before, the short but bloody fight at Rutherford's Farm was a Federal victory, sending the Confederates scampering off to Winchester and beyond. Ramseur probably lost around 500 men, while Averell lost about 242 in his infantry units alone. (Patchan, 15–22)

What units participated in the battle of Second Kernstown, July 24, 1864?
Early's Army of the Valley District was composed of Maj. Gen. John C. Breckinridge's Corps, containing two divisions commanded by Brig. Gen. Gabriel C. Wharton and Maj. Gen. John B. Gordon. Maj. Gen. Robert E. Rodes's and Maj. Gen Stephen D. Ramseur's divisions reported directly to Early. Also included was a cavalry division under Maj. Gen. Robert Ransom. The Federal Army of West Virginia was commanded by Brig. Gen. George Crook and contained the divisions of Col. Joseph Thoburn, Col. Isaac H. Duval, Col. James A. Mulligan, and two cavalry divisions under Brig. Gen. Alfred N. Duffié and Brig. Gen. William Averell. The Union force was led by Maj. Gen. Horatio Wright and contained the Sixth Corps and a portion of the Nineteenth Corps. When Wright crossed the two corps over the Shenandoah, he did a cursory reconnaissance and decided Early was retreating to Richmond, so he led the Sixth and Nineteenth to Washington, there to be transferred to Petersburg. (Patchan, 23, 42)

What future famous feuding families were with the 45th Battalion, Virginia Infantry, at Kernstown?
On the rolls were seventeen Hatfields and eleven McCoys. (Patchan, 43)

What was the final tally for the battle of Second Kernstown, July 24, 1864?
It was a victory for Jubal Early's army. With losses of only about 600 men, his soldiers managed to inflict 1,185 casualties on Gen.

Crook's Army of West Virginia. Changes were to come, however, as Gen. Grant sent Maj. Gen. Philip H. Sheridan to the valley to take command of the newly formed Army of the Shenandoah. Along with him Sheridan also brought the cavalry divisions of Brig. Gen. Wesley Merritt and James H. "Henry" Wilson. (Patchan, 50)

What was the outcome of the fighting at Third Winchester (Opequon Creek) on September 19, 1864?
It was the first of two staggering losses for Jubal Early's army. Though initially gaining some success, flank attacks by Crook's Eighth Corps and two Federal cavalry divisions (Merritt's and Averell's) drove the Confederates through town and south. It was the first time the Second Corps had been driven from the field. (Faust, 835)

Who was Col. George S. Patton's famous grandson?
General George S. Patton of World War II tank fame. The grandfather-colonel was mortally wounded while leading a brigade at Winchester. His brother, Walter Tazewell Patton, was mortally wounded at Gettysburg, fighting with the 7th Virginia Infantry. The two brothers lie side by side in Winchester's Stonewall Cemetery. (Delauter and Beck, 85–86; Coco, n.p.)

What happened on September 22, 1864, at Fisher's Hill in the Shenandoah Valley?
Early's Army of the Valley was routed by Philip Sheridan and his commanders, Maj. Gen. Horatio Wright, Maj. Gen. William Emory, and Maj. Gen. George Crook. Wright and Emory's troops assaulted the Confederates on Fisher's Hill from the front while Crook marched his men into a position on the flank and rear of Early's army. When Crook's men attacked perpendicularly to the Confederate line, the Rebels broke and ran. The only thing that saved the Confederate army was darkness. Union losses were 528 and the Confederate casualties totaled 1,255. (Faust, 260–261)

What two former West Point classmates and friends fought each other at the battle of Tom's Brook, also known as the "Woodstock Races," on October 9, 1864?
Union Gen. George Armstrong Custer and Confederate Gen. Thomas L. Rosser. When the two men's brigades had deployed, Custer rode to the front of his and, close enough to the Confederate line to be recognized, he doffed his hat and bowed. The Union casualties were fifty-seven while the Confederates lost 550. (Heidler and Heidler, 1960)

Following his victory at Tom's Brook, where did Sheridan set up his headquarters?
At the "Belle Grove" plantation east of Cedar Creek near Middletown. (S. Patchan, 8)

Where did Early cross the North Fork of the Shenandoah River early on the morning of October 19, 1864?
Gordon's wing marched along the northern base of Massanutten Mountain and crossed at both Bowman Ford and McInturff's Ford. Wharton and Kershaw skirted the river by moving up the Valley Pike. Kershaw eventually crossed Cedar Creek at Bowman's Mill Ford and Wharton at the Stickley House and Mill. (Patchan, 13, 16 maps)

When Early attacked the unsuspecting Federal camp at Cedar Creek, how did he deploy his troops?
On the right was Gordon's Corps, made up of Ramseur's, Evans's, and Pegram's divisions. These units attacked Crook's camp from the southeast. Kershaw led his division against Thoburn from the south. Wharton brought his division up the Valley Pike and attacked the area beyond Stickley House and Mill on Cedar Creek. (S. Patchan, 18, map)

By 1:00 p.m., what was the position of the two armies?
The Confederate attack had pushed the Federals north of Middletown where they formed a line about two miles north of the town, their left hugging the Valley Pike. The Confederate line extended

westward from Middletown along the Old Forge Road. Retreating Federal troops had made it almost to Winchester and lined the Valley Pike, reaching back to the battlefield. As Sheridan rode toward Cedar Creek, he cursed the men, and then pleaded with them to turn and follow him back, telling them they had more fight in them. (S. Patchan, 63, map, 43–44)

Which distinguished Confederate general was mortally wounded in the Federal counter-attack at Cedar Creek?
Maj. Gen. Stephen Dodson Ramseur. As the general was mounting his horse (two others having been shot out from under him), a ball entered his right side, passed through both lungs and lodged below the left arm. He received the wound on a slope west of Miller's Mill, just northwest of Middleburg. His men began to take him off the field on a horse but he was soon transferred to an ambulance. Captured before he was able to be taken across Cedar Springs Run, Ramseur was taken to Belle Grove where his wound was pronounced mortal. He died on October 20. Coming to visit him in his last hours were many old West Point comrades, including Bvt. Maj. Henry A. DuPont, George Custer, Wesley Merritt, and Philip Sheridan. Ramseur had just become a new father, but died not knowing if he had a son or a daughter. The final casualty list for the battle was Union 5,672 and Confederate 2,910. (Gallagher, 163–165; S. Patchan, 19, 48; Sifakis, 120)

On November 25, 1864, Confederate Col. Robert M. Martin brought a team of men into New York City with the intention of doing what?
Burning the city down in retaliation for Sherman's march through Georgia. Spreading out, they set fires at the La Farge House, Astor House, St. Nicholas, Metropolitan, and nine other hotels, as well as Phineas T. Barnum's Museum. None of the fires were serious, in part because the arsonists kept the room doors shut so they would not be detected, limiting the amount of oxygen in the room—no oxygen, no fire. It is interesting to note that when they tried to set the La Farge House ablaze, next door at the Winter Garden Theatre a benefit performance of *Julius Caesar* was being held. The three main stars were Edwin Booth (cast

as Brutus), Junius Brutus Booth Jr. (cast as Cassius), and John Wilkes Booth (cast as Mark Antony). (Livingston, 66–68)

Who was Capt. Robert Cobb Kennedy?
He was the only member of Martin's raiders who got caught. He was kept at Ft. Lafayette for four months and then, on March 25, 1865, executed, the last Confederate to be executed before the war's end. (Livingston, 68)

What incident on September 16, 1864, involved cattle rustling?
The Hampton-Rosser cattle raid. With Grant's lengthening lines around Petersburg, the Confederate food supply was becoming critical. A Confederate scout happened to find a herd of between 2,500 and 3,000 head of lightly guarded cattle at Coggin's Point, six miles south of City Point. Maj. Gen. Wade Hampton, the Confederate cavalry commander, received permission to try to take the herd. Hampton rode out of camp with 4,000 troopers and was joined two days later by Brig. Gen. Thomas Rosser's Laurel Brigade. The combined forces attacked the 1st DC Cavalry and then the 13th Pennsylvania Cavalry, which was actually guarding the cattle. The Confederates calmed the herd, then started them back to their lines via the same route they had come. They had taken almost 2,500 head and, along with the Confederate "cowboys," the column stretched almost seven miles. Finally, on the morning of September 17, the troopers reached their lines, having suffered only sixty-one casualties. (Faust, 336–337)

What happened in Centralia, Missouri, on September 27, 1864?
The town was raided by William "Bloody Bill" Anderson and his gang, accompanied by Thomas Todd and Si Gordon. They first looted the town and held up a stagecoach, then stopped a train and captured twenty-four unarmed Union soldiers, twenty-three of which they shot down in cold blood. The one remaining soldier they used to exchange for one of their own captured men. The group then killed over one hundred Union soldiers who were chasing them, then went back into town where they killed more soldiers before riding off. Anderson was eventually killed on October 7, 1864. (Heidler and Heidler, 47–48)

UNITS

Who made up most of Co. K, 1st Michigan Sharpshooters?

Native Americans. The company was comprised mostly of Ottawa and Chippewa (Ojibwa) Indians. The regiment participated in the assault after the Crater explosion, taking heavy casualties. (Catton, 435)

What distinction does the 1st Maine Heavy Artillery hold?

During the assault on Petersburg on June 16, 1864, the regiment suffered 580 casualties out of the unit's 850 men, giving it the distinction of suffering the greatest loss in one engagement of any Union regiment in the war. Of the 2,047 regiments in the Union Army, the 1st Maine sustained the greatest loss in battle. (Dickson, 248; Fox, 125, 451)

~⌒ CHAPTER 6 ⌒~

1865

THE ASSASSINATION

Who were the men John Wilkes Booth recruited to help him kidnap the president?
Samuel B. Arnold, Michael O'Laughlen, John H. Surratt, George Atzerodt, David E. Herold, and Lewis Thornton Powell (Paine or Payne). (Henig, 344)

Who were the couple who sat with President Lincoln and his wife Mary at Ford's Theater on the evening of April 14, 1865?
Maj. Henry Rathbone and Miss Clara Harris.

Who was sitting outside the presidential box and let Booth pass into the box?
Charles Forbes, a White House valet. (Kauffman, 46)

Who was William H. Crook?
Crook was a White House guard whose shift on April 14 was from 8:00 a.m. to 4:00 p.m. His relief, John F. Parker, was three hours late so he was still at the White House when President Lincoln left for the theater. Crook remembered that Lincoln, on his way out said, "Goodbye, Crook," rather than "Good night, Crook." Parker had deserted

his post and Crook always regretted not having been there himself. Parker was tried but found not guilty of deserting his post. (Sifakis, 95; Kauffman, 393)

Who was the first doctor to attend Lincoln after he was shot?
Charles A. Leale, an army surgeon. Leale was also taking Lincoln's pulse when he died the next morning. (Catton, 589; Craughwell, 1)

Where was the president taken after he was shot?
Across the street to the William Petersen house at 453 Tenth St. (Catton, 589)

Who was Robert King Stone?
Lincoln's personal surgeon. He did not reach the president until he had been moved to the Petersen House. At Mary Lincoln's request, Stone took charge of the case but soon determined that there was no hope for the president. (Sifakis, 393)

It is estimated that how many people visited the president's room as he lay dying?
At least fifty-seven. There were about twelve in the room when he died, including his son Robert, Edwin M. Stanton, Charles Sumner, Surgeon-General Joseph K. Barnes, and James Tanner (a stenographer). (Craughwell, 2)

Who had procured the pine box Lincoln's body was placed in when they removed him from the Peterson House?
Assistant quartermaster Gen. Daniel Rucker. (Craughwell, 4)

Who performed Lincoln's autopsy?
Two assistant army surgeons, J. Janvier Woodward and Edward Curtis. Also present in the room during the autopsy were Surgeon General Barnes, Dr. Robert Stone, Dr. Charles Crane, Dr. Charles S. Taft, Dr. William M. Notson, Gen. Daniel Rucker, and Orville H. Browning. (Craughwell, 5)

What were the names of the undertakers who took care of Lincoln after his autopsy and what was the name of the embalmer who embalmed Lincoln?
Charles D. Brown and Joseph B. Alexander. These two men had also arranged the funeral of Lincoln's eleven-year-old son Willie. Henry P. Cattell was the master embalmer who worked for Brown and Alexander. (Craughwell, 5–6)

Who was Laura Keene?
Keene was the star of *Our American Cousin*, which Lincoln was watching when he was assassinated. (Boatner, 450)

What line in *Our American Cousin* made up the last words that Abraham Lincoln ever heard?
"Don't know the manners of good society, eh? Wal, I guess I know enough to turn you inside out, you sockdolagizing old mantrap!" (Foote, 980)

What does "Sockdolager" mean?
In the case of the aforementioned line, it refers to a very aggressive woman who dominated men with force, who charmed them and teamed them with a heavy hand or, its feminine equivalent, a sharp tongue. (Quigley, 147)

Who was Joseph B. Stewart?
Stewart was seated in the front row at Ford's Theater when Booth leaped onto the stage. As Booth ran off, Stewart gave chase but was slowed when, as he testified, Edmund Spangler slammed the door on him. He eventually made it into the alley but by then Booth was mounted and Stewart could not get hold of the reins. (Sifakis, 390–391)

Who was Edmund Spangler?
Following the assassination, Spangler was convicted for a "role" in the plot that he had actually never performed. It was alleged that he held Booth's horse while the killing took place. He was sentenced to six

years and sent to the Dry Tortugas, where he served only two-thirds of his sentence. Spangler had been a scene-shifter in Ford's Theater, so after Booth entered the theater, Spangler went back to work, asking the theater "grunt," "Peanuts" Burroughs, to hold Booth's horse, which he did. (Sifakis, 381; Kanazawich, 11, 31)

What did John Wilkes Booth shout when he jumped to the stage at Ford's Theater after shooting the president?
"Sic Semper Tyrannis!" ("Thus always to tyrants!")

Name the four Lincoln conspirators who were hanged at the Old Washington Arsenal on July 7, 1865?
Pictured below just after the hanging are, left to right, Mary Surratt, Lewis Paine (Powell), David Herold, and George Atzerodt. (Kanazawich, 69–70; Davis, 378)

When did Booth break his left leg?
Since the assassination, it has been thought that Booth broke his leg when jumping from Lincoln's booth to the stage; however, a number

Execution of Lincoln Conspirators. USAMHI

of eyewitnesses indicate a far more likely possibility. Booth told several people during his escape that he broke the leg when his horse fell on him. David Herold backed up this story, saying that he was with Booth when it happened and helped him back onto his horse. No one who saw him just following the deed made any mention of Booth being in pain or favoring his right leg. (Kauffman, 17)

Who was Dr. Samuel A. Mudd?
Dr. Mudd set John Wilkes Booth's leg on April 15, 1865, then gave him and David Herold lodging, a meal, and some material assistance in their flight from Washington. He was arrested on April 21 and later tried for involvement in the plot to assassinate the president. He was sentenced to life imprisonment at Ft. Jefferson in the Dry Tortugas. (Faust, 516)

What did Samuel Mudd do while he was imprisoned at Ft. Jefferson?
At first he tried to escape, but was caught and held in irons until January 1866. He then became a model prisoner, tending to the sick during the August–September 1867 yellow fever outbreak. As a reward for his service in the epidemic, President Johnson pardoned him and he was released in March 1869. (Faust, 516)

When did President Lincoln die?
At 7:22 a.m. on April 15, 1865. (Denney, 559)

What did Secretary of War Edwin Stanton reportedly say when Lincoln died?
"Now he belongs to the ages." (Catton, 590)

Where was John Wilkes Booth cornered?
At the Garrett farm two and one half miles south of Port Royal, Virginia. (Denney, 563)

Who reputedly mortally wounded John Wilkes Booth when he refused to surrender?
Sgt. Boston Corbett of the 16th New York Cavalry. (Denney, 563; Kauffman, 49)

What happened to Boston Corbett prior to his wounding of Booth?
He was an evangelical Christian who was born in England in 1832.
To help himself avoid the temptation of women he castrated himself
in 1858. He was captured on June 23, 1864, by Mosby's partisans in
a skirmish near Chantilly, Virginia, and sent to Andersonville Prison.
Following his exchange in March 1865, he became part of the detachment that pursued Booth. (Thompson, 56)

**Who commanded the detachment of New York cavalry that caught
up with and ultimately killed Booth?**
Lt. Edward P. Doherty. (Kauffman, 46)

Who was in charge of the expedition that found and killed Booth?
Everton J. Conger, a civilian detective. He received $15,000 in reward
money. (Kauffman, 47)

Where is Booth's final resting place?
He is buried in the Booth family plot in Green Wood Cemetery in
Baltimore, Maryland. There is a small, unmarked stone in the plot
that is said to be his grave. My warning to those readers who wish
to visit the cemetery and Booth's grave: the last time this researcher
was in the cemetery, he was shot at from outside the grounds, so care
should be taken when visiting the site.

**Who was named to head the commission that was to try the assas-
sination conspirators?**
Maj. Gen. David Hunter. (Denney, 567)

What happened to Boston Corbett?
He became the doorkeeper for the Kansas state legislature, where
one day he drew a pistol on some of the members. Committed to an
insane asylum, he escaped and disappeared. (Kauffman, 49)

**After Lincoln's funeral train left Washington on April 21, where
did it stop before reaching Springfield?**
Baltimore, Harrisburg, Philadelphia, New York, Albany, Buffalo,
Cleveland, Columbus, Indianapolis, and Chicago; generally, except

for the stop in Chicago, it retraced the route Lincoln took when he traveled to Washington as the president-elect. (Catton, 595)

How many photographs of Lincoln's body were taken?
One, taken by Jeremiah Gurney Jr. Secretary of War Edwin Stanton thought that the photograph was inappropriate so he ordered the negative destroyed along with all known copies of the image. One did survive, but did not surface until 1952. (Catton, 596)

What two other politicians were to be assassinated at the same time as Lincoln, and who was to do the job?
Vice-President Andrew Johnson was to be murdered by George Atzerodt, who chickened out at the last moment. Secretary of State William Seward was to be killed by Lewis Powell (Paine). Powell successfully reached Seward's room and, though he wounded the secretary and four others, the wound was not fatal.

PERSONALITIES

Always the focus of controversy, what happened to "Beast" Butler in January 1865?
Heeding a request from Grant, Lincoln relieved Butler of command of the Army of the James. (Denney, 512)

Who replaced Butler as the commander of the Army of the James?
Maj. Gen. E. O. C. Ord. (Denney, 512)

In January 1865, who became an assistant adjutant general of Grant's staff?
Capt. Robert Todd Lincoln, the president's son. (Denney, 519)

Who was the first black staff officer in the U.S. military?
Maj. Martin R. Delany, who attained the rank on February 26, 1865. (Catton, 379)

Whom did Jefferson Davis appoint secretary of war on February 6, 1865?
Maj. Gen. John C. Breckinridge. (Boatner, 83)

What new position did Robert E. Lee assume on February 9, 1865?
Commander of all Confederate Armies. (Denney, 529)

What was Vice President Andrew Johnson's problem when he took the oath of office?
Allegedly he was drunk. His acceptance speech was slurred and close to being incoherent. (Denney, 542)

Who was in the crowd listening to Lincoln's Second Inaugural Address, standing below the podium?
John Wilkes Booth.

Who was William Wing Loring?
By the end of the war, William Wing "Old Blizzards" Loring was the senior Confederate major general on active field duty. He had served in western Virginia, Vicksburg, then in Mississippi and Georgia, where he took over command of Polk's Corps when the general was killed. On June 23, 1864, he was replaced as a corps commander by Lt. Gen. A. P. Stewart, who led the corps in the Atlanta and Carolinas Campaigns. (Faust, 447)

Who was the last Confederate general to surrender his troops and on what date did he do it?
Brig. Gen. Stand Watie, on June 23, 1865, in Doaksville, Indian Territory. (Faust, 737)

Who did Gen. Watie surrender to?
Watie surrendered a battalion of Union Creek, Seminole, Cherokee, and Osage Indians to Lt. Col. Asa C. Matthews. (Faust, 736)

What was Stand Watie's major claim to fame?
He was the only Indian to become a general in the Civil War. Though Eli Parker, Grant's military secretary, did become a brigadier general, his commission did not come until after the war had ended. Parker was a Seneca; Watie was a Cherokee. (Faust, 557–558, 807–808)

What was President Davis wearing when he was captured?
He was wearing regular men's clothing but when he tried to slip away he put his wife's shawl over his head. It fooled no one. (Bradley, 55)

Who administered the oath of office to Abraham Lincoln at his second inaugural?
Newly appointed Chief Justice Salmon P. Chase. (Holzer and Shenk, 187)

Who was Christian Rath?
The hangman for the Lincoln conspirators. He prepared the nooses and put the hoods over the prisoners' heads, making sure that the rope was in the proper position. (Sifakas, 327)

Who was Union Brig. Gen. Frank Wheaton's father-in-law?
The Confederate adjutant general Samuel Cooper, the first full Confederate general. (Green, 18; Faust, 165)

Whose life did Edwin Booth save at the railroad terminal in Jersey City?
Robert Lincoln, the president's son. (Livingston, 68)

Who was the only Federal soldier to be awarded two Medals of Honor during the Civil War?
Sgt. Thomas W. Custer, George Armstrong Custer's brother. The first he received for capturing a Confederate flag during the fighting near Namozine Church. The second he received was also for the capture of Rebel colors at Sailor's Creek, but for this he paid a price; the color bearer shot Custer in the face, the ball entering his cheek and passing out behind his ear. When his brother saw him, he ordered the younger Custer to see a surgeon. Flushed with courage, Custer gave the flag to someone and headed back into the battle, forcing Gen. Custer to place his brother under arrest and have him then taken forcibly to seek medical attention. (Urwin, 244, 246–248)

EVENTS

When did the Naval Academy move back to Annapolis from Newport, Rhode Island?
Summer 1865. (Faust, 522)

What was the first state to ratify the Thirteenth Amendment passed by Congress on February 1, 1865?
Illinois. (Denney, 525)

What five men met on a Federal steamer at Hampton Roads, Virginia, on February 3, 1865, to informally discuss peace negotiations?
Confederate Vice President Alexander Stevens; R. M. T. Hunter, president pro tem of the Confederate Senate; Judge John A. Campbell, formerly of the U.S. Supreme Court; President Lincoln and Secretary of State William H. Seward. (Catton 551)

What was the outcome of the conference?
The members had a nice chat but accomplished nothing. The president insisted that there would be no peace until the Confederate armies were disbanded and the national government recognized in the South. In addition, the Southerners would have to accept the abolition of slavery. (Catton 551)

When was Abraham Lincoln inaugurated to his second term?
March 4, 1865. (Catton 555)

MISCELLANEOUS

What happened to the USS *San Jacinto* of *Trent* Affair fame?
On January 1, 1865, she ran aground at Green Turtle Bay, Abaco, in the Bahamas. The crew managed to salvage most of the armament, ammunition, rigging, cables, and copper bottom, following which the hulk was abandoned. (Denney, 512)

What did Robert E. Lee hope to accomplish by evacuating his lines in Petersburg?

Lee hoped that he could get away from Grant and take his troops into North Carolina, where he would link up with Johnston's army. The combined armies would then defeat Sherman and turn back against Grant in Virginia. (Catton, 557)

What was the fate of the CSS *Shenandoah*?

Because the *Shenandoah* was in the Bering Sea capturing whaling ships, her crew did not know the war was over until August 2, 1865. The captain, Lt. James Waddell, sailed the ship back to Liverpool and surrendered to British authorities on November 6, 1865. The ship itself finally sank in 1879; at the time, it belonged to the Sultan of Zanzibar. (Denney, 577; Faust, 793–794)

Where was Gen. Lee's headquarters from November 1864 until April 2, 1865?

The home of William Turnbull in Petersburg. (Calkins, 19)

What was (and is) Juneteenth?

It is the oldest known celebration of the end of slavery. On June 19, 1865, Union soldiers commanded by Maj. Gen. Gordon Granger landed in Galveston, Texas. They brought with them the news that the war was over and that all slaves were now free. Upon hearing the news, many blacks left the area, going in search of family members. The celebration on that date was a time for reassuring, for prayer, and for gathering remaining family members. Many former slaves made an annual pilgrimage back to Galveston on June 19. (elecvillage)

BATTLES

Wilmington–Ft. Fisher, 1865

What comprised the Federal attack force that arrived at New Inlet, south of Ft. Fisher, on January 12, 1865?

There were fifty-eight naval warships and fourteen army transports.

The army troops, led by Brig. Gen. Alfred H. Terry, included Adelbert Ames's Division, Charles J. Paine's Division, and the Second Brigade, First Division, Twenty-fourth Corps, commanded by Joseph C. Abbott. (Fonvielle, 52)

When did Terry land his men in the second attempt to take Ft. Fisher?
On January 13. Despite heavy seas, Terry managed successfully to get his men ashore at Federal Point, about four miles north of the fort. Here he dug a line of entrenchments with little fire from the Confederates. By 8:00 a.m. January 14, Terry had a secure foothold on Federal Point. (Fonvielle, 52)

What did Braxton Bragg do to assist his commanders at Ft. Fisher?
Nothing. He ignored the Confederate commander's telegraphs and pleas for assistance. In addition, he had assumed field command at the Sugar Loaf and declined to attempt to drive the Federal infantry out of their entrenchments. He eventually sent reinforcements, but in attempting to land and get to the fort, the Federal artillery fire became so heavy that the transports were forced to retire. In all, only 350 men had been unloaded and they had to run almost two miles to reach the fort. (Fonvielle, 53–54)

In addition to the infantry, what other force was sent onto the beach to attack the fort?
Porter sent 2,261 sailors and Marines: the blue jackets armed with cutlasses and pistols, and the Marines with rifle-muskets, under the command of Fleet Capt. K. Randolph Breese. When they attacked, they were slaughtered. They were raked with canister and case shot as well as small-arms fire of hundreds of Confederates in the fort. When someone started talking about a retreat most of the sailors and Marines turned into a mob and headed back for the beach. Some sixty men, including Breese, took shelter behind the palisade fence and were forced to remain there until darkness gave them the chance to sneak away. The Federals suffered 284 casualties in just thirty minutes of fighting. (Fonvielle, 54–55)

Where did the Federals break through at the fort?

As the sailors and Marines were attacking so were Adelbert Ames's three brigades at the west end of Ft. Fisher. General Curtis, followed by Cols. Louis Bell and Galusha Pennypacker, had managed to move up the western beach and plant their flags. Curtis led his men through the gate at the foot of Shepherd's Battery but Confederate artillery fire forced him to switch to the east and enter the fort through the palisade. More Federals joined the attack and managed to push the Confederates out of the fort southward and into Battery Buchanan. Here transports were supposed to be waiting to embark the survivors out, but the battery captain had abandoned the garrison and left with the boats. By 10:00 p.m. the battle was over and the Federals were in possession of Ft. Fisher. (Fonvielle, 54–56)

Following the Federal victory, what unfortunate accident occurred on January 16 at Ft. Fisher?

Two drunk Marines looking for booty entered the fort's magazine and set off 13,000 pounds of gunpowder. The explosion killed an unknown number of Union and Confederate soldiers. (Fonvielle, 56)

What did Bragg do following the fall of Ft. Fisher?

At first, he was contacted by President Davis telling him to immediately retake the fort. Bragg chose not to, as he thought that Porter was still strong enough to destroy his army. He ordered all the forts on the mainland and islands south of Ft. Fisher to be abandoned, then concentrated his remaining troops at Ft. Anderson across the river from Sugar Loaf. Bragg then turned the command of the troops over to Maj. Gen. Robert Hoke and returned to Richmond to reorganize his staff. (Fonvielle, 56–57)

What were the final movements in the capture of Wilmington?

Terry and Porter were joined by troops of Maj. Gen. John Schofield's Twenty-third Corps. The advance on Wilmington began on February 11 when Schofield ordered Terry to move on Sugar Loaf. On February 16, Schofield redeployed Maj. Gen. Jacob Cox's division to the west side of the Cape Fear River with orders to advance on Ft. Anderson.

Ft. Anderson, a formidable earthwork, and Sugar Loaf—one on the east side of the Cape Fear River and the other on the west side—now anchored the defenses of the river approach to Wilmington. Rather than assault the fort directly, Cox sent his men on a twelve-mile circuitous march around Orton Pond and onto the rear of the fort. When the Ft. Anderson commander, Gen. Johnson Hagood, discovered that a strong Federal force was bearing down on his rear he requested permission to abandon the fort, which was granted. When Cox attacked Ft. Anderson, his troops found the fort evacuated. At the same time, Terry discovered that the Rebels had abandoned Sugar Loaf. The Federals continued to push the Confederates back toward Wilmington and eventually into the city. Bragg returned and on February 22 ordered his troops to retreat. Just as his rear guard cleared town, Schofield's Corps marched in. (Fonvielle, 57–62)

What was the symbolic value of the city of Columbia, South Carolina, to the Confederacy?
Other than being the state capital, the Secession Convention had first met in the chapel of the First Baptist Church before relocating to Charleston. (Elmore, 7)

What happened during the day of February 17, 1865, in Columbia?
Mayor Thomas Jefferson Goodwyn surrendered the town to Federal forces. This was preceded by Confederate forces pulling out of the city and heading northeast. (Elmore, 14)

What was the last official act by the Confederate States in Columbia?
General Butler's men setting fire to the Charlotte Railroad depot. (Elmore, 14)

Who were the first Federals into the city of Columbia?
Those of Col. George Stone who, with sixty men, had crossed the Broad River the night before and set up a beachhead. The next day Stone marched his men into the city and at 10:00 a.m. was met by Mayor Goodwyn, who surrendered to him. (Elmore, 13, 16)

Who raised the U.S. colors over the State House during the initial Federal occupation?
Col. Justin C. Kennedy, 13th Iowa Infantry. These colors were later cut down by Col. Stone's people and replaced with Fifteenth Corps banners. (Elmore, 16)

Who set fire to the city of Columbia?
At first it was blamed on the Confederates who were said to set the fires as they evacuated the city. However, the main fire that destroyed the city did not begin until between 7:00–8:00 p.m., long after the Confederates had left. It is thought that the main culprit was liquor. As the Federal troops marched into Columbia, crowds along the street handed out liquor in an attempt to appease the invaders. The soldiers had not eaten or slept well for the last two days and the effects of the "fighting whiskey" did not take long to appear. Later in the night, hundreds of drunken soldiers roamed the town looting, pillaging, and setting fires. Many sober soldiers brought in to quell the disturbance were soon drunk themselves and of no use. (Elmore, 16–24)

What were the two Union armies responsible for the taking of Richmond and Petersburg?
The Army of the Potomac under Maj. Gen. George Gordon Meade and the Army of the James commanded by Maj. Gen. E. O. C. Ord. These two were joined on March 26 by Maj. Gen. Philip Sheridan, who had wintered in and around Winchester, Virginia. Sheridan, accompanied by two divisions of cavalry (Custer's and Devin's) had left Winchester on February 27, crossed the James and reported to General in Chief Grant. (Greene, 7–8)

What is considered to be Lee's "Last Grand Offensive"?
The battle of Ft. Stedman, on March 25, 1865. The Confederates, under Maj. Gen. John B. Gordon, began their attack at 4:00 a.m. and captured Ft. Steadman and batteries No. Ten, Eleven, and Thirteen. Then it was found that satellite forts the attackers planned to take did not exist. Retreating back into Ft. Stedman, the slow initial Federal response finally began in earnest. By 8:00 a.m., rather than risking a retreat, many of the Confederates surrendered and the assault was

over. Confederate casualties were 2,681, while the Federals suffered about 1,017. (Faust, 279)

During the Federal breakthrough on April 2, 1865, who was the first Federal soldier to cross the Confederate works?
Credit for this has been given to Capt. Charles G. Gould of the 5th Vermont. Once across he was bayoneted twice and bashed over the head, but managed to get back into Union lines. He was eventually awarded the Medal of Honor for his exploits. (Greene, 18)

What did Maj. Clifton K. Prentiss and Pvt. William S. Prentiss have in common?
They were brothers, the major fighting for the Union while the private fought for the Confederacy. They were both wounded during the fighting on April 2 and were treated in the same field hospital. Unfortunately, neither survived his wound. (Green, 21)

Who killed Lt. Gen. Ambrose Powell Hill?
Cpl. John W. Mauk. He and Pvt. Daniel Wolford were members of the 138th Pennsylvania and, following the breakthrough on April 2, were wandering around behind the Confederate lines. When Hill and his aide Sgt. George W. Tucker reached the edge of a wood line along Long Road near Heth's headquarters the two Yankee soldiers fired; one shot, Mouk's, severed Hill's left thumb before going through his heart and out his back. (Greene, 22, 24)

What disease did A. P. Hill have that may have soon killed him if not for the Yankee lead that actually did?
Gonorrhea, contracted while on furlough, probably in New York City when he was attending the U.S. Military Academy. While in most people gonorrhea runs its course and leaves no lasting effects, in the case of Hill it, as "old soldiers" would say, went down on him causing severe adhesions, resulting in a severe case of prostatitis that tormented him the rest of his life. (Robertson, 11–12)

Who took over command of Hill's Corps after he was killed?
Maj. Gen. Henry Heth. (Greene, 45)

During the breakthrough on April 2 what happened at Ft. Gregg and Ft. Whitworth?
The Confederates managed to throw together a force of about 1,000 men and were able to hold off 7,000 Federals for more than two hours, thus allowing Gen. Lee to evacuate his army from the Petersburg defenses. (Greene, 45–46, 63)

What was the nickname of Confederate Battery 29 (Ft. Mahone)?
Ft. Damnation. (Greene, 49)

What Federal regiment was the first to fly the United States flag over Petersburg on April 3, 1865?
The 1st Michigan Sharpshooters. (Greene, 52)

Where did Gen. Grant and President Lincoln meet on the morning of April 3?
At Grant's headquarters at the Thomas Wallace residence, 21 South Market Street. The two men sat on the porch for about an hour and a half discussing reconstruction. (Greene, 53)

Who commanded the army during the January 15, 1865, assault on Ft. Fisher, North Carolina?
Brig. Gen. Alfred H. Terry. (Denney, 512)

What was the last major action fought in the Shenandoah Valley on March 2, 1865?
A battle at Waynesboro, Virginia, fought between Jubal Early's infantry, Brig. Gen. Gabriel C. Wharton's 1,700-man division, and Union cavalry under Brig. Gen. George A. Custer. The Confederates were defeated and although Early and his staff managed to escape, Custer's men took 200 wagons, fourteen stands of colors, and more than 1,000 prisoners. (Denney, 541)

On April 1, 1865, who was the Confederate commander at Five Forks and what was he doing while his men were being attacked by Sheridan's Yankees?
Maj. Gens. George Pickett and Fitz Lee were at a shad bake hosted by Maj. Gen. Tom Rosser. By the time Pickett made it back to his

troops, they had been routed, losing about 3,000 men. (Weeks, 260–262)

Who replaced Maj. Gen. Gouverneur Warren following the fighting at Five Forks?
Brig. Gen. Charles Griffin. Though the battle had been won Gen. Sheridan thought that Warren had brought his corps up late and that he had mishandled his troops. (Weeks, 262; Faust, 803)

What was the last land battle of the Civil War?
Palmito Ranch, Texas, on May 12–13, 1865. Between Brazos Santiago, off the coast of Texas, and Brownsville is a small rise known as Palmito Ranch. There had existed an unofficial truce between the Union and Confederate troops in the area since March 1865. Unfortunately, the Union troops were commanded by an inexperienced and ambitious colonel, Theodore H. Barrett. (Faust, 556)

What happened at the battle of Palmito Ranch?
Col. Barrett decided to attack the Confederates at Brownsville on May 12. With a force of about 800 men, the Federals, on May 13, came upon the "Cavalry of the West" at Palmito Ranch. The Confederates were led by a former Texas Ranger, John S. "Rest in Peace" Ford. The Confederates opened with artillery fire, then Ford and his cavalry charged, causing Barrett to call a retreat. The Confederates chased and harassed the Yanks all the way back to Boca Chico, killing, wounding, or capturing 118 Federals. The Confederates listed five casualties. Thirteen days after the battle, Ford learned the war was over and, rather than surrender, disbanded his cavalry. (Faust, 556)

The Retreat to Appomattox

On what date did Lee pull his army out of Petersburg and begin his retreat west?
April 2, 1865. (Catton, 564)

Who commanded the troops at the battle of Sutherland Station and what was the outcome?
Maj. Gen. Nelson Miles's division attacked four Confederate brigades led by Brig. Gen. John R. Locke. The Confederates, after repulsing two frontal attacks by Miles's people, were unable to cope with a flank attack and gave way. The Confederates lost about 600 prisoners and two cannon. This victory enabled the Federals to block the South Side Railroad. (Faust, 737–738; Calkins, 19)

What four bridges over the Appomattox River did the Army of Northern Virginia use to evacuate Petersburg on the night of April 2–3, 1865?
Pocahontas bridge, Richmond and Petersburg Railroad bridge, Battersea Pontoon bridge (which Robert E. Lee used), and Campbell's bridge. The Pocahontas and Campbell bridges were destroyed after the crossing. (Calkins, 19)

Who were the eight Confederate generals captured at the battle of Sailor's Creek?
Lt. Gen. Richard Ewell; Maj. Gen. George Washington Custis Lee, the son of Robert E. Lee; and Brig. Gens. Eppa Hunton, Seth Barton, James P. Simms, Dudley M. DuBose, Joseph B. Kershaw, and Montgomery Corse. (Faust, 249, 429, 377; Calkins, 31)

On April 3, 1865, who raised the first Union flag over the city of Richmond?
Maj. Atherton H. Stevens Jr., an aide to Brig. Gen. Godfrey Weitzel. (Denney, 554)

What was the last major battle between the Army of Northern Virginia and the Army of the Potomac?
Sailor's Creek, April 6, 1865. (Denney, 555)

Who was the last Union general mortally wounded in the Civil War?
Brig. Gen. Thomas Alfred Smyth. Smyth was shot in the mouth on April 7, 1865, near Farmville, Virginia, and died two days later on April 9, the day Lee surrendered. (Faust, 700)

What did Lee expect to find at Amelia Court House when his army arrived there?
Much-needed supplies of food. Unfortunately, there had been a mix-up, and the trains sent were loaded with artillery ammunition but no rations and fodder. It was Lee's plan that, after leaving Amelia Court House, the army would move down the Richmond & Danville Railroad to Danville, Virginia. The Army of Northern Virginia remained in the Amelia Court House area on April 4. (Calkins, 23)

What happened at Painesville, Virginia, on April 5, 1865?
There was a skirmish, during which Federal cavalry under Brig. Gen. Henry E. Davies attacked a Confederate wagon train, destroying it. The Yankees burned 200 wagons and took eleven battle flags, 320 prisoners, 310 teamsters, and five English Armstrong cannons. Unfortunately, a number of wagons were loaded with records belonging to the Confederate government and their destruction, and what has been lost, is rued by historians. (Calkins, 26)

Who was the last Confederate general to be mortally wounded in the war?
Brig. Gen. James Dearing, who was wounded during the fight at High Bridge on April 6, 1865, and died at Lynchburg on April 23. A Federal bridge-burning party was sent to torch and destroy High Bridge across the Appomattox River, then stop the Confederates from crossing the river. Near the bridge, the party ran into Confederate cavalry, who killed or captured the Northern troops. Also killed during the fighting was Col. Theodore Read (Gen. E. O. C. Ord's chief of staff). (Calkins, 32)

What was High Bridge?
High Bridge spanned the Appomattox River just four miles east of Farmville, Virginia. The Southside Railroad ran across the bridge. It was built in 1852 and was between 2,400 and 2,500 feet long. It was built on twenty-one brick piers and was 126 feet high. During the retreat, Confederate forces under Maj. Gens. William Mahone and John B. Gordon used the bridge to cross the river. After their crossing, they burned four of the bridge's spans. (Calkins, 32)

What was the significance of Cumberland Church, north of Farmville?

This was Gen. Mahone's headquarters and possibly also Gen. Lee's. It was here that Lee got the first note from Gen. Grant concerning the surrender. Lee showed the note to Gen. Longstreet, who commented, "Not yet." (Calkins, 33)

Where was Gen. Grant's headquarters on the night of April 8?

"Clifton," near Sheppards along the Richmond-Lynchburg Stage Road. Generals Grant and Rawlins slept in one bed while his staff used the floor in the parlor. About midnight Grant received a letter from Gen. Lee in which he suggested a meeting place to discuss surrender terms. (Calkins, 35)

Upon reaching New Store, whom did Gen. Lee relieve of command?

Generals Pickett, Bushrod Johnson, and Richard H. Anderson. Most of the men in these three commands were gone and there was no further reason to keep them in the army. They were told to go home and wait for orders. There is some evidence Gen. Pickett never got the order, and remained with the army. This caused Lee to remark, "Why is that man still with the army?" (Calkins, 35)

A few miles west of Walker's Church Gen. Grant received a message from Gen. Lee that alleviated what problem?

The migraine headache he had been suffering during the entire night of April 8–9, 1865. (Marvel, 179)

Who accompanied Gen. Lee to the meeting with Grant at the McLean House in Appomattox Court House?

Col. Charles Marshall and Pvt. Joshua O. Johns, along with Union Lt. Col. Orville Babcock and one of his lieutenants. (Bearss, 408; Marvel, 179)

How long did Gen. Grant and Gen. Lee meet to work out the surrender terms?

Approximately three hours, a half hour of which was taken up by Grant's lateness in getting to the meeting. (Foote, 949)

How many Union officers were in the room during the meeting between Grant and Lee?

The number varies depending on the source. Some say that they included Maj. Gen. Philip Sheridan, Lt. Col. Orville Babcock, Lt. Col. Horace Porter, Maj. Gen. E. O. C. Ord, Brig. Gen. Seth Williams, Lt. Col. Theodore S. Bowars, and Lt. Col. Ely S. Parker. Some sources add Brig. Gen John Rawlins, Brig. Gen. Rufus Ingalls, Brig. Gen. Michael Morgan, Brig. Gen. George H. Sharpe, Lt. Col. Adam Badeau, and Capt. Robert T. Lincoln. Gen. George A. Custer was also in the house but in an outside hallway where he could only occasionally open the door and check in on the proceedings. (Appomattox Surrender)

What happened to the furniture in Wilmer McLean's parlor following Lee's departure?

General Ord took the marble-topped table that was near Lee's chair on which the surrender terms were signed. Custer took the table on which Grant wrote his draft of the surrender terms, Sherman had ostensibly paid twenty dollars in gold for the table as a gift to Custer's wife. Custer's quartermaster peeled the paper cover off the table as his prize. Lt. Col. Edward W. Whitaker, Custer's inspector general, took the chair in which Lee sat. Basically everything in the room that could be removed, was. (Marvel, 181)

What incident took place between Brig. Gen. Joshua Chamberlain and Maj. Gen. John B. Gordon on April 12, 1865?

Chamberlain lined his division on both sides of the Richmond-Lynchburg Stage Road leading into the Court House. The Confederates marched up the road from the east with flags flying, led by Maj. Gen. John B. Gordon. Gordon, saddened and humiliated by the pending surrender, rode with his head low and face downcast. As he reached the Union line, the order was given to the Union troops to shift from order arms to carry, "the marching salute." When Gordon heard the sound of the shifting arms he "looks up, and taking the meaning, wheels superbly [toward Chamberlain], making with himself and his horse one uplifted figure, with profound salutation as he drops the point of his sword to the boot toe; then facing to his own command, gives word for his successive brigades to pass us with the same position of the manual,—honor answering honor." (Chamberlain, 259, 261)

How many Confederates were paroled at Appomattox Court House?
28,231. (Calkins, 44)

Who owned the house where Gen. Lee surrendered to Gen. Grant?
Wilmer McLean, the same man whose home was the Confederate commander's command post at First Manassas. Thus the war began in his front yard and ended in his parlor.

The March to Bennett Place

Who surrendered the largest number of Confederate troops at the end of the war, and where?
Gen. Joseph E. Johnston, on April 26, 1865, surrendered all Confederate forces in the Carolinas, Georgia, and Florida—a total of 89,270 men. (Weeks, 214)

Where did Gen. Johnston surrender his army and to whom?
Johnston surrendered to Maj. Gen. William T. Sherman at the James Bennett home near Durham Station, North Carolina. (Faust, 736)

Where did Sherman camp his army following his march through the Carolinas, and where did he make his headquarters?
Goldsboro, North Carolina, and he made the Richard Washington house his headquarters. (Bradley, 7–8)

What four Union leaders met aboard the *River Queen* in City Point on March 28, 1865?
Gen. Grant, Gen. Sherman, Adm. Porter, and President Lincoln. They met to discuss military and political matters, such as what was to be done with the Rebel armies after they were defeated. (Bradley, 14–15)

What did Sherman hope to accomplish by attending the meeting in City Point?
He wanted Gen. Sheridan to join him in North Carolina and he wanted Grant to postpone his campaign until the middle of April. He failed on both accounts, as Grant told him that he was going to begin his next offensive within a few days and Sheridan refused to join him in the Carolinas. (Bradley, 14)

Where did Joseph Johnston have his army and headquarters?
Smithfield, North Carolina, about thirty miles northwest of Sherman. (Bradley, 16)

At the end of March 1865, what was the strength of the two armies in North Carolina?
Sherman had about 89,000 men camped around Goldsboro, while Johnston had a mere 13,900 infantry at Smithfield. In early April, Johnston was joined by Lt. Gen. Stephen D. Lee and his men, raising the Confederate number to 32,500. (Bradley, 16, 18)

When Sherman's armies began their march toward Raleigh on April 10, what Hoosier regiment was credited with capturing Smithfield?
Moving back slowly, Confederates under Wade Hampton were able to burn the bridge across the Neuse River. Unable to save the bridge, members of the 75th Indiana were able to take the town, including three barrels of applejack, which they eagerly consumed. (Bradley, 23)

What three armies were under Sherman's command in his movement on Raleigh?
On the Left Wing was the Army of Georgia, commanded by Maj. Gen. Henry W. Slocum. The Right Wing, the Army of the Tennessee, was led by Maj. Gen. Oliver O. Howard. Brig. Gen. Judson Kilpatrick's Third Cavalry Division screened Slocum's right. Finally, the Center, the Army of the Ohio, was commanded by Maj. Gen. John M. Schofield. (Bradley, 20)

When Sherman took Raleigh, where had Johnston moved his army?

The Hillsborough area, west-northwest of Durham Station. (Bradley, 47)

What was the sequence of events between April 13 and April 17 when Sherman and Johnston met at the Bennett Place?

April 13—At a meeting with President Davis and his cabinet Johnston and Beauregard press for negotiations between the Confederates and Sherman discussing cessation of hostilities. Davis writes a letter to Sherman, which is then taken to Wade Hampton's headquarters for delivery to the Union commander.

April 14—Sherman receives the letter and writes a reply, which is sent to Kilpatrick for delivery back to the Confederate lines.

April 15—Sherman's letter reaches Hampton's headquarters that evening. Meanwhile, Kilpatrick has moved his cavalry to Durham's Station.

April 16—Johnston receives Sherman's letter in the morning. He then orders his generals to halt their movements and await further orders. Kilpatrick tries to sabotage the negotiations but Sherman sees through the cavalryman's plan.

April 17—Sherman leaves Raleigh and goes to Durham Station, then rides west on the Hillsborough Road. At 10:00 a.m. Johnston leaves Hampton's headquarters and rides east. Just after noon, the two army commanders meet, then ride back to the Bennett Place. (Bradley, 46–48)

How many times did Sherman and Johnston meet to negotiate the Confederate surrender?

Three times: April 17, April 18, and April 26. (Bradley, 49–51)

Who joined Sherman and Johnston during the April 18 meeting at the Bennett Place?

Confederate Secretary of War John C. Breckinridge. Breckinridge was attending because he was a major general and Sherman refused to negotiate with any member of the Confederate government. (Bradley, 50)

Who came to visit Sherman on April 24, 1865?
Lt. Gen. Ulysses S. Grant. Grant informed Sherman that President Johnson had rejected his proposed surrender terms and was ordering him to resume hostilities. While this was happening, Johnston received notification of President Davis's approval of Sherman's terms. An hour later, Johnston received a letter from Sherman ending the truce, canceling the agreement, and demanding that Johnston surrender under the same terms given to Lee at Appomattox. (Bradley, 50)

What happened at Sherman and Johnston's third meeting?
Gen. Schofield attended the third meeting and suggested that two documents be written: one resembling the terms of Lee's surrender; and a second specifying those wanted by Johnston. The documents were drawn up and signed. The next day Johnston made a list of eight "Supplemental Terms," which Schofield revised, making a list of six. (Bradley, 55)

When, where, and to whom did Lt. Gen. Richard Taylor surrender his Confederate forces?
At the end of the war, Taylor commanded the department of Alabama, Mississippi, and East Louisiana, containing some 12,000 troops. He surrendered his command at Citronelle, Alabama, about forty miles north of Mobile, on May 4, 1865. Prior to the surrender, Taylor and Maj. Gen. E. R. S. Canby had established a truce, but when Canby terminated the truce Taylor thought it best to surrender. The men were given the usual terms, with officers being able to keep their sidearms and mounted men their horses. (Faust, 736)

What do some consider the last shot of the Civil War?
On June 22, 1865, the *Shenandoah* came upon the bark *Jerah Swift* in the Bering Straits, and after a three-hour pursuit, the Confederate fired a round from a 32-pounder Whitworth across her bow. The captain of the *Jerah Swift* decided to save his crew and gave up the vessel.

The next day, the *Shenandoah* came upon a trading vessel that had a newspaper stating that Lee had surrendered, Richmond had fallen, and the Confederate government had fled. Despite this, Capt. Waddell continued his voyage and captured and burned several more vessels, but no shots were fired. (Foote, 1029–1030)

UNITS

What was the first Federal regiment to enter Charleston after it fell on February 17, 1865?
The 55th Massachusetts, a black regiment that had spent much of their enlistment on the islands south of Charleston.

Where and by what regiment was President Jefferson Davis captured on May 10, 1865?
Near Irwinville, Georgia, by the 4th Michigan Cavalry. (Denney, 569)

Whom have some identified as the last Union soldier to be killed in the Civil War?
Pvt. William Montgomery, serving in the 155th Pennsylvania at Appomattox Court House on April 9, 1865. Unfortunately, there were other Union soldiers killed later; for example, in the attack on Ft. Blakely later in the day on April 9. There were also the attacks at Columbus, Georgia, on April 15, 1865, and Palmito Ranch, Texas, May 12–13, 1865. (Davis, 166; Faust, 556)

~⁀ CHAPTER 7 ⌣~

POSTWAR

PERSONALITIES

Who was the last Confederate general to die?
Felix Huston Robertson, on April 20, 1928, at the age of eighty-nine.
(Faust, 637)

What role in the Lincoln assassination did former Iron Brigade commander Rufus King perform while he was acting as the minister to the Papal States following the war?
He helped secure the arrest and extradition of Lincoln conspirator John H. Surratt. (Faust, 418)

Following a visit to Robert E. Lee after the war, what comment did George Pickett make to John S. Mosby and what was Mosby's reply?
"That old man . . . had my division massacred at Gettysburg!" To which Mosby replied, "Well, it made you famous." (Mark Hughes, 4)

Who led the Irish Fenian invasion of Canada in 1866?
Former Union Brig. Gen. Thomas Sweeny. (Davis, 177; Faust, 739)

What was the fate of British adventurer Percy Wyndham after the Civil War?
After joining the Garibaldi Guard in 1866 he went to South Asia in an attempt to make a living. He was killed when a balloon he was riding in crashed in Mandalay, Burma, in 1879. (Beattie, 89)

What became of Samuel Mudd following his release from the Dry Tortugas?
He returned to his medical practice and died in 1883. In 1979, President Jimmy Carter announced that it was his opinion that Mudd was not one of the Lincoln conspirators. (Faust, 516)

Who were the only two Civil War generals, who were brothers, to be killed during the war?
Federal Brig. Gen. William Rufus Terrill was killed at Perryville, Kentucky, on October 8, 1862, and Confederate Brig. Gen. James Barbour Terrill was killed at Bethesda Church, Virginia, on May 30, 1864. (Mark Hughes, 11; Faust, 748)

Name the general who was promoted from captain to brigadier general on June 29, 1863, who went on to become the superintendent of the U.S. Military Academy?
Wesley Merritt.

Who was the Confederate cavalryman who went on to command troops in the U.S. Army during the Spanish-American War?
Joseph Wheeler. President William McKinley appointed Wheeler a major general of volunteers and he commanded cavalry in Cuba. He was then sent to the Philippines and commanded a brigade before returning to the United States, where he was named a brigadier general in the Regular Army.

Who was the last Union Civil War soldier to die, and when?
The last Union soldier to die was Albert Woolson, who passed away on August 2, 1956, at the age of 109. Woolson was a drummer in Co. C., 1st Minnesota Heavy Artillery. The company never saw action.

What happened to General Meade's horse Old Baldy following his retirement?

Baldy retired to a farm outside of Philadelphia where the general continued to visit him. The horse participated in memorial parades, including the funeral of his master, Gen. Meade. Outliving the general by ten years, Baldy was finally put to sleep on December 16, 1882, when he became too feeble to stand. A week later two of Meade's veterans (Messers. Hervey and Johnston) dug up the horse and severed his head, which was then taken to a "first-class taxidermist." Old Baldy's head hung for many years in a GAR museum in Philadelphia until he was sent out for a face lift. While the head was being treated, an argument erupted between members of the post and certain members who were forced out. The forced-out members, however, had the claim ticket for Baldy's head, and when they collected it they took it to the Civil War Library and Museum, also in Philadelphia. There Old Baldy remained on display until 2008, when the museum closed to move to a new location. As of the writing of this volume, Old Baldy remains in storage. However, efforts are under way to return Baldy's head to the GAR museum. (Magner, 7)

What happened to Traveller after the Civil War?

Traveller remained with General Lee after the war, following him to Washington College. The horse followed his master to his final resting place when Lee died in 1870. Traveller died the next year and his skeleton was placed on display until 1970, when it was finally buried on the Lee Chapel grounds, not far from his master. (Magner, 5)

Who was the last Confederate Civil War soldier to die?

Pleasant Crump, Thomas Riddle, John B. Salling, and Walter Williams; the reader can take his pick as there seems to be no definitive record as to who was the last Confederate to die. Crump died on December 31, 1951, and he was at one point definitely a Confederate soldier. Salling died on March 16, 1958; Riddle died in 1954; and there is scant evidence that either one of them was a Confederate soldier. Williams was reputedly only four at the outbreak of the war, so his claim is suspect.

What did the firing on Ft. Sumter and the battle at Palmito Ranch, Texas, on May 12–13, 1865, have in common?
Ft. Sumter, the first battle of the Civil War, was a Confederate victory; Palmito Ranch, the last battle of the Civil War, was also a Confederate victory. (Mark Hughes, 13)

What famous horse's head is pictured below?
Old Baldy, General Meade's horse.

What did fire-eater Edmund Ruffin do after the end of the war?
Despondent over the outcome of the war, and refusing to live under a Union government, on June 17, 1865, he committed suicide in Amelia County, Virginia. (Faust, 646)

Old Baldy.
USAMHI

After the Civil War Judson Kilpatrick was appointed minister to what South American country?
Chile. After he failed to be elected to Congress in 1880 he returned to his diplomatic post and died in Santiago of Bright's disease on December 4, 1881.

What Confederate general is buried in a traffic circle in the northern part of Richmond?
General Ambrose Powell Hill. His body was removed from Hollywood Cemetery in 1891 and placed at the intersection of Laburnam Avenue and Hermitage Road. (Owen and Owen, 279; Greene, 24)

What Civil War general played a small part in the downfall of the Boss Tweed ring in New York during the initial part of the Grant administration?
Former Maj. Gen. Francis Channing Barlow, who was at the time the United States marshal for the southern district of New York. Refusing the take the "honest graft" that came with the office, Barlow cleaned his office of bribetakers and replaced them with competent and honorable men. This caused a storm of outrage with New York City Republicans, who called for his removal. Barlow later supported deputy attorney general Charles S. Fairchild for refusing to accept Tweed's jailhouse confession. (Welch, 212, 239–240)

What Vermont-born and short-time Gettysburg attorney became one of the most "unrelenting of Radical Republicans?"
Thaddeus Stevens.

What did David Dixon Porter, Fitz John Porter, William D. "Dirty Bill" Porter, and David G. Farragut have in common?
Three of them were naval officers and one an army officer, but their major connection was that they were all related. David Dixon Porter's brother was William D. Porter, his cousin was Fitz John Porter, and his adopted brother was David G. Farragut. (Faust, 594–595)

To what position did President U. S. Grant appoint Eli Parker in 1869?
Commissioner of Indian Affairs. (Faust, 557)

In what political capacity did Ambrose Burnside serve following the war?
He was elected governor of Rhode Island three times, then became a United States senator from Rhode Island and served in the Senate until his death. (Warner, 58)

What did George McClellan do after he was replaced by Ambrose Burnside?
He retired to New Jersey to await orders that never came. In 1864 he unsuccessfully ran on the Democratic ticket against Lincoln; he then served as governor of New Jersey from 1878 to 1881. (Warner, 292)

What Union general is credited with establishing Memorial Day?
Maj. Gen. John A. Logan. (Faust, 443)

What political office did former general George Stoneman hold after the war?
He was the governor of California from 1883 to 1887. (Faust, 721)

Following the war, what did former Maj. Gen. John White Geary do?
He was elected governor of Pennsylvania and served two consecutive terms. (Faust, 302)

What two presidents served in the ranks of the 23rd Ohio?
William McKinley and Rutherford B. Hayes. (Faust, 463)

What future presidents served in the Civil War?
Ulysses S. Grant, James A. Garfield, Benjamin Harrison, Rutherford B. Hayes, William McKinley, and though not a military figure, Andrew Johnson. Chester A. Arthur served in a variety of administrative posts between 1861 and 1863. (Boatner, 668)

How did Dorothea Dix spend her years following the war?
She crusaded to improve care for the insane and founded a hospital in Trenton, New Jersey. (Faust, 222)

What organization did Clara Barton found in 1881?
The American Red Cross. (Faust, 43)

Who was the last full-rank Union general to die?
Adelbert Ames, on April 13, 1933, at the age of ninety-seven. (Faust, 11)

What did Frederick Douglass do following the Civil War?
In 1877 he was appointed U.S. marshal for the District of Columbia and in 1881 he became the recorder of deeds in the district. In 1889 he was appointed the U.S. Minister to Haiti. (Boatner, 245)

What happened to Rose O'Neal Greenhow's daughter following the war?
She became an actress. (Boatner, 356)

What did Robert E. Lee do following the war?
He became the much-beloved president of Washington College in Lexington, Virginia. Following his death the school changed its name to Washington and Lee College.

What did Lincoln's secretary John Hay do after the war?
He was assistant secretary of state in 1878, and the secretary of state in the McKinley and Roosevelt administrations. He also served as ambassador to Great Britain. On November 13, 1903, he signed the Jay-Bunau-Varilla Treaty that provided for the construction and operation of a canal in Panama. He also coauthored with John Nicolay the ten-volume *Abraham Lincoln: A History*. (Boatner, 388; Graff, 711)

What did the ring that President Theodore Roosevelt wear contain?
A lock of President Abraham Lincoln's hair. (H. Holzer, xxxii)

When Gen. Henry Morris Naglee left the banking business, in what new profession did he engage?
He bought a fifty-acre vineyard in San Jose, California, and began growing riesling and charbonneau grapes. He even produced his own brandy. (Magner, 35)

What did Robert Todd Lincoln, the president's son, do following the Civil War?
He became a corporation lawyer in Chicago and Washington. He dabbled in railroading, becoming president of the Pullman Company from 1897 to 1911. He served as the secretary of war in the Garfield and Arthur administrations and also served as the minister to Great Britain under Harrison. (Boatner, 485)

What was Henry Wirz's fate?
On November 10, 1865, he became the only man executed for war crimes due to his mistreatment of Union prisoners at Andersonville. (Boatner, 941–942)

James B. Eads, known for building the USS *Cairo*, later became famous for the construction of what?
The first steel bridge over the Mississippi River. (Henig, 119)

What did Brig. Gen. Benjamin H. Grierson do after the Civil War?
He remained in the army and as a colonel commanded the 10th U.S. Cavalry, one of two U.S. Cavalry regiments whose enlisted men were African Americans. While leading the regiment he participated in numerous actions against the Indians in the West. (Faust, 326)

What happened to Mathew Brady following the Civil War?
He became a drunk and died in 1896, a nearly blind pauper. (Henig, 250)

What did P. G. T. Beauregard do following the war?
He served for a time as a railroad president, then as a supervisor of the Louisiana State Lottery and as state adjutant general. (Faust, 52)

Where did Richard S. Ewell retire to?
A farm in Spring Hill, Tennessee, the site of an action prior to the battle of Franklin, Tennessee.

What happened to Col. (later Maj. Gen.) Edward R. S. Canby following the Civil War?
He commanded the Department of Columbia on the Pacific coast where, on April 11, 1873, he was murdered by Modoc Indians during peace negotiations. (Klinger, 59)

What happened to Col. (later Brig. Gen.) John P. Slough after the war?
He served on the panel that tried Henry Wirz and later became Chief Justice of New Mexico Territory. On December 15, 1867, he was shot and killed by political rivals in Santa Fe's La Fonda's billiard room. (Klinger, 59)

What did Phil Sheridan do in his postwar career?
In 1869 he was promoted to lieutenant general and succeeded Sherman as General in Chief in 1884. He became a full general in 1888. He wrote a two-volume *Personal Memoirs*, a work he completed just three days before his August 5, 1888, death. (Faust, 680)

What did John M. Schofield do following the war?
At first he commanded the First Military District in Virginia. He served for a short time as secretary of war in the Johnson administration. He was the superintendent of West Point for five years and finally he succeeded Philip Sheridan as commanding general of the army in 1888. (Faust, 667)

Following the war what did former Brig. Gen. Samuel Wylie Crawford do for the Gettysburg battlefield?
He purchased the land in Plum Run Valley where his division attacked on July 2, 1863, saving it from development.

Who became the first chief of the United States Secret Service on July 5, 1865?
William P. Wood, former superintendent of the Old Capital Prison and the first man appointed to chase down counterfeiters. (Craughwell, 44)

Who began the war as a private and rose through the ranks to lieutenant colonel?
Washington Roebling. Roebling served at various battles, including Antietam, Chancellorsville, The Wilderness, and Spotsylvania. At Gettysburg he was an aide to Brig. Gen. Gouverneur K. Warren who, hearing fire from the area of Little Round Top, caused Warren to ride to the hill and thus into history. Roebling at one point led Col. Patrick O'Rorke's 140th New York up the hill and to O'Rorke's destiny. Roebling's greatest claim to fame, however, is the building of the Brooklyn Bridge. (Pfanz, 201, 226; Terdoslavich, 98)

Who, perhaps, saved Mary Todd Lincoln's life on her return trip to the United States after her self-imposed exile to France?
Mrs. Lincoln had been walking the deck of the ship she was sailing on and, as she was about to go down a steep staircase, the ship lurched, causing her to lose her balance. Luckily she was being followed by a woman who reached out and grabbed her skirt. The woman was Sarah Bernhardt. (Craughwell, 165)

Who was the last person to die who had looked at the face of Abraham Lincoln before he was buried for the fourth time on September 26, 1901?
Fleetwood Lindley, son of Joseph Lindley, a member of the Lincoln Guard of Honor, who died on February 1, 1963. (Craughwell, 197)

When did Mary Todd Lincoln die and what happened to her body upon her death?
July 15, 1882. After an elaborate funeral her body was placed in a crypt next to her three sons, Edward, William, and Thomas, and near the empty sarcophagus that had once held Lincoln's body. During the evening following the funeral her body was taken to the basement and placed in a shallow grave next to her husband. (Craughwell, 166–167)

Who was Paul Philippoteaux?
Philippoteaux was a cyclorama painter who was born in Paris, France, and who learned at least part of his trade from his father. Without a doubt the cyclorama he is best known for is the *Battle of Gettysburg*.

There were more than one version of the painting but the one that ended up in Gettysburg was the one on display in Boston and thus is known as the "Boston version." In preparing to do the painting Philippoteaux spent time in Gettysburg having William H. Tipton take a number of now-famous photographs of The Angle and Copse of Trees. The artist also talked to such generals as Winfield Scott Hancock, Alexander Webb, and Abner Doubleday. The painting was displayed in two buildings before its, hopefully, final move to the new park visitor center, that being in a building on East Cemetery Hill and then the Mission 66 building that has housed the cyclorama since the war's centennial. (Boardman and Porch, 23; 38–39)

How big is the *Battle of Gettysburg*, painted by Paul Philippoteaux?
It is 377 feet long by 42 feet high. Its volume is the equivalent of three Olympic-size swimming pools and it weighs approximately four tons. When the artist originally created it he used between four and five tons of paint. There are approximately 20,000 men and horses painted onto the canvas. (Boardman and Porch, 69)

What happened to Clara Harris, who sat with President Lincoln the night he was shot?
Miss Harris married Maj. Henry R. Rathbone, her escort. The couple moved to Germany, where he went insane and murdered her. (Sifakis, 179)

Who was Ira Harris?
The father of Clara Harris of Lincoln's assassination fame, who was a Republican United States senator. The New York cavalry regiment the "Ira Harris Guard" was named for him. (Sifakis, 179–180)

What did Winfield Scott Hancock do following the war?
During Reconstruction he commanded the Fifth Military District. Made a major general in the Regular Army in 1866, he eventually commanded the Department of the East, spending most of his time on Governor's Island near New York City. In 1880 he was nominated for president as part of the Democratic ticket; however, he lost to James A. Garfield by a few thousand votes. (Faust, 337–338)

What did Maj. Gen. John Gibbon do after the war?
He remained in the army, ultimately rising to the rank of brigadier general and retiring in 1891. During the 1876 campaign where Custer and his troopers met their fate, Gibbon was with the relief column commanded by Brig. Gen. Alfred H. Terry that was first on the field, saving the survivors and burying the dead. He eventually became commander in chief of the Loyal Legion of the United States. (Boatner, 340)

MISCELLANEOUS

What were the first four National Military Parks established by Congress in the 1890s?
Chickamauga-Chattanooga, Shiloh, Gettysburg, and Vicksburg. (Sword, 57)

What is MOLLUS?
The Military Order of the Loyal Legion of the United States. A group of Union veterans came up with the idea of forming an organization made up of former Union officers. Meeting in Philadelphia, Pennsylvania, on April 15, 1865, the group wrote a constitution and bylaws. Members would be army, navy, and Marine Corps officers who had served the Union honorably, their descendants and collateral descendants. There were local, state, and national headquarters or "commanderies." (Faust, 494)

What was the War Library and Museum?
The War Library was founded in Philadelphia in 1922 by members of MOLLUS for the purpose of displaying artifacts that belonged to members. At its height the museum housed a 13,000-volume library and memorabilia from such notables as Grant, Meade, Reynolds, Slocum, and many more. It also contained weapons, regimental colors, political banners, and Medals of Honor. Located on Pine Street, the museum has unfortunately, as of this writing (2010), closed. The collection was placed in storage and a new site for the museum is being sought. The books are now in the possession of the Philadelphia Union League, while the collection languishes waiting for a new

home, though plans are presently being made to disperse the holdings to other venues for three years. (Kaufman, Civil War News)

What is the oldest monument on the Gettysburg battlefield?
The Minnesota Urn, which sits in the Minnesota section of the National Cemetery. The monument was dedicated in 1867 by the survivors of the 1st Minnesota. (Magner, 111)

Where are the bodies of the Lincoln conspirators now buried?
Powell, Atzerodt, Herold, and Mrs. Surratt were initially buried where they were executed. The bodies were then, along with those of Booth and Henry Wirz, buried under the floor of a warehouse at the Washington Arsenal. In 1869 President Andrew Johnson released the bodies to the families for burial elsewhere. Mary Surratt was taken to Mt. Olivet Cemetery, David Herold was taken to Congressional Cemetery, George Atzerodt was buried under an assumed name in St. Paul's Lutheran Cemetery in Baltimore. Booth's remains finally ended up in the family plot in Green Mount Cemetery in Baltimore. Where Lewis Powell's remains went remained a mystery for more than a century. Initially buried in Washington's Holmead Cemetery, they disappeared when the cemetery was decommissioned. Finally in 1993 an anthropologist located Powell's skull in the Smithsonian Institution and after the FBI confirmed the identification, at least that part of the remains was taken to Geneva, Florida, where they were once again buried. (Kauffman, 391)

Who was the first person to come up with the idea of stealing Lincoln's body and holding it for ransom?
Supposedly an unnamed Springfield attorney, but the plan failed when the two men he hired to help him backed out of the deal due to their honesty. (Craughwell, 79)

Who was the second man who decided to steal Lincoln's body?
Big Jim Kennally, a small-time counterfeiter who had heard of the earlier scheme and thought that taking the body and ransoming it would aid in the release from jail of a big-time counterfeiter. (Craughwell, 80–81)

After the attempt to steal Lincoln's body was foiled and the thieves jailed, what happened to Lincoln's body?
It was first hidden behind a stack of wood in the basement of his tomb; then, after two years, it was buried in a shallow grave. (Craughwell, 158)

What was the Lincoln Guard of Honor?
Nine men, several of whom had buried Lincoln in his tomb's basement, formed the guard to protect the remains of Abraham Lincoln and dedicate themselves to keeping the secret of Lincoln's grave. (Craughwell, 162)

Where is Abraham Lincoln's body today?
In the Lincoln Memorial in Oak Ridge Cemetery in Springfield, Illinois. Lincoln's remains are encased in a steel cage ten feet below the monument floor, sealed within a ten-foot-deep solid block of concrete. (Craughwell, 210)

The *Sultana*

Who was the captain of the USS *Sultana*?
Capt. J. Cass Mason. (Potter, 10)

When the USS *Sultana* left Camp Fisk near Vicksburg, Mississippi, what was it carrying?
1,866 troops, seventy-five cabin passengers, eighty-five crewmembers, sixty horses and mules, and more than one hundred hogs. Some estimates put the number of soldiers on board as being as high as 2,100 and the total number on board close to 2,500. The *Sultana* was originally designed to carry 376 passengers. (Faust, 731; Potter, 17, 20)

Besides the *Sultana*, what other ships were scheduled to transport troops up the Mississippi?
The *Olive Branch*, the *Henry Adams*, and the *Pauline Carroll*. (Faust, 731)

The passengers onboard the *Sultana* were comprised mostly of what?
Former prisoners of war who had been at Andersonville and Cahaba prison camps. They were headed for Camp Chase where they were to be mustered out of the army. (Potter, 8)

What happened to the *Sultana* about 3:00 a.m. on April 27, 1865?
Three of the ship's four boilers exploded near Hen and Chickens Island just upriver from Memphis, Tennessee. More than 2,000 of the crew and passengers were lost. Some estimates put the number of dead at 1,800. The destruction of the *Sultana* is still considered the worst maritime disaster in the United States and one of the worst on record. (Faust, 731; Potter, 8)

What was "fishy" about the number of men on the *Sultana*?
Only 1,000 men were supposed to be placed on the steamer. Capt. Mason, in collusion with Reuben Hatch, a brother of Ozias M. Hatch, a Lincoln crony and Illinois secretary of state, was to be paid extra for any troops he could pack onto the ship above the allotted number, therefore making a tidy profit. (Potter, 10, 12)

What was so special about the actions of Frances Ackley the night the *Sultana* burned?
Mrs. Ackley was the wife of Charles Ackley, the acting executive officer of the gunboat *Tyler*. As survivors were floating past the tied-up *Tyler*, Frances took command of one of the *Tyler*'s cutters, went to the river, and rescued between forty and fifty people. For this she was proclaimed a heroine and was awarded a special pension by the U.S. Congress. (Potter, 20)

Who was the only person tried for the *Sultana* disaster?
Capt. Frederick Speed, who had been ordered to prepare the rolls of prisoners prior to their being placed on private steamboats. On the orders of Secretary of War Stanton, he was court-martialed and found guilty. He was sentenced to be dismissed from the service until the Judge

advocate general reviewed the transcript of the trial and concluded that he had been railroaded. The sentence was overturned and he was publicly exonerated. He was later given an honorable discharge. (Potter, 54)

Where are the remnants of the *Sultana* today?
Under a bean field near Mound City, Arkansas. (Potter, 59)

When did President Andrew Johnson officially declare the Civil War was over and the insurrection was at an end?
April 2, 1866. (Denney, 577)

When the Thirteenth Amendment to the Constitution became law on December 18, 1865, what did it do?
By stating "Neither slavery nor involuntary servitude, except as a punishment for crime whereof the party shall have been duly convicted, shall exist within the United States, or any place subject to their jurisdiction," it abolished slavery. (Faust, 242; "The Constitution of the United States of America")

What states voted against the ratification of the Thirteenth Amendment?
Mississippi, Texas, Florida, Oregon, California, Iowa, Kentucky, New Jersey, and Delaware. (Faust, 752; Denney, 541)

What was the Grand Review?
The War Department ordered the two major Union armies to march in a grand review in Washington. On May 23, 1865, the 80,000 men of George Gordon Meade's Army of the Potomac marched down Pennsylvania Avenue. The next day, May 24, starting at 9:00 a.m., the 65,000 men of Sherman's group, led by Sherman, his staff and Maj. Gen. O. O. Howard marched the same route. The last regiment of Sherman's army passed the reviewing stand and President Johnson at 4:30 p.m. (Faust, 319)

What was a carpetbagger?
Northerners who went south during Reconstruction and took over control of many of the Southern state and local governments for

financial gain. They got their names from their luggage, which was known as "carpetbags." (Boatner, 127)

Following the war, what did the war correspondent GATH build?
He bought a tract of land on the Crampton's Gap battlefield just west of Burkittsville, Maryland. There he built a number of buildings that he called Gapland. Among the structures was a stone arch monument that looks like a one-walled castle. On this are inscribed the names of 157 reporters, newspaper and army artists, both North and South, who covered the Civil War. The monument was dedicated on October 16, 1896. GATH died in 1914 and was laid to rest in Laurel Hill Cemetery in Philadelphia, Pennsylvania. (Magner, 69)

What was the Gillmore Medal of Honor?
Quincy Gillmore had 400 bronze medals made that were given to the enlisted men who had distinguished themselves in the operations around Charleston, South Carolina, between July and September 1863. The front of the medal had Gillmore's signature, with the words "For Gallant and Meritorious Conduct." The reverse side had a representation of Ft. Sumter in ruins and the date "Aug. 23rd 1863." Each medal was also engraved with the name of the recipient. (Boatner, 343)

What, as some at the time said, was the boneheaded purchase made by Secretary of State William Henry Seward in 1867?
"Seward's Folly": the purchase of Alaska from Russia. (Boatner, 732)

What significant event took place in Charleston Harbor on April 14, 1865?
Gen. Robert Anderson raised the same flag over Ft. Sumter that he had lowered exactly four years earlier. (Faust, 15)

Who was Ft. Sill, Oklahoma, named for?
In 1869, Philip Sheridan named the fort for Brig. Gen. Joshua Woodrow Sill, who was killed at the battle of Stones River. Sheridan and Sill were classmates at the Military Academy. (Boatner, 762)

What was the Joint Committee of Fifteen?
The popular name for the Joint Congressional Committee on Recon-struction. It was appointed in December 1865 and was principally made up of Radical Republicans who worked out the punitive Reconstruction measures imposed on the former Confederacy. (Boatner, 442)

What publication did journalist Sumner A. Cunningham establish in January 1893?
The Confederate Veteran Magazine. Cunningham ran the publication until his death in December 1913, publishing biographies and mem-oirs of Southern soldiers, reunion and monument dedication informa-tion and general information about the life of the Confederate soldier. When Cunningham died, Edith Pope took over publication of the periodical and continued it until December 1932. (Faust, 157)

Who published Grant's memoirs and how much money did they make?
Samuel Clemens, aka Mark Twain. The volumes ultimately made approximately $450,000. (Terdoslavich, 121)

To what office was former Maj. Gen. Benjamin F. Butler elected in 1882?
Governor of Massachusetts. In 1884 he unsuccessfully ran for president in the Anti-Monopoly and Greenback parties. (Boatner, 109–110)

What did "Prince John" Magruder do after the war was over?
Refusing to apply for a parole, he went to Mexico and fought for Maximilian. When Maximilian fell, Magruder returned and settled in Houston, Texas. (Faust, 468)

What were the *Alabama* Claims?
When Ulysses S. Grant became president in 1869 he inherited an international problem; the demand that the United States be compen-sated for shipping losses caused by Confederate cruisers that had been built and outfitted in England. The majority of the claims were against

the CSS *Alabama*. The sticking point was that Britain wanted to only recognize terms of existing correspondence. When the U.S. Congress failed to agree, the British submitted a revised treaty where new evidence would be included and that a neutral head of state would oversee binding arbitration. The major fly in the ointment was Secretary of State William Seward, who hated Grant and made demands the British would not agree to. When Seward was replaced by Hamilton Fish, an agreement was finally hammered out and ratified on May 24, 1871. A settlement was finally reached in September 1872 giving the United States $15.5 million in gold and Great Britain $1,929,819 for wartime losses to its subjects. (Faust, 4)

What was the Freedmen's Bank?
The Freedmen's Savings and Trust Company was chartered by Congress in early 1865, opening its first bank in New York on April 4, 1865. Only blacks were permitted to make deposits of monies to be used to buy homes and land. By 1872 there were thirty-four branches, all but two in Southern cities. Unfortunately, poor management, lousy bookkeeping, and an incompetent staff, in addition to bad loans, were the downfall of the institution. Even with the help of Frederick Douglass the bank could not recover from the Panic of 1873, and it closed in June 1874 with thousands of investors losing their money. (Faust, 290)

᪗ CHAPTER 8 ᪖

TODAY

What marks the site of the battle of Wauhatchie?
A single monument to the New York units of Ireland's Brigade of Geary's division. The entire site has been eaten up by modern development. (Author's personal observations)

How many equestrian statues are on the Gettysburg battlefield?
Seven traditional and one modern. They are Gen. Lee atop Traveller on the Virginia Monument, Gen. Meade atop Old Baldy, Gen. Reynolds, Gen. Hancock, and Gen. Sedgwick atop Handsome Joe, Gen. Slocum, and Gen. Howard. A modern "equestrian" monument to Gen. Longstreet has been placed on the field but it is not a true equestrian in the sense of the others dotting the battlefield. (Author's personal observations)

What is the condition of today's Salem Church battlefield?
It, since the mid-1970s, does not exist. The church remains, along with a few monuments, but the battlefield itself is gas stations and strip malls. (Author's personal observations)

Today, where do Gen. Meade, Gen. Crawford, and Gen. Pemberton lie?
Laurel Hill Cemetery in Philadelphia. (Author's personal observations)

Who is Judson Kilpatrick's great-great-grandson?
Anderson Cooper, of CNN fame. Gloria Vanderbilt, Cooper's mother and the 1970s and 1980s fashion designer, was Kilpatrick's great-granddaughter. (Bull Runnings)

Are there any truly pristine Civil War battlefields left?
Unfortunately, probably not. There are many that can be called close to pristine but there is always a modern building, road, or tower dotting the local landscape. (Author's personal observations)

What regimental monument is found in the Cold Harbor National Cemetery?
A monument to the 8th New York Heavy Artillery honoring the 137 members of the regiment who were killed or mortally wounded during the battle. It is one of only two regimental monuments on the Cold Harbor battlefield. The other honors the 2nd Connecticut Heavy Artillery. (Richmond, 55, 60)

What is considered by many to be the most dangerous concussion fuse handled by collectors and relic hunters?
The Tice fuse. Extreme caution must be used when handling one. Probably the best suggestion is to not purchase one. (Dale Beiver, Boyertown, PA)

Where are the shattered tibia and fibula bones of Maj. Gen. Daniel Sickles's lower right leg that was amputated at Gettysburg after he was wounded?
The Armed Forces Medical Museum in Washington, D.C. It was said that after the war the general went to visit his leg once a year. (Coco, 82)

Whatever happened to the statue of George Armstrong Custer that was located at the edge of the Plain at West Point that was dedicated in 1879?
Well, it's only a story, but when the statue was erected, Libby Custer hated it so much, saying it did not look like any pose that her husband would have taken, that she asked to have it taken down. She appealed to Gen. Sheridan but finally, with the help of Secretary of

War Robert Todd Lincoln, the monument was removed. The pedestal was moved to Custer's grave where it rests today. The statue itself was later scheduled to be cut off at the waist, saving the arms and torso to be made into an "excellent work of Art." The monument was shipped to New York and dismembered. However, the project was never finished because the designer was murdered by the husband of his former mistress. What ultimately happened to the statue—some West Point tales say that it now lies at the bottom of the Hudson River. There does exist a photograph of the monument—and yes, it is a pretty bad likeness. (Robbins, 405–408)

Who is buried in Custer's grave?
Libby Custer, for sure. George Armstrong Custer, maybe; maybe not. In June 1877, a year after the battle of the Little Big Horn, a detachment of 7th Cavalry troopers returned to the battlefield to retrieve bodies. In all, ten bodies were retrieved, but was Custer's one of them? They could not positively identify one as being the Lt. Col. (General). One archaeologist suggests, ". . . there exists the possibility, at least, that one or more unknown troopers may be perpetually doomed to the commission of that most cardinal of military sins: impersonating an officer." And it is interesting to think, had not the Indians removed all the bodies of their dead, might it be an Indian warrior buried next to Libby? (Barnard, *Custer*, 66–74)

During the period 1857 to 1879, who were the three cadets to receive the most demerits at the Military Academy?
The winner was Marcus Reno (Class of 1855), who over six years earned 1,031 demerits. The next, and at a surprisingly disappointing second, was George Armstrong Custer (Second Class of 1861), who gathered a mere 726. The last, who did not graduate until well after the war, was Philadelphian Benjamin "Benny" Hodgson (Class of 1870), who garnered 747 in five years. It is interesting to note that all three were with the 7th Cavalry at the Little Big Horn. The only one to survive was Reno. Two other cadets did in fact receive more demerits, George "Poet" Patten (1,077) and Charles H. Larnard (1,658), but they received those demerits as members of earlier classes before the 200 point per year limit was imposed. (Robbins, 188–189, 377)

What five cemeteries contain the most Civil War generals' graves?
Arlington National Cemetery (183); Greenwood Cemetery, Brooklyn, New York (54); Post Cemetery, West Point, New York (45); Spring Grove Cemetery, Cincinnati, Ohio (39); Laurel Hill Cemetery, Philadelphia, Pennsylvania (30).

Who were the two Civil War soldiers most recently buried?
As of this writing (2010)—Union: On September 17, 2009, the remains of an unknown New York soldier were laid to rest in the General B. H. Solomon Saratoga National Cemetery. The soldier, who died while fighting in or near Miller's Corn Field at Antietam, had lain next to a limestone outcropping until being found in October 2008. Extensive archeological and forensic studies looking at the remains determined that the soldier was between seventeen and nineteen years of age. Confederate/perhaps Federal: In the spring of 2009 the remains of an unknown soldier were found during construction in a portion of the Franklin, Tennessee, battlefield. The soldier was laid to rest in Rest Haven Cemetery where soldiers from both sides are buried. Attending the funeral were honorary pallbearers Harold Becker and James Brown Sr., both sons of Civil War soldiers. (Civil War News, 4–5; 22–23)

How does one become a Civil War reenactor?
First, you have to decide what regiment you wish to reenact with. Then you can go on the Internet to find out if that regiment has reenactors. Another possibility is a once-a-year issue of the *Civil War News* that has advertising for every group, be it reenacting or Round Table or museum or whatever, looking for members. The newspaper also has monthly advertising for groups looking for members. Potential recruits, however, should show caution as to what groups to join; there are some who just like to get together, shoot off some black powder, then party all night. There are other groups that are very strict in recruiting members, making sure that their uniforms are correct even down to the stitching of the cloth. These are the groups this author recommends, because it is where the reader will get the most knowledge of what it might have been like to be a Civil War soldier.

Today the remaining earthworks of Ft. Walker lie in Grant Park in Atlanta. Who is the park named for?

Not for Ulysses S. Grant, but for Lemuel Grant, a Confederate engineer who donated the land for the park. (S. Davis, 26)

What is Pamplin Historical Park and the National Museum of the Civil War Soldier?

A 1991 effort to preserve a threatened battlefield near Petersburg, Virginia, which has evolved into what today is a 422-acre "historical campus" featuring museums, antebellum homes, a Civil War battlefield, and a slave life exhibit, along with educational programs. The battlefield consists of where on April 2, 1865, the Army of the Potomac broke through Lee's defense line, setting in motion the Appomattox Campaign. Dr. Robert B. Pamplin Jr., a businessman and philanthropist from Oregon, was told that a tract of land that had belonged to his ancestors during the Civil War was available for sale. The property was acquired along with an adjacent tract, and the Pamplin Park Civil War Site was opened in 1994. The park has continued to expand, becoming a world-class Civil War site and educational center. (Pamplin Park)

How many monuments are on the Gettysburg battlefield today (2010)?

1,325. (John Heiser, GNBP)

The Father Corby monument on the Gettysburg battlefield has a twin—where is it?

On the campus of Notre Dame University in South Bend, Indiana, where it is referred to as "Fair Catch Corby."

Which are the three monuments on the Gettysburg battlefield sculpted by Henry Kirke Bush-Brown?

The equestrian statue of John Sedgwick on the northern slope of Little Round Top along Sedgwick Avenue; the John Fulton Reynolds monument, located along the Chambersburg Pike on McPherson's Ridge; and the George Gordon Meade monument on Cemetery Ridge overlooking the field of the Pickett-Pettigrew-Trimble Assault. In addition, he also sculpted the head of Abraham Lincoln on the Lincoln Speech Memorial in today's Gettysburg National Cemetery. (Magner, 9, 10, 12; Hawthorne, 130)

Who sculpted the North Carolina Monument at Gettysburg and for what other work is he best known?
Gutzon Borglum. Borglum also began the work on what was to become the monument to Lee, Jackson, and Stuart carved into the side of Stone Mountain near Atlanta, Georgia, but he did not finish the work. He is best known for the four colossal presidential heads found at Mount Rushmore National Memorial. (Hawthorne, 36)

What is the largest monument on the Gettysburg battlefield today?
The Pennsylvania monument, which contains 1,252 tons of cut granite, 1,410 tons of broken stone, 740 tons of sand, 366 tons of cement, 50 tons of steel bars, and 22 tons of bronze. The monument contains bronze tablets with the names of more than 34,500 Pennsylvania soldiers who served at the battle of Gettysburg. (Hawthorne, 82)

What bronze portrait statues adorn the Pennsylvania Monument?
Abraham Lincoln, Andrew Curtin, George Gordon Meade, John Reynolds, Winfield Scott Hancock, David Birney, Alfred Pleasonton, and David Gregg. (Hawthorne, 82)

Who was the sculptor of the Winfield Scott Hancock statue on the Pennsylvania Monument?
Cyrus Dallin, who also sculpted the famous Paul Revere Monument seen today in Boston, Massachusetts. (Kay Jorgensen, Tunbridge, Vermont; Hawthorne, 82)

How many monuments are on the Antietam battlefield?
According to the Antietam NPS web site, there are ninety-six monuments on the battlefield, most of which are Union monuments. There are regimental (1st Delaware, Irish Brigade) and individual (Clara Barton, William McKinley), as well as monuments to the six generals killed during the battle. These do not include the 300 War Department tablets that describe the action on various areas of the battlefield. (Antietam)

～ CHAPTER 9 ～

OTHER "STUFF"

GENERAL "STUFF"

The pictured bones belong to what famous Civil War horse?
Traveller.

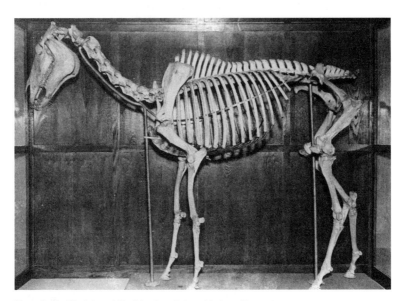

Traveller's Skeleton. Washington & Lee University

How long was Thomas J. "Stonewall" Jackson a general in the Confederate Army?
Twenty-three months. (J. Robertson, 17)

What were the two most popular handguns during the Civil War?
The Model 1860 Army Colt and the Colt Model 1861 Navy revolvers. The Army Colt was a .44-caliber six-shot weapon that weighed two pounds, eleven ounces. There were approximately 200,000 of them produced between 1860 and 1872, the majority of which were purchased by the U.S. government. The Navy Colt was similar except it was a .36-caliber handgun. Approximately 38,000 of these weapons were produced, though the government purchased very few. The majority of the Navy Colts were privately purchased. The weapons were not specific to either branch of the military, as the Navy used Army models and the Army used Navy models. (Faust, 152)

Over the course of his administration, how many books did Abraham Lincoln charge to his library account at the Library of Congress?
One hundred and twenty five. (Holzer and Shenk, viii)

How many times did Abraham Lincoln leave Washington to visit the troops in the field?
Eleven. (Cramer, x)

What is the most identifiable characteristic of the July 1864 Federal cartridge box?
An embossed "US" on the flap as opposed to the earlier brass "US" plate. (Dale Beiver, Boyertown, PA)

Who was known as the "Cyclone in Calico"?
Mary Anne Ball Bickerdyke, who was a nurse in the Western Theater, serving in the armies of U. S. Grant during the Vicksburg Campaign and William T. Sherman in the Atlanta Campaign. She served in field hospitals near the fighting and cut through red tape getting supplies as well as cleaning up dirty hospitals. (Faust, 58)

What was special about Norwich University in Norwich, Vermont, during the war?
Only West Point and Annapolis supplied more Union Civil War officers. The school was also a military academy, and of the 1,013 students who attended the institution between 1835 and 1865, two-thirds of them served in the war. Of the school's alumni, seven became major generals, sixteen brigadier generals, six commodores, and one rear admiral. Five of the former students were brevetted major general, nineteen brigadier generals, and four received the Medal of Honor. Four of the alumni served as generals or flag officers in the Confederacy. The secretary of the Navy, Gideon Welles, attended Norwich. (Faust, 539)

Who was Timothy O'Sullivan?
A photographer who began the Civil War working with Alexander Gardner and Mathew Brady. He was one of Brady's ablest field photographers. For a time he was attached to the topographical engineers, then traveled along the South Carolina coast recording images. After Fredericksburg, when Gardner set up his own studio, O'Sullivan joined him and became his chief of field operations. He photographed the Chancellorsville battlefield as well as Gettysburg, Spotsylvania, The Wilderness, and Petersburg. When Richmond fell he was there to record the devastation. After the war he went west and then went to work for the Treasury Department. He died on Staten Island of tuberculosis in 1882. (Faust, 550–551)

What did Maj. Gen. George Thomas, General Winfield Scott, and Admiral David Farragut all have in common?
They were Southern-born.

Who was Ambrose Bierce?
A soldier and later author who served in the Western Theater in the 9th Indiana. He eventually was promoted to first lieutenant and was wounded at Kennesaw Mountain. After the war he wrote numerous works that were adapted by the media. Perhaps one of his best-known works was "An Occurrence at Owl Creek Bridge," which became an

episode on Rod Serling's *The Twilight Zone*. Bierce disappeared in 1913 while covering Pancho Villa's fighting in Mexico. (Faust, 58–59)

How many men did Delaware provide the Federal government?
Approximately 12,000 men for service in the army, which included nine infantry regiments and one regiment of cavalry.

How many prisons were established during the Civil War?
One hundred and fifty, of which only two were considered bearable, the rest being plagued by filth, disease, illness, and death. (Davis, 438)

How many general hospitals were established in Washington, D.C., and how many patients could they treat?
There were sixteen, and each had a bed capacity of between three and four thousand. (Davis, 420)

What was the largest Union prisoner of war camp?
The Federal prison at Point Lookout, located where the Potomac River enters the Chesapeake Bay. (Davis, 441)

What were the names of some of the regimental newspapers printed during the war?
Union: the *Buck and Ball*, the *Camp Kettle*, and the *Unconditional S. Grant*. Confederate: the *Mule*, the *Wood Chuck*, and the *Rapid Ann*. (Davis, 204)

What was the southernmost Federal prison camp?
Ft. Jefferson in the Dry Tortugas off Key West, Florida. (Davis, 442)

How many prisoners were taken during the Civil War?
Approximately 647,000, or about 16 percent of all enlistments. (Davis, 467)

How many prisoners died in prisoner of war camps during the war?
56,014 died while in prison. Union troops suffered 30,218 deaths or 15 percent of those in confinement, while Confederates lost 25,976

deaths or 12 percent of those taken prisoner. The death rate for prisoners was about 13 percent, while the chance of dying on the battlefield was only 5 percent. (Davis, 467)

What were the two most popular weekly newspapers printed during the war?
Frank Leslie's Illustrated Newspaper and *Harper's Weekly.* (Davis, 206)

Who were the four most popular illustrators covering the war?
Alfred R. Waud, Winslow Homer, Edwin Forbes, and Thomas Nast. (Davis, 214–219)

What was the largest hospital in the Confederacy?
Chimborazo Hospital in Richmond. It contained 150 one-story buildings, situated on 125 acres. The hospital housed more than 4,800 patients and it is estimated that over the course of the war it treated 76,000 patients. There was a bakery that delivered 1,000 loaves of bread per day, an ice house, soup kitchens, a farm with 200 cows, and a large goat herd. (Davis, 420)

What was the Tredegar Iron Works?
Located in Richmond, Virginia, the Tredegar Iron Works was the major manufacturer of cannon for the Confederacy. Tredegar was a private firm that had been run by Joseph R. Anderson since 1843. It was the only antebellum rolling mill that had the ability to not only produce cannon but railroad rails. During the course of the war it produced around 1,100 cannons, including 3-inch ordnance rifle guns, 12-pounder Napoleons, and heavy cannons used in costal defense, more than any other works in the Confederacy. By 1863 the works had 2,500 employees and supported shoemaking shops, a firebrick factory, sawmill, a tannery, and nine canal boats. By early 1865 the production of cannon at Tredegar had all but ceased. (Faust, 761–762)

What future president of the United States hired a substitute so that he could stay home and care for his mother and sisters?
Grover Cleveland. (Terdoslavich, 99, 179)

What were the casualty rates for doctors who served in the Union Army?
Forty-two were killed in battle, eighty-three wounded, 290 died of disease or accidents, and four died in prison. (Davis, 421)

How long did the average amputation take?
About fifteen minutes. (Davis, 423)

How many Northern women volunteered to serve as nurses during the war?
More than 3,000. (Davis, 430)

What was the down side of the painkillers administered to patients during the Civil War?
Though many of them were effective during surgery and recovery, many, such as morphine and opium, were addictive, leading to many Civil War veterans becoming drug addicts. (Davis, 431)

What was "Old Soldier's disease"?
Drug addiction. (Davis, 432)

What modern death practice essentially got its start in the Civil War?
Embalming. Though the practice stemmed from ancient times, Civil War embalmers improved the process, pumping the blood out of the cadaver's circulatory system and replacing it with a liquid to prevent decay. (Davis, 433)

What Confederate medical corps procedure dramatically reduced the infection rate in their patients?
The use of horsetail hairs as sutures. Because the horse hairs were brittle they were first boiled to make them more pliable. The act of boiling (thus sterilization) reduced infections. (Davis, 432)

What medical procedure used maggots?
Doctors found that patients with wounds that had flies land and lay eggs, forming maggots, did not develop gangrene as readily. The mag-

gots only ate dead tissue, and thus infected tissue. When this author was in Viet Nam he learned that, if isolated with a wound, maggots could possibly save his life. In a worst-case scenario and you were starving, you could also eat them. (Davis, 432)

Because of the shortage of medical supplies in the Confederacy due to the blockade, what did doctors use to treat patients?
A vast variety of home cures and herbal medicine. Some of the most-used herbs, roots, bark, and leaves included partridgeberry, sassafras, lavender, tulip tree, bearberry, sumac, white oak leaves, hops, white cherry, blackberry, and sage. Of course the one remedy used on both sides was whiskey, rum, and brandy. (Davis, 433)

What surgery did a rat perform?
One patient at Chimbarazo had a bad wound in his instep from which a tangled mass of flesh protruded. A matron, Mrs. Phoebe Pember, recalled seeing the soldier, on whom doctors refused to operate. One morning when Mrs. Pember passed the soldier he was all smiles and, looking at the wound, found it to be gone with nothing but a large, clean hole remaining. The procedure of removing the mass was done during the course of the night by a rat. (Davis, 434)

What was Ambrose Burnside's major claim to fame?
His whiskers. He had a bald head but bushy whiskers that extended from his ears down his cheeks to a sweeping mustache. Thus his name and whiskers, somewhat corrupted, have become what we know today as sideburns. (Dickson, 175)

What units made up a Civil War army?
Army—7,000–100,000+ men commanded by major generals, lieutenant generals, or full generals (Confederate).

Corps—Two or more divisions.

Division—Two or more brigades—Union averaged 6,200 men, Confederate 8,700 men.

Brigades—Two or more regiments—Union averaged 2,000 men, Confederate 1,850 men.

Regiment—Originally consisted of 1,000 (ten companies) men but as the war progressed the numbers were consistently reduced. By Gettysburg, Union regiments only averaged 350 men. A regiment was usually commanded by a colonel or lt. colonel, but later in the war, often by lesser-ranking officers.

Company—Was initially made up of 100 men commanded by a captain. (Boatner, 611–612)

What were the three major causes of death in Civil War armies?
Disease, killed in action, and accidents.

Who was known as the "Queen of the Confederacy"?
Lucy Holcombe Pickens, the wife of Francis W. Pickens of South Carolina. Pickens was the governor of the state when it seceded from the Union. Mrs. Pickens was from La Grange, Tennessee, where Grierson's Raid began, and she was the only woman to have her image on Confederate money. (Roth, 17)

Abraham Lincoln shared his birthday, February 12, 1809, with what other famous personality?
Charles Darwin. (Quammen, 20)

What are the top six Civil War movies? (This is the author's list; others might disagree.)
The Horse Soldiers: A classic John Wayne movie the author has watched for over forty years; a takeoff on Grierson's Raid and for the most part totally inaccurate, I love this movie.

Glory: This movie is about the 54th Massachusetts and the strife African Americans went through to gain their freedom. It is a classic and should be viewed by every Civil War buff.

Gone With The Wind: Margaret Mitchell's classic Civil War novel; it ranks among the best.

Gettysburg: Michael Shaara's Civil War novel of Gettysburg is filled with errors, but this adaptation still gives the watcher a taste of what Civil War combat was like.

Red Badge of Courage: The original with Audie Murphy is an interesting tale of the Union soldier's view of combat.

The Birth of a Nation: Though quite racist, this movie is classic in the sense that men who fought in the war were still alive. Many of the uniforms in the movie were remnants from Civil War storage.

How much food did it take to keep a Civil War horse healthy?
Each horse would consume ten gallons of water per day, five in the morning and another five at night. He ate twelve pounds of grain (oats preferred) and fourteen pounds of hay per day. (Magner, 47)

What state supplied more troops to the Confederate cause than any other?
North Carolina. (Faust, 777)

How many men did the state of Connecticut contribute to the war effort?
Approximately 55,000. The state sent thirty infantry regiments, one cavalry regiment, two heavy artillery units, and three light artillery units. Approximately 3,000 men served in the U.S. Navy. Of the men sent, approximately 20,000 had become casualties by war's end. (Faust, 159)

Are all the burials in Gettysburg's Soldiers' National Cemetery Yankees?
Probably not. Some of the possible mistakes include: Milton F. Knott, Co. F, 1st Maryland or 1st Maryland Potomac Home Brigade could be Minion F. Knott, Co. F, 1st Maryland Battalion, C.S.A.; John Johnson, Co. K, 11th Massachusetts, could be John T. Johnson, Co. K, 11th Mississippi; E. T. Green, Co. E, 14th Pennsylvania, could be Eli T. Green, Co. E, 14th Virginia. (Magner, 108)

What is strange about the monument to Co. H, 1st United States Artillery, that sits near the fence in the Gettysburg National Cemetery?
The cannon was made by the "Revere Copper Co.," founded by Paul Revere after the American Revolution. The piece served at Gettysburg

and was hit and dented by a Confederate shell. What is strange, however, is that if one looks closely at the tube he will see that it was placed on the carriage upside down. (Magner, 110)

What's odd about the grave of Maj. Gen. Henry Tucky Collis in the Gettysburg National Cemetery?
Only special permission got him buried in the cemetery. Though his regiment, the 114th Pennsylvania, fought at Gettysburg, he was not with them. He did live in Gettysburg for a short time, building a home on Seminary Ridge that he named "Red Patch." His grave sits at the head of the Pennsylvania section, not in the semicircle of graves. (Magner, 111)

What were the most popular newspapers of the Civil War era?
New York *Herald*, New York *Times*, New York *Tribune*, Richmond *Daily Dispatch*, Charleston *Mercury*, Richmond *Enquirer*, and *Harpers Weekly*. (Flagel, 173–180)

Ft. Pulaski near Savannah was named for whom?
Brig. Gen. Casimir Pulaski, a Polish patriot and aide to General George Washington. During the British occupation of Savannah during the Revolution, the Americans tried to retake the city. During the final assault, Pulaski was mortally wounded. (Durham, 8)

What was the most popular smoothbore cannon of the Civil War?
The 12-pounder Napoleon. The gun was named for French emperor Napoleon III, who was instrumental in its development. It had a 66-inch tube with a caliber of 4.62 inches that weighed 1,227 pounds. The piece had a maximum range of 1,680 yards but its effective range was between 800 and 1,000 yards. It could fire canister, spherical case shot, shell, or shot. It was most effective at close range, firing canister. (Boatner, 578)

Who was Rufus Barringer?
Barringer was one of the better cavalry officers to hail from North Carolina during the war. His service began with the 1st North Carolina and during the war he served in all of the battles involving the

Army of Northern Virginia. Slow to gain rank, he did not become a brigadier general until after the battle of Yellow Tavern in May 1864. He later covered Robert E. Lee's withdrawal from Petersburg in April 1865 and was captured at Namozine Church on April 3, 1865. (Faust, 41)

What distinction does the town of Matamoros, Mexico, hold?

A port just south across the Rio Grande from Brownsville, Texas, it served as a place for blockade runners from Cuba to land. Mexico's nonbelligerent status meant that Union warships could not interfere with Confederate ships that were in Mexican waters. It was known as being the least efficient of the blockade-running ports but it did have the distinction of being the only one never to be closed by the Union navy. (Faust, 480)

What did Abner Doubleday have to do with the national pastime of baseball?

Despite being given credit for devising the game and for perfecting the rules and having ballfields named after him at places like West Point and the Baseball Hall of Fame in Cooperstown, New York, Abner Doubleday had absolutely nothing to do with baseball. He may have watched the game and perhaps even played it, but that was the extent of his involvement in baseball.

How many troops did Illinois provide to the Union Army?

In total, almost 260,000 men, most of whom served in the 150 regiments that fought in the Western Theater. Illinois also provided seventeen cavalry regiments, two light artillery regiments, and eight independent batteries. Some 2,200 men also served as sailors and marines. More than 1,800 men also served in black regiments. (Faust, 378)

How many men from Iowa served in the Union forces?

Some 76,000 men served in the forty-six Iowa army regiments. The state also provided four batteries of light artillery and nine regiments of cavalry. In proportion to its population, it is estimated that Iowa supplied more men to the Union forces than any other state. (Faust, 383)

What was a "coal torpedo"?
A device made of cast iron and filled with powder. It was painted to resemble a piece of coal, and then placed at ship refueling stations. When put in the ship's boiler, it would explode, damaging or sinking the ship. (Denney, 360)

What is a salient?
A salient is a portion of a defensive line or fortification that sticks out from the main works. This extension was probably the closest to the enemy's position. Two of the most famous salients during the war were the "Mule Shoe" at Spotsylvania and Elliott's Salient in Petersburg, where the Crater was formed. (Faust, 652)

What is a trunnion?
Trunnions are the two cylindrical pivots attached to the center of gravity of a cannon or mortar. They sit on the field carriage or platform carriage of the gun and allow it to be elevated or depressed. (Faust, 764)

What is odd about Gilbert Moxley Sorrel's home in Savannah, Georgia?
Today it is said to be the most haunted house in the city.

How many African Americans served during the war?
In the Federal armies there were approximately 186,000 blacks who served. In the South it was not until February 1865 that Southern leaders finally authorized the recruitment of blacks, but it came too late, as Robert E. Lee and the Army of Northern Virginia had already surrendered on April 9, 1865. (Faust, 63–64)

Who were Ranald Slidell Mackenzie's Confederate relatives?
His uncle was Confederate diplomat John Slidell, and he was a nephew by marriage to Gen. P. T. G. Beauregard. (Faust, 463)

Who were some of the other members of William Quantrill's band?
"Bloody" Bill Anderson, Cole Younger, and Frank and Jesse James. (Weeks, 20)

What is lob-scouse?
Slang for a soldier's dish made of baked or stewed salt meat with vegetables and hardtack. It was actually a naval dish called "lob's course" that used a ship's biscuit rather than hardtack. (Boatner, 486)

What is a "Pook Turtle"?
Pook Turtle was the name given to seven Federal ironclads that were designed by Samuel M. Pook. The ironclads included the *Cairo, Carondelet, Cincinnati, Louisville, Mound City, Pittsburg,* and *St. Louis* that fought on the Mississippi and western waters.

What federal building in Washington, D.C., now sits on the site of the Old Capital Prison where Belle Boyd and Rose Greenhow were imprisoned?
The Supreme Court building.

Who was the youngest Union Civil War general?
Galusha Pennypacker. When Pennypacker became a general he was not old enough to vote for the president who appointed him.

What was a "Hardee Hat"?
A black 1858 army hat with a tall, round crown and wide brim. The right side of the brim was usually rolled up on the right and fastened to the crown with a brass eagle. A black plume often decorated the left side. It was regulation Army headgear until the beginning of the Civil War, when it was replaced, for the most part, with kepis. Some units, mostly volunteer and regular units, continued to use it during the war. Probably the most famous unit to continue to use the hat was the Iron Brigade, also known as the "Black Hats." William J. Hardee was on the army board that reviewed the pattern in 1855 and, though his involvement in adopting the hat was minimal, his name stuck with it. It was also known as the Jeff Davis hat because Davis was secretary of war at the time the hat was being considered. (Faust, 338)

Which Civil War Union general lies in the largest and most ornate mausoleum in the Post Cemetery at the U.S. Military Academy?
Egbert Ludovicus Viele. Viele's pyramid-shaped tomb is perhaps thirty feet tall with four Egyptian columns surrounding the doors, plus two sphinxes guarding the entrance.

What was a "bishop"?
It was a small round cushion worn at the back of a woman's belt that was used to lift the hoops. Quite often these were used to smuggle home quinine or morphine when the lady visited the North. When crossing between Northern and Southern territory, the bishops were inspected by sticking a long pin through them. If the pin passed through the ladies were allowed to continue. (Catton, 448)

Who were the only subordinate generals whom Robert E. Lee called by their first name?
Brig. Gen. Henry Heth and Edward "Old Allegheny" Johnson.

What Confederate general was known to his close aides as "Tycoon"?
Gen. Robert E. Lee. (Faust, 444)

What was the first building to occupy the site of Ford's Theater?
The first building was erected in 1833–1834 and was the home of the First Baptist Church of Washington. The building was purchased by John Thomson Ford in 1861 after the church merged with another and relocated. Ford turned the property into a theater that was in part gutted by a fire nine months after its opening. Ford rebuilt the theater, which was completed on August 27, 1863, and was the theater in which Abraham Lincoln was mortally wounded. (Faust, 267–268)

Who was Postmaster Montgomery Blair's brother-in-law?
Gustavus Vasa Fox, for whom Lincoln created the position of assistant Navy secretary in 1861. (Faust, 283)

Soldiers from what state were known as Tarheels?
North Carolina. It is said that they received this nickname because many of the state's population made pine tar and pitch for export in

colonial times. The Tarheels always boasted that they were "First at Bethel, furthest forward at Gettysburg and Chickamauga, and last at Appomattox." (Faust, 742)

What is a haversack?
A canvas bag that a soldier wore via a strap over the right shoulder. It would carry the man's rations as well as other assorted items the soldier wanted close at hand.

What were "Galvanized Yankees"?
Captured Confederate soldiers sent to serve on the Western Frontier. (Faust, 296)

What is a vivandiere?
Women who were unofficially attached to a regiment and served doing various camp chores and acting as nurses. Two of the best known vivandieres were Marie Tebe and Bridget Divers. (Faust, 789)

What well-known vivandiere served with the 2nd, 3rd, and 5th Michigan?
Annie Etheridge, also known as "Gentle Annie" or "Michigan Annie." (Faust, 247)

Where was Robert E. Lee's home prior to the Civil War?
The Custis estate of "Arlington," which is located on the Virginia side of the Potomac River opposite Washington, D.C.

What happened to Arlington during the Civil War?
In 1864 it became a cemetery for the war dead. It was a deliberate plan on the part of the Federal government to ensure that the traitor Robert E. Lee would never live there again.

Who was the first soldier buried at Arlington?
William Henry Christman, a laborer from Lehigh County, Pennsylvania, who had died of peritonitis on Wednesday May 11, 1864. His burial was on May 13, 1864, followed by another later in the day. Six more were buried on May 14, and another seven on May 15. By the

time the war ended in April 1865, 15,000 graves were spread over the grounds of Arlington. (*Where Valor Rests*, 21)

What was Admiral John Dahlgren's major contribution to Civil War navies?
He was responsible for the invention of three types of ordnance, bronze boat howitzers, iron smoothbore shellguns, and iron rifled guns. The iron shellgun known as the Dahlgren gun became one of the standard guns of Civil War navies. The USS *Monitor* carried two eleven-inch Dahlgren guns. (Faust, 202–203)

What was the name of the training camp for African American soldiers located outside of Philadelphia, Pennsylvania?
Camp William Penn. (Jeffry Wert, Centre Hall, PA)

Why was Joseph Hooker called "Fighting Joe" Hooker?
During the Peninsula Campaign a press wire to a Northern paper read "Fighting—Joe Hooker." The dash was dropped when the quote was put in the newspaper, thus giving Hooker his nom de guerre. (Frye, 53)

Beginning with the (First Bull Run) Manassas Campaign, who were the generals who commanded the principal Union armies that operated in the Virginia Theater?
Brig. Gen. Irvin McDowell, Maj. Gen. George B. McClellan (twice), Brig. Gen. John Pope, Maj. Gen. Ambrose Everett Burnside, Maj. Gen. Joseph Hooker, and Maj. Gen. George Gordon Meade.

Which is it, rifled-musket or rifle-musket?
The proper term is rifle-musket. (Jeffry Wert, Centre Hall, PA; Coggins, 32)

How many men did Minnesota send off to the war?
Approximately 24,000; they were used in Union service and in Indian fighting. (Faust, 498)

What was the second most popular rifle-musket used during the Civil War?
The .577-caliber Enfield rifle-musket. Some 800,000 Enfields were imported by both sides during the war. They were made in London and Birmingham, England, by private contractors. (Faust, 243–244)

During the Civil War, what was the most widely used rifle-musket?
The .58-caliber Springfield, named for its production at the Springfield Arsenal in Springfield, Massachusetts.

Who was Abraham Lincoln's railroad "genius"?
Col. Herman Haupt. Though appointed a brigadier general on September 5, 1862, he did not accept the commission, preferring to serve without rank or pay. He resigned on September 14, 1863, and returned to private life. (Warner, 218)

At what college did Herman Haupt teach civil engineering, architecture, and mathematics following his graduation from the Military Academy?
Pennsylvania College (now Gettysburg College) in Gettysburg, Pennsylvania. (Faust, 351)

Who were Copperheads?
Northern Democrats who were more conciliatory toward the South than were Republicans. They got the name Copperhead as some of them wore copper pennies as identification badges. (Faust, 564)

What was panada?
A combination of crumbled hardtack and medicinal whiskey or water given to weak patients. It got its start during the Mexican War but was also used during the Civil War. (Faust, 556)

How many men from Kentucky served during the Civil War?
Almost 76,000 served in the Union forces, while 25,000 served the Confederate cause. (Faust, 414)

What was the ultimate fate of "Old Abe" the war eagle?
In 1864 he was presented to the state of Wisconsin, where he lived in a cage in the state capital. Unfortunately he died of smoke inhalation during a fire in the capitol on March 28, 1881. He was then stuffed and mounted and once again placed on display until another fire destroyed him. (Faust, 544)

What is a "shad-belly" truss?
Prefabricated segments used in the repair or building of railroad bridges. (Catton, 276)

What Hollywood movie was based on the raid led by Col. Benjamin H. Grierson in 1863?
John Wayne's *The Horse Soldiers*.

Who was Brig. Gen. Randolph Barnes Marcy's son-in-law?
George McClellan, for whom Marcy served as chief of staff in 1861. (Boatner, 512)

What is a gabion?
A cylindrical wicker basket used to reinforce fieldworks. They stood three to four feet tall and were several feet in diameter, filled with dirt and stones. (Faust, 295)

What job did a musician have when his regiment went into battle?
He was a stretcher-bearer and helped the wounded.

How many men from Kansas served during the war?
Just over 20,000, though most of those served either in-state or nearby states. (Faust, 407)

How many men served in the military during the Civil War?
The figures are difficult to determine. Some figures indicate that in the Union Army there may have been as many as 2,900,000, while the Confederate Army may have had 1,300,000. Due to different types of enlistment, these numbers must include duplications. The Union

probably had 1,500,000 three-year enlistments and the Confederacy around 1,000,000, so these are probably the best numbers to go on. (Catton, 356)

How many men died during the war?
Today the best estimate of the number who died is approximately 621,000. At least this is the number most commonly used. It should be noted that death came from not only bullets but also disease and accidents.

What is an abatis?
An obstacle made of fallen trees that faced away from the defenders and pointed toward the enemy.

What are accouterments?
The items carried by a soldier other than his weapons and clothing that included things like a cartridge box, canteen, cap box, and so on. (Boatner, 2)

What was a "housewife"?
A sewing kit that the soldier carried in his haversack or knapsack.

What was "slosh" or "Coosh"?
A Confederate dish made of flour, water, and boiled bacon grease. (Terdoslavich, 7, 111)

What is an acoustic shadow?
The phenomenon where sound, such as artillery or infantry combat, cannot be heard a short distance from the fighting but might be heard as much as one hundred miles away. Cases of acoustic shadow were reported at such battles as Seven Pines, Gaines' Mills, Iuka, Perryville, and Chancellorsville. (Boatner, 2)

Maj. Henry Burroughs Holliday was the major of the 27th Georgia. Who was his son?
Doc Holliday, of western gunfighter fame. (Krick, 196)

What is an Agnew?
The dress worn by nurses from the Sanitary Commission during the Peninsula Campaign. They consisted of a man's shirt with an open collar, sleeves rolled up, shirttails out, worn over a skirt with no hoops. (Boatner, 4)

What was a Brooke gun?
Developed by J. M. Brooke, it was a rifled gun that resembled a Parrott. One caliber was a 3-inch field piece that weighted 900 pounds. It fired a ten-pound projectile and had a range of 3,500 yards. (Boatner, 88)

What was "Buck and Ball"?
A musket round used in .69-caliber smoothbores that was comprised of a round .69-caliber ball and three buckshot. (Boatner, 94)

What is "Buck and Gagging"?
A form of punishment where a soldier is gagged. He is then seated with his knees drawn up, the arms passed around them and a rod inserted horizontal to the ground, completely immobilizing him in a very uncomfortable position. (Boatner, 95)

What was canister?
An artillery projectile consisting of a tin can filled with twenty-seven small cast-iron or lead balls packed in sawdust. Usually used in smoothbore cannon, it made the artillery piece into a huge shotgun. Canister could be used up to 400 yards but was most lethal at between 100 and 200 yards. (Boatner, 119)

What was a carcass?
A hollow cast-iron shell filled with burning material. The flame would exit through four fuse holes and set fire to any combustible material it came into contact with. (Boatner, 122)

In what capacity did the future steel magnate Andrew Carnegie serve during the war?
He worked in the transportation division of the Union War Department. (Boatner, 123)

What 1999 horror movie was set in Burkittsville, Maryland, near the Crampton's Gap battlefield?
The Blair Witch Project, directed by Daniel Myrick and Eduardo Sánchez.

What two shoulder weapons did President Lincoln fire during his administration?
The Henry and the Spencer. (Dale Beiver, Boyertown, PA)

Who were the Knights of the Golden Circle?
A secret society of Southern sympathizers found in the North. They were originally organized in the South in the 1850s in an attempt to spread slavery. They ultimately became the Peace Democrats who were opposed to the war. In 1863 they changed their name to Order of American Knights and then in 1864 they changed it again to Sons of Liberty. (Boatner, 466)

Brig. Gen. Hugh Mercer engaged John Norris to design what?
His home on Monterey Square, along Bull Street in Savannah, Georgia. The house was not completed during the war and Mercer sold it to John R. Wilder in 1866, never having lived in it due to ill health and a pending court martial. (Kingery, 133, 140)

What was the ultimate fate of Hugh Mercer's Savannah "home"?
Over the years it fell into disrepair, until 1969 when Jim Williams, a man noted for his preservation efforts in not only Savannah but in other Georgia cities, bought it and restored it. Today it is one of the premier homes in Savannah and a favorite stop for visitors to the city, but for a different reason. The house and Jim Williams became major characters in the best-selling novel and Clint Eastwood movie *Midnight in the Garden of Good and Evil*.

Who was Hugh Mercer's great-grandson?
The composer of such songs as "Moon River," lyricist and Academy Award–winner Johnny Mercer.

Who was William Reynolds?
Naval Commander Reynolds was the brother of Maj. Gen. John Fulton Reynolds, who was killed at Gettysburg. He became a midshipman in

1833 and was part of Wilkes's expedition to the Antarctic in 1838. He retired in 1855 but later served as a storekeeper in Hawaii. In 1862 Reynolds was reactivated and later assigned to command the area of Port Royal, South Carolina. (Boatner, 695; Sifakis, 333)

How many chaplains served during the Civil War?
Approximately 2,600. The majority, 2,500, were Protestant ministers while Catholic, Jewish, and African Americans made up the other one hundred. (Henig, 62)

What happened out on the American Plains on October 7, 1861?
After eighteen months, the Pony Express was discontinued. (Denney, 85)

What did John C. Frémont do following the Civil War?
Frémont was an explorer, charming and loyal; however, his Civil War career proved to be a military embarrassment for the Union. He served as the territorial governor of Arizona from 1878 to 1883. When his personal fortune disappeared he was forced to depend on his wife's writing for his income in his later years.

Who was Thomas Morris Chester?
He was the first African American war correspondent for a major daily newspaper, the *Philadelphia Press*. When Maj. Gen. Godfrey Weitzel's Twenty-Fifth's Corps' black troops marched triumphantly into Richmond on April 3, 1865, Chester accompanied them. (Henig, 226)

Who was Alexander T. Augusta, M.D.?
The first African American commissioned as a surgeon, with the rank of major in the U.S. Army. (Henig, 208)

Who was Dr. Mary Walker?
The first woman to become a U.S. Army physician. She was also the recipient of the Medal of Honor in "recognition of her services and sufferings." Unfortunately the medal was taken away in 1917 but was restored posthumously in 1977. (Henig, 205, 208)

What was the largest Confederate ironclad built?
The CSS *Tennessee*. She was 209 feet long with a beam of 48 feet. She had a draft of 14 feet, carried six inches of armor plating forward and two inches on the deck, and had six guns. (Faust, 746)

What joint resolution did Senator John B. Henderson propose as an amendment to the Constitution that would abolish slavery on January 11, 1864?
What was to eventually become the Thirteenth Amendment. (Denney, 359)

Who commanded the CSS *Tennessee* during its fight with Farragut on August 5, 1864?
Admiral Franklin Buchanan. (Faust, 86)

What carbine is often found with a leather-covered barrel?
The Sharps and Hankins Navy. (Dale Beiver, Boyertown, PA)

Of the six Confederate secretaries of war, who held the job the longest?
James A. Seddon of the Virginia planter aristocracy. (Catton, 456, 457)

Who was perhaps the most famous artist-correspondent of the Civil War?
Alfred Waud. An Englishman who worked for *Harper's*, he covered the war from First Manassas to Appomattox Court House. (Catton, 460)

Who was the best known Union "secret" agent?
Allan Pinkerton, a private detective who established a detective agency. (Catton, 462)

How many men served as prisoners of war during the Civil War?
It has been estimated that 194,000 Federals became prisoners of war while 215,000 Confederates suffered the same fate. (Catton, 470)

How many men died in prisoner of war camps?
Figures suggest that as many as 30,000 Union troops died, as did 26,000 Confederates. (Catton, 470)

When you read that an army goes "up" the Shenandoah Valley, in what direction are they moving?
South!

What arms manufacturer was the major supplier of pistols to the Union Army?
Samuel Colt of Hartford, Connecticut. (Catton, 499)

What were "Sherman's neckties"?
As Sherman's army marched to the sea one of the major targets for destruction was the railroads. What the soldiers would do was take the tracks, lift the ties, knock off the rails, then take the ties and put them into piles that they set on fire. The men set the rails on top of the fires and when they became red hot they took the rails and wound them around trees or telegraph poles, forming what was known as "Sherman's neckties."

Who was Capt. Andrew J. Russell?
He was the only official military photographer during the Civil War. (Henig, 252)

Which Union general was known as the "Russian Thunderbolt"?
John Basil Turchin (born Ivan Vasilovich Turnchinoff), the only Russian-born officer in the Union Army. Turchin spent most of his time in the armies of the West where he eventually gained brigade command in the Army of the Ohio. He was at one point court-martialed because of his military methods but a visit to President Lincoln by his wife changed things. Lincoln was so impressed by the visit of Mme. Turchin that he promoted Turchin to brigadier general. He resigned due to health reasons on October 4, 1864, and died in an asylum on June 19, 1901. Turchin was also called "the Mad Cossack." (Faust, 766; Davis, 193)

Who were the original owners of the White House, McClellan's supply depot on the Pamunkey River?
The house had been owned by Martha Dandridge Custis, George Washington's wife. It was then owned by George Washington Park Custis, Martha's grandson and father of Robert E. Lee's wife, Mary.

Upon Custis's death the 4,000-acre farm passed to Lee's son Henry Fitzhugh "Rooney" Lee. (Mewborn, 7)

What German regiment did Lew Wallace use as a model for his descriptions of the Roman legions marching into Rome in his book *Ben Hur*?
The 32nd Indiana, from Wallace's memory of them at the battle of Shiloh. (Davis, 183)

Who were three foreign soldiers of fortune who served during the Civil War, and how did they perform?
Lionel Jobert D'Epineuil (French, a fraud, and failed miserably); Alfred N. A. Duffié (French, qualified but not a good commander, captured in the autumn of 1864 by Confederates near Bunker Hill, West Virginia, due to his own stupidity); Sir Percy Wyndham (British, despite being captured by Turner Ashby at Harrisonburg, Virginia, on June 6, 1862, he gained a credible military reputation). (Davis, 184–187)

Who was Franklin Thompson of the 2nd Michigan?
Thompson was actually Canadian-born Sarah Edmonds. She had dressed like a boy since childhood growing up on her father's farm. She ran away from home when she did not like who her father had chosen as her husband. First taking a job as a Bible salesman, she joined the Union army when the war broke out. She fought at Antietam and was called the "hairless boy" by members of her regiment. Edmonds did not reveal her true identity until an 1884 reunion of the Second. (Davis, 188)

What foreign country contributed the most people who fought for the Confederacy?
France. (Davis, 189)

What Frenchman fought for the Confederacy and rose to the rank of major general?
Prince Camille Armand Jules Marie de Polignac. He was initially commissioned a lieutenant colonel and at the battle of Shiloh was on

P. T. G. Beauregard's staff. He served during the Red River Campaign and at the battle of Mansfield, Louisiana. Because his last name was so difficult to pronounce, his Texas men called him "Polecat." (Davis, 190–191)

Who was the last Confederate major general to die?
Prince Camille Armand Jules Marie de Polignac, on November 15, 1913, in France. (Davis, 191)

Who was the most successful French born-officer in the Union Army?
Phillippe Régis Dénis de Keredern de Trobriand. He had been an author, poet, novelist, philanderer, and duelist before he married an American heiress. At the outbreak of the Civil War he became colonel of the 55th New York ("Lafayette Guard") and finished the war as a major general. (Davis, 191)

What was the most multinational unit to serve in the Union Army?
The 39th New York, also known as the Garibaldi Guard and named for the Italian patriot Guiseppe Garibaldi. The regiment contained Hungarians, Italians, Poles, Germans, Czechs, Spaniards, French, and Portuguese.

Who was the Garibaldi Guard's first colonel and what happened to him?
Col. Frederic D'Utassy. He was caught selling government horses to civilians, prosecuted and imprisoned. (Davis, 192)

What were the most common diseases known to the Civil War soldier?
Measles, mumps, typhoid, typhus, smallpox, malaria, and yellow fever. Smallpox was the most feared despite the fact that a vaccine had been developed more than eighty years before the Civil War broke out. (Davis, 410)

An "Old Soldier" was Civil War slang for what?
A malingerer. (Davis, 411)

What was the most common surgery performed by Civil War surgeons in the field?
Amputations—almost three-quarters of the surgeries performed cut off a limb. (Davis, 411)

What was a barbette?
A raised wooden platform that allowed an artillery piece to fire over the protecting wall of the piece. They were usually only found in permanent or semipermanent fortifications. In temporary fortifications, a mound of dirt was often used in place of the wooden platform. (Faust, 38–39)

What was the strength of a Union Civil War artillery battery?
One hundred fifty-five men, consisting of one captain, four lieutenants, two staff sergeants, six sergeants, twelve corporals, six artificers, two buglers, fifty-two drivers, and seventy cannoneers. (Faust, 45)

Besides its men, what made up an artillery battery?
Six guns, a limber drawn by six horses, and six or more caissons each attached to a limber and drawn by six horses. In addition, each battery would carry between 1,218 and 1,344 rounds of ammunition. Confederate batteries often only had four or five guns and fewer horses. (Faust, 45, 46)

Who were the "Fighting McCooks"?
They were fourteen members of the McCook family of Ohio who fought for the Union during the war. Seven were sons of Maj. Daniel McCook and the other seven were cousins. Daniel led a unit of Ohio Home Guards; three of his sons, Alexander McDowell McCook, Robert Latimore McCook, and Daniel McCook Jr., became generals during the war. Another son, Roderick Sheldon McCook, became a lieutenant in the U.S. Navy. One cousin, Edward Moody McCook, became a major general of volunteers. (Faust, 258–259)

What was Florida's contribution to the war effort?
Florida supplied between 14,000 and 15,000 men to the Confederate war effort in twenty-one military organizations. The state also provided about 2,500 blacks and whites to the Union side. (Faust, 264)

How many men from Maine served in the Civil War?
Sixty-seven thousand men served in some thirty-five military regiments, special units, or in the navy or Marines. Some of the more famous men who served from Maine were Lincoln's first vice president, Hannibal Hamlin, and officers such as Maj. Gen. Oliver O. Howard, Brig. Gen. Joshua L. Chamberlain, and Brig. Gen. Adelbert Ames. (Faust, 469)

How many men served in the military from Massachusetts during the war?
The Bay State sent 152,048 men off to war in seventy-seven infantry regiments as well as cavalry and artillery units. The state also had the Springfield Arsenal, which produced 800,000 .58-caliber rifle-muskets during the war. (Faust, 479)

Michigan supplied how many men to the war effort?
Eighty-seven thousand. (Faust, 489)

In the television series *The Rebel* who played Johnny Yuma?
Nick Adams. (Terdoslavich, 182)

In the *Twilight Zone* episode "The Passerby," who was the last person to walk down the road?
Abraham Lincoln. (Terdoslavich, 182)

Who wrote *Gone With The Wind*?
Margaret Mitchell.

Who were the four major characters in *Gone With The Wind* and what actors played the roles in the movie?
Scarlett O'Hara—Vivien Leigh; Rhett Butler—Clark Gable; Melanie Hamilton—Olivia de Havilland; and Ashley Wilkes—Leslie Howard.

What did Missouri do for troops in the war?
For the Federal side, the state provided 109,000 men, who served in 447 different military organizations. On the Confederate side, some 40,000 men served in one hundred units. (Faust, 501–502)

What was New Hampshire's contribution of men to the war?
Some 36,000 men from New Hampshire served in the Federal forces, comprising eighteen infantry regiments, one cavalry regiment and one battery of light artillery. The state also provided men for three sharpshooter companies. Almost 6,700 men also served in the navy and the Marines. (Faust, 525)

How many men from New Jersey served in the war?
Around 80,000, in forty infantry regiments, three cavalry regiments and five batteries. (Faust, 526)

For what battle were the most Medals of Honor awarded to African American troops?
Chaffin's Farm, on September 29, 1864. There were a total of twelve Medals of Honor awarded, which is more than half of the number of medals given to African Americans during the entire Civil War. The recipients included William Barnes (38th U.S. Colored Troops); Powhatan Beaty (5th U.S. Colored Troops); James H. Bronson (5th U.S. Colored Troops); James Gardiner (36th U.S. Colored Troops); Thomas R. Hawkins (6th U.S. Colored Troops); Alfred B. Hilton (4th U.S. Colored Troops); Milton Murry Holland (5th U.S. Colored Troops); Miles James (36th U.S. Colored Troops); Alexander Kelly (6th U.S. Colored Troops); Robert Pinn (5th U.S. Colored Troops); Edward Ratcliff (38th U.S. Colored Troops); and Charles Veal (4th U.S. Colored Troops). (Medals)

What was the nickname of the M1840 cavalry saber?
"Old Wrist Breaker." It was replaced with the M1860 light saber for obvious reasons. (Dale Beiver, Boyertown, PA)

How many men did New York send to fight the Civil War?
New York sent the largest number of men to fight in the war, almost 475,000. (Faust, 531)

What are the *Official Records*?
The Federal government began collecting government papers pertaining to the war in 1864. The papers were cataloged and the government

began publishing them in book form. By 1877, thirty-seven Union volumes and ten Confederate volumes had been printed. Because of the sheer number of papers the officer in charge, Capt. Robert N. Scott, organized the way the volumes would be presented. There would be four series; Series I would contain campaigns and theaters of operation in chronological order; Series II relates to prisoners of war and political prisoners; Series III contains the reports and correspondence of Federal and state officials; while Series IV does the same for the Confederacy. The production of the volumes continued between 1880 and 1900 and ultimately totaled 128 volumes plus one atlas that contained 1,006 maps and sketches. An index volume was published in 1901. The official titles of the volumes are *War of the Rebellion Official Records of the Union and Confederate Armies* and *Official Records of the Union and Confederate Navies in the War of the Rebellion*. There was also a thirty-one-volume set of the naval *Official Records*. In recent years a one-hundred-volume *Supplement to the Union and Confederate Official Records* has been published, containing material that has surfaced since the publication of the original set. (Faust, 802)

What was important about the Orange & Alexandria Railroad?
The 170-mile-long railroad stretched from Lynchburg, Virginia, through Gordonsville, where it intersected with the Virginia Central Railroad, then on to Alexandria on the Potomac River. The rail line was used by both Union and Confederate troops during the war. Until 1862 the railroad was mostly used by the Confederates. Following the Second (Bull Run) Manassas Campaign the northern part of the line remained in Federal hands. (Faust, 547)

What was Oregon's contribution to the war effort?
Probably the most notable contribution was Edward D. Baker, who had been elected to fill the state's empty U.S. Senate seat. Of course Baker's moment was short-lived as he was killed at the battle of Ball's Bluff on October 21, 1861. The primary military contribution of the state was protection from marauding Indians and to help support army posts when regular troops went east to fight in the war. (Faust, 548)

Who was Albert J. Cashier?

Cashier was a private in the 95th Illinois whose name is on the Illinois Monument in Vicksburg. He enlisted in Co. G and after Vicksburg he participated in the Red River Campaign and at Nashville. Following the war Cashier returned to private life where, in 1911, he was involved in an automobile accident and was sent to a hospital where it was discovered that he was really a woman. Apparently her real name was Hodgers or Hadges and she had been born in Ireland. (Sifakis, 70)

Who were Angelina and Sarah Grimké?

Southerners who opposed slavery. Moving to Philadelphia they became involved with the Quakers but found their teachings too confining. Angelina went on to teach in New Jersey and Massachusetts; Sarah taught in Massachusetts. (Sifakis, 167)

Who was Ethan Allen Hitchcock?

Hitchcock was the grandson of Ethan Allen. Too old for field duty, he spent the Civil War as a staff officer. He served as commissioner for exchange of war prisoners and commissary general of prisoners. (Sifakis, 196)

Who was Donehogawa?

Donehogawa is Eli Parker's Indian name. Parker was on Grant's staff. (Sifakis, 115)

Who was Maria Lydig Daly?

Daly was the North's equivalent to Mary Boykin Chesnut, writing *Diary of a Union Lady, 1861–1865*. Critical of Lincoln and his generals, she referred to the president as "Uncle Ape." Today her diary is almost forgotten. (Sifakis, 104)

Who was Titian J. Coffey?

Though in an acting capacity, Coffey served the shortest tenure of any cabinet official in the Lincoln administration. During much of the Civil War he served as an assistant attorney general. When Edward

Bates resigned on November 24, 1864, as attorney general Coffey was placed in the position, which he held for one week before James Speed was permanently named to the position. (Sifakis, 81)

Who was Henry Burden?
Burden invented a horseshoe-making machine in 1834. During the Civil War his company produced 600,000 shoes a year in thirteen sizes. (Sifakis, 55)

What was the fate of Florena Budwin?
She disguised her identity as a woman and joined the Union Army with her husband. She, along with her husband, was captured and sent to Andersonville Prison. There her husband died. She was later transferred to the Confederate prison at Florence, South Carolina, where she fell sick. During her treatment it was discovered that she was a woman. Despite the care given to her she died on January 25, 1865, probably the only woman to die in a Confederate prison camp. (Sifakis, 52)

Who was Benjamin William Brice?
The last officer to hold the post of Federal paymaster general during the war. (Sifakis, 45)

Who was the "Florence Nightingale of America"?
Mary O'Connell, also known as Sister Anthony. Educated in Massachusetts, she joined the American Sisters of Charity and became involved in hospital work. She and her fellow sisters cared for Ohio soldiers in both camp and field during the war. (Sifakis, 8)

What is presently the only wartime building within the Vicksburg NBP?
The James Shirley house, simply called the "white house," which served as the headquarters of the 45th Illinois Infantry during the siege. (Winschel, 9)

What is a brevet rank?
This rank is honorary and is awarded to an officer for valor or for meritorious service. Though the rank was higher than the officer's reg-

ular rank it held none of the authority or the pay of the higher rank. Brevets were used by the British prior to the Revolutionary War and were picked up by the Americans soon afterward. During the Civil War there was a glut of brevet promotions, 1,400 in all. The last brevet promotion was issued in 1900 for service in the Philippine Islands. (Heidler and Heidler, 281; Hunt and Brown, xiii, xx)

What ship served as a U.S. revenue cutter, a Confederate blockade runner and as a warship in both the Union and Confederate navies?
The *Harriet Lane*. (Heidler and Heidler, 933)

Who was the *Harriet Lane* named for?
James Buchanan's niece. (Heidler and Heidler, 933)

What is the monument pictured below, where is it, and who sculpted it?
The Shaw Memorial can be found in Boston Common at Beacon Street, Boston, Massachusetts. It was sculpted between 1884 and

Shaw Memorial. Saint-Gaudens National Historic Site

1897 by Augustus Saint-Gaudens. The monument depicts Col. Robert Gould Shaw leading the men of the 54th Massachusetts. This image is of a bronze that was cast in 1997 by the Trustees of the Saint-Gaudens Memorial. It is located at the Saint-Gaudens National Historic Site in Cornish, New Hampshire. (Dryfhout, 222–229)

What other sculptures of famous Civil War personalities did Augustus Saint-Gaudens produce?

Some of his other major works include: *Abraham Lincoln: The Head of State ("Seated Lincoln")*, located in Grant Park in Chicago, Illinois; *Sherman Monument*, Grand Army Plaza, New York, New York; *General John A. Logan Monument*, Grant Park, Chicago, Illinois; *General William T. Sherman Bust*, *Abraham Lincoln: The Man ("Standing Lincoln")*, Lincoln Park, Chicago, Illinois, and the *Farragut Monument*, Madison Square Park, New York. (Dryfhout, 111, 124, 168, 230, 253, 278)

Name the five known Chinese who served in the Union army and navy?

Hong Neok Woo (50th Pennsylvania), Cpl. John Tommy (70th New York), Joseph Pierce (14th Connecticut), Antonio Dardell (27th Connecticut), Ah Mei (U.S. Navy). There were undoubtedly more but the research and information are so scant that it seems these are the only five names that come up the most. (Heidler and Heidler, 434; Magner, unpublished manuscript).

Who was the highest-ranking Hispanic in the Civil War?

Adm. David Glasgow Farragut. George Farragut, Farragut's father, was born in Minorca and came to America during the Revolutionary War. He later married a woman of Scotch-Irish ancestry and on July 5, 1801, David Farragut was born. He eventually went under the foster care of Com. David Porter, father of David Dixon Porter, and the future commodore obtained an appointment as a midshipman in the U.S. Navy, despite being only nine years old. (Ted Alexander, Antietam National Battlefield; Heidler and Heidler, 682–683)

Who were the "Forty-eighters"?
Germans who served in the Civil War who had fought in the 1848–
1849 revolutions to establish a democratic and unified Germany.
(Heidler and Heidler, 823)

What is unusual about the medals given to the MacArthur's?
Arthur MacArthur, Jr. was awarded the Medal of Honor for his actions
at the battle of Missionary Ridge. His son Douglas MacArthur was
awarded a Medal of Honor during World War II. They are the only
father/son combination to be awarded Medals of Honor. (Heidler and
Heidler, 1237)

What was *Maum Guinea*?
Maum Guinea, by Metta Victoria Fuller Victor, was a novel. It was
so popular that many soldiers, both North and South, read it and
it could be found in homes both in America and Europe. It was an
antislavery book like *Uncle Tom's Cabin* but some have said that it
helped create the pro-Union sentiment in the British Isles. (Heidler
and Heidler)

What was one of the effects of Union occupation on the environment of Chattanooga?
To provide firewood for the men, so many trees were chopped down
that by 1865 there were only fifty-one remaining shade trees in the
city. (Sword, 8)

What was the first bolt-action rifle adopted by Federal Ordnance?
The Greene breech-loading rifle. A number of these weapons were
purchased by Russia. (Dale Beiver, Boyertown, PA)

What was a whip pennant baseball game?
The Civil War era's version of the World Series. (Livingston, 54)

What was an Identification Disc?
The Civil War forerunner of the dog tag worn by today's soldiers.
These were small coin-sized discs that had on one side an image.

These images included Winfield Scott, George McClellan, eagles, and George Washington, along with many other images. The reverse side was blank and on that side either the soldier himself or a jeweler or perhaps someone working for a sutler stamped the soldier's name and data. The information provided often included the soldier's name, company, regiment, and hometown. (Maier and Stahl, 9, 12)

How many monitors did the U.S. Navy build during the Civil War?
After the success of the John Ericsson–built *Monitor* in its fight with the Confederate *Merrimack* (CSS *Virginia*), the U.S. Navy instituted a major building program of monitors. The *Roanoke* was a cut-down steam frigate; *Orondaga* was a double-turret monitor. The *Passaic* class included ten vessels; *Canonicus* class, nine vessels; *Monadnock* class, four vessels; *Casco* class, twenty vessels, *Dictator*; *Puritan*; *Kalamazoo* class, four vessels (never launched or commissioned). (Patrick Purcell, Wayne, PA)

What is interesting about the military career of Samuel Wylie Crawford?
Crawford graduated from the University of Pennsylvania's medical school in 1850. He joined the army and became an assistant surgeon and served on the western frontier until 1861. April 1861 found him in command of an artillery battery at Ft. Sumter. Following this he was commissioned a major of the 13th U.S. Infantry, now an infantry officer. On April 25, 1862, he was promoted to brigadier general. In May 1863 he was placed in command of the Pennsylvania Reserves. During the course of the war he was brevetted through all grades to major general in the Volunteer and Regular armies. He served at First Winchester, Cedar Mountain, Antietam, Gettysburg, the Overland Campaign and the siege of Petersburg. Following the war he lived in Philadelphia and is buried in that city's Laurel Hill Cemetery. (Magner, 7–8)

What was the American Letter Express Company?
It was a postal service that allowed letters to cross between the lines. Initially the Southern Express Co. took mail to Louisville, Kentucky, which at the beginning of the war was neutral territory. There, the Adams Express Co. would take the mail for dispersal in the North.

The American Letter Express Co. was formed and offices were kept in Louisville and Nashville, delivering the mail in both directions at a cheaper rate than had been charged before. Unfortunately, due to the military actions of the armies, the operation lasted for only a short time. (Faust, 17)

What were the Federal weapons that the Confederates said were loaded on Sunday and fired the rest of the week?
The seven-shot repeating Spencer carbines and rifles.

Besides Raphael Semmes, who was one other Civil War participant who was both a general and an admiral?
Samuel Powhatan Carter. A native of Tennessee, at the beginning of the war he was serving as a lieutenant in the U.S. Navy. He was sent back to Tennessee as an army recruiter and eventually became the colonel of the 2nd Tennessee Infantry Regiment. Carter was then promoted to brigadier general on May 1, 1862, and was named a brevet major general, U.S. Volunteers, in 1865. Returning to the Navy, he retired as a commodore in 1881 and was promoted to rear admiral on the retired list on May 26, 1882. (Patrick E. Purcell, Wayne, PA)

What five Union states infantry regiments suffered the most deaths during the war?
Kentucky—Of 43,550 enlisted there were 10,774 deaths, or 24.7 percent

Vermont—Of 26,355 enlisted there were 5,224 deaths, or 19.8 percent

Michigan—Of 76,218 enlisted there were 13,855 deaths, or 19.3 percent

Iowa—Of 68,118 enlisted there were 13,001 deaths, or 19.0 percent

Maine—Of 49,635 enlisted there were 9,398 deaths, or 18.9 percent

These numbers include killed and mortally wounded as well as death from other causes. (Fox, 526)

Who were the eighteen Union Army Corps and Division general officers killed or mortally wounded during the war, and where?

Maj. Gen. James B. McPherson—Atlanta.
Maj. Gen. Joseph K. Mansfield—Antietam.
Maj. Gen. John F. Reynolds—Gettysburg.
Maj. Gen. John Sedgwick—Spotsylvania.
Maj. Gen. Isaac I. Stevens—Chantilly.
Maj. Gen. Philip Kearny—Chantilly.
Maj. Gen. Jesse L. Reno—South Mountain.
Maj. Gen. Israel B. Richardson—Antietam.
Maj. Gen. Amiel W. Wipple—Chancellorsville.
Maj. Gen. Hiram G. Berry—Chancellorsville.
Bvt. Maj. Gen. James S. Wadsworth—The Wilderness.
Bvt. Maj. Gen. David A. Russell—Opequon.
Brig. Gen. William H. Wallace—Shiloh.
Brig. Gen. Thomas Williams—Baton Rouge
Brig. Gen. James S. Jackson—Chaplin Hills.
Brig. Gen. Isaac P. Rodman—Antietam.
Brig. Gen. Thomas G. Sevensen—Spotsylvania.
Bvt. Brig. Gen. James Mulligan—Winchester (1863).

In addition, there were thirty-three brigade commanders and an additional twenty-three bvt. brigadiers (who were without brigade commands) were killed. (Fox, 40–41)

Who were the eleven Confederate Army Corps and Division commanders killed or mortally wounded during the war?

Gen. Albert Sydney Johnston—Shiloh.
Lt. Gen. Thomas J. Jackson—Chancellorsville.
Lt. Gen. Leonidas Polk—Pine Mountain.
Lt. Gen. Ambrose P. Hill—Petersburg.
Maj. Gen. William D. Pender—Gettysburg.
Maj. Gen. J. E. B. Stuart—Yellow Tavern.
Maj. Gen. W. H. Walker—Atlanta.
Maj. Gen. Robert E. Rodes—Opequon.

Maj. Gen. Stephen D. Ramseur—Cedar Creek.
Maj. Gen. Patrick R. Cleburne—Franklin.
Brig. Gen. John Pegram—Hatcher's Run.

In addition there were sixty-two brigade commanders with a rank of brigadier general killed during the war. (Fox, 571–572)

When was the USS *Cairo* recovered and where is she now?
The USS *Cairo*, pictured below, was initially found on Veteran's Day 1956 by Edwin C. Bearss, Warren Grabau, and M. Don Jacks who went looking for her in the Yazoo River near Benson Blake's 1860s lower plantation. They found a large metal object buried in the silt but it wasn't for another four years that there was a dive on the site to confirm if it was the *Cairo*—which it was. Later, with the help of a tug, a portion of the wreck (the pilothouse) was raised and a number of items known to belong to men on board were recovered. Problems delayed the excavation but finally in October 1965, with the help of several vessels including the dredge *Cairo*, part of the USS

USS *Cairo*. USAMHI

Cairo's hull broke the surface of the river. The ship was finally placed on an underwater barge that, when its 750,000 gallons of water were expelled, brought the *Cairo* to the surface. In the late winter of 1965 the recovered *Cairo* was taken to Pascagoula on the Mississippi Gulf Coast and offloaded at the Ingalls Shipbuilding Corp., where a preservation process was begun. Finally in 1977 the *Cairo* was taken back to Vicksburg, where the National Park Service took over the task of restoration, preservation and interpretation. Since the mid-1980s the restored *Cairo* has been on display at the Vicksburg National Military Park. (Bearss, 420–431)

Bibliography

BOOKS AND ARTICLES

Aimone, Alan, and Barbara Aimone. "Much to Sadden and Little to Cheer: The Civil War Years at West Point." *Blue & Grey Magazine*. Volume IX, Issue 2. December 1991.

Allen, Stacy D. "Shiloh! We Must This Day Conquer or PERISH!" *Blue & Gray Magazine*. Volume XIV, Issue 3. February 1997.

———. "Shiloh!: The Second Day's Battle and Aftermath." *Blue & Gray Magazine*. Volume XIV, Issue 4. April 1997.

Barnes, Frank. *Fort Sumter National Monument South Carolina*. Washington: National Park Service. 1961 reprint.

Bearss, Edwin C. *Fields of Honor: Pivotal Battles of the Civil War*. Washington: National Geographic Society. 2006. 448 pp.

———. "The Vicksburg Campaign: Grant Moves Inland—The Crossing of Big Bayou Pierre, and the Battles of Raymond and Jackson." *Blue & Gray Magazine*. Volume XVIII, Issue 1. October 2000.

———. "The Vicksburg Campaign: Grant Marches West—The Battles of Champion Hill and Big Black Bridge." *Blue & Gray Magazine*. Volume XVIII, Issue 5. June 2001.

Beatie, Dan. *Brandy Station 1863: First step toward Gettysburg*. Oxford: Osprey Publishing. 2008. 96 pp.

Benedict, G. G. *Vermont in the Civil War. A History of the Part Taken By The Vermont Soldiers and Sailors in the War For The Union 1861–1865*. (Two Volumes). Burlington: The Free Press Association. 1888.

Bergeron, Arthur W., Jr. "The Battle of Mobile Bay and the Campaign for Mobile, Ala. 1864–65." *Blue & Gray Magazine*. Volume XIX, Issue 4. April 2002.

Boardman, Sue, and Kathryn Porch. *The Battle of Gettysburg Cyclorama: A History and Guide.* Gettysburg: Thomas Publications. 2008. 79 pp.

Boatner, Mark Mayo III. *The Civil War Dictionary.* New York: David McKay Company, Inc. 1959. 974 pp.

Bogle, James G. "The Great Locomotive Chase or, The Andrews Raid." *Blue & Gray Magazine.* Volume IV, Issue 6. June–July 1987.

Bradley, Mark L. "The Road to Bennett Place, North Carolina, 1865." *Blue & Gray Magazine.* Volume XVII, Issue 1. October 1999.

Calkins, Chris. "The Apple Jack Raid, December 7–12, 1864: 'For This Barbarism There Was No Real Excuse.'" *Blue & Gray Magazine.* Volume XXII, Issue 3. Summer 2005.

———. "The Battle of Weldon Railroad (or Globe Tavern), August 18–19, 1864." *Blue & Gray Magazine.* Volume XXIII, Issue 5. Winter 2007.

Catton, Bruce. *The American Heritage New History of The Civil War.* New York: Penguin Books USA Inc. 1996. 630 pp.

———, (ed). *The Battle of Gettysburg by Frank A. Haskell.* Boston: Houghton Mifflin Company. 1958 reprint. 169 pp.

Cavanaugh, Michael A., and William Marvel. *The Petersburg Campaign: The Battle of the Crater. "The Horrid Pit." June 25–August 6, 1864.* Lynchburg: H. E. Howard, Inc. 1989. 181 pp.

Chamberlain, Joshua Lawrence. *Passing of the Armies: An Account of the Final Campaign of the Army of the Potomac, Based upon Personal Reminiscences of the Fifth Army Corps.* Dayton: Morningside Bookshop. 1982 reprint. 392 pp.

Coco, Gregory A. *A Vast Sea of Misery: A History and Guide to the Union and Confederate Field Hospitals at Gettysburg, July 1–November 20, 1863.* Gettysburg: Thomas Publications. 1988. 208 pp.

———. *Gettysburg's Confederate Dead.* Gettysburg: Thomas Publications. 2003. 127 pp.

Coddington, Edwin B. *The Gettysburg Campaign: A Study in Command.* Dayton: Press of Morningside Bookshop. 1979 reprint. 866 pp.

Cole, James M., and Rev. Roy E. Frampton. *Lincoln and the Human Interest Stories of The Gettysburg National Cemetery.* Hanover: The Sheridan Press. 88 pp.

Cooling, Benjamin Franklin. "Monocacy: The Battle That Saved Washington." *Blue & Gray Magazine.* Volume X, Issue 2. December 1992.

Corby, William, C. S. C. *Memoirs of Chaplain Life: Three Years with the Irish Brigade in the Army of the Potomac.* New York: Fordham University Press. 1992 reprint. 412 pp.

Cozzens, Peter. *No Better Place To Die: The Battle of Stones River.* Urbana: University of Illinois Press. 1990. 281 pp.

Cramer, John Henry. *Lincoln Under Enemy Fire: The Complete Account of His Experiences During Early's Attack on Washington.* Knoxville: The University of Tennessee Press. 2009 reprint. 138 pp.

Craughwell, Thomas J. *Stealing Lincoln's Body.* Cambridge: The Belknap Press of Harvard University Press. 2007. 250 pp.

Davis, Stephen. "Atlanta Campaign: Hood Fights Desperately. The Battles for Atlanta. Actions From July 10 to September 2, 1864." *Blue & Gray Magazine.* Volume VI, Issue 6. Special Issue.

Davis, William C. *Battle at Bull Run: A History of the First Major Campaign of the Civil War.* Garden City: Doubleday & Company, Inc. 1977. 298 pp.

Davis, William C., Brian C. Pohanka and Don Troiani, (eds.). *Civil War Journal: The Legacies.* Nashville: Rutledge Hill Press. 1999. 515 pp.

Davis, William C. *Jefferson Davis: The Man and His Hour—A Biography.* New York: HarperPerennial. 1992 reprint. 784 pp.

———. (ed.). *The Image of War 1861–1865: The End of An Era.* Garden City: Doubleday & Company, Inc. 1984. 496 pp.

Delauter, Roger U., and Brandon H. Beck. *Early's Valley Campaign: The Third Battle of Winchester.* Lynchburg: H. E. Howard, Inc. 1997. 127 pp.

Denney, Robert E. *The Civil War Years: A Day-by-Day Chronicle of the Life of a Nation.* New York: Sterling Publishing Company, Inc. 1992. 606 pp.

Dickson, Keith D. *The Civil War for Dummies.* Hoboken: Wiley Publishing, Inc. 2001. 384 pp.

Dizikes, John. *Opera in America: A Cultural History.* New Haven: Yale University Press. 1993. 628 pp.

Donald, David Herbert. *Lincoln.* London: Jonathan Cape. 1995. 714 pp.

Dryfhout, John H. *The Works of Augustus Saint-Gaudens.* Hanover: University Press of New England. 1982. 356 pp.

Durham, Roger S. "Savannah: Mr. Lincoln's Christmas Present." *Blue & Gray Magazine.* Volume VIII, Issue 3. February 1991.

Elmore, Tom. "The Burning of Columbia South Carolina, February 17, 1865." *Blue & Gray Magazine.* Volume XXI, Issue 2. Winter 2004.

Faust, Patricia L. (ed.) *Historical Times Illustrated Encyclopedia of the Civil War.* New York: Harper & Row, Publishers. 1986. 850 pp.

Flagel, Thomas R. *The History Buff's Guide to the Civil War.* Nashville: Cumberland House. 2003. 400 pp.

Fonvielle, Chris. "The Last Rays of Departing Hope: The Fall of Wilmington, Including the Campaigns Against Fort Fisher." *Blue & Gray Magazine.* Volume XII, Issue 2. December 1994.

Foote, Shelby. *The Civil War: A Narrative—Red River to Appomattox,* Vol. 3. New York: Random House. 1974. 1106 pp.

Fox, William F. *Regimental Losses in The American Civil War 1861–1865.* Dayton: Morningside Bookshop. 1995 reprint. 595 pp.

Frassanito, William A. *Antietam: The Photographic Legacy of America's Bloodiest Day.* New York: Charles Scribner's Sons. 1978. 304 pp.

Freeman, Douglas Southall. *Lee of Virginia.* New York: Charles Scribner's Sons. 1958. 243 pp.

Frye, Dennis E. *Antietam Revealed: The Battle of Antietam and the Maryland Campaign as You Have Never Seen It Before.* Collingswood: C.W. Historicals, LLC. 2004. 198 pp.

———. "Purged Away with Blood: John Brown's War." *Hallowed Ground.* Volume 10, Number 3. Fall 2009.

Gallagher, Gary W. *Stephen Dodson Ramseur: Lee's Gallant General.* Chapel Hill: The University of North Carolina Press. 1985. 232 pp.

Goodwin, Doris Kearns. *Team of Rivals: The Political Genius of Abraham Lincoln.* New York: Simon & Schuster. 2005. 916 pp.

Graff, Henry F. (ed.) *The Presidents: A Reference History.* New York: Simon & Schuster. 1997. 815 pp.

Greater Chambersburg Chamber of Commerce. *Southern Revenge: Civil War History of Chambersburg, Pennsylvania.* Shippensburg: White Mane Publishing, Inc. 1989. 192 pp.

Greene, A. Wilson. "April 2, 1865: Day of Decision at Petersburg." *Blue & Gray Magazine.* Volume XVIII, Issue 3. February 2001.

Hawthorne, Frederick W. *Gettysburg: Stories of Men and Monuments—As Told By Battlefield Guides.* Hanover: The Sheridan Press. 1988. 140 pp.

Haythornthwaite, Philip J. *Uniforms of the Civil War, 1861–65,* 1st American Edition. New York: Macmillan, 1975. 192 pp.

Heidler, Davis S., and Jeanne T. Heidler (eds.) *Encyclopedia of the American Civil War: a Political, Social, and Military History.* New York: W. W. Norton & Company. 2000. 2733 pp.

Hennessy, John. "The Second Battle of Manassas: Lee Suppresses the 'Miscreant' Pope." *Blue & Gray Magazine.* Volume IX, Issue 6. August 1992.

Hessler, James A. *Sickles At Gettysburg: The Controversial Civil War General Who Committed Murder, Abandoned Little Round Top, and Declared Himself the Hero of Gettysburg.* New York: Savas Beatie. 2009. 490 pp.

Hicks, Brian, and Schuyler Kropf. *Raising the Hunley: The Remarkable History and Recovery of the Lost Confederate Submarine.* New York: Ballantine Books. 2002. 301 pp.

Holzer, Harold, and Joshua Wolf Shenk. *In Lincoln's Hand: His Original Manuscripts.* Washington: The Library of Congress. 2009. 196 pp.

Holzer, Harold (ed.). *The Lincoln Anthology: Great Writers on His Life and Legacy from 1860 to Now*. New York: The Library of America. 2009. 964 pp.

Hughes, Mark. *The New Civil War Handbook: Facts and Photos for Readers of All Ages*. New York: Savas Beatie. 2009. 158 pp.

Hughes, Michael A. "Pea Ridge, or Elkhorn Tavern Arkansas—March 7–8, 1862: The Campaign, the Battle, and the Men Who Fought for the Fate of Missouri." *Blue & Gray Magazine*. Volume V, Issue 3. January 1988.

Hunt, Roger D., and Jack R. Brown. *Brevet Brigadier Generals in Blue*. Gaithersburg: Old Soldier Books. 1990. 700 pp.

Jeal, Tim. *Stanley: The Impossible Life of Africa's Greatest Explorer*. New Haven: Yale University Press. 2007. 579 pp.

Jordan, Weymouth T., Jr. *North Carolina Troops 1861–1865: A Roster—Vol. VI, Infantry*. Raleigh: North Carolina Office of Archives and History. 2004 reprint. 770 pp.

Kanazawich, Michael. *Remarkable Stories of the Lincoln Assassination*. Orrtanna: Colecraft Industries. 2008. 102 pp.

Kauffman, Michael W. *American Brutus: John Wilkes Booth and the Lincoln Conspiracies*. New York: Random House. 2004. 508 pp.

———. "John Wilkes Booth and the Murder of Abraham Lincoln." *Blue & Gray Magazine*. Volume VII, Issue 4. April 1990.

———. "Booth's Escape Route: Lincoln's Assassin On the Run." *Blue & Gray Magazine*. Volume VII, Issue 5. June 1990.

Kelly, Dennis. "Atlanta Campaign: Mountains to Pass, A River to Cross. The Battle of Kennesaw Mountain, And Related Actions From June 10 to July 9, 1864." *Blue & Gray Magazine*. Volume VI, Issue 5. June 1989.

Kingery, Dr. Dorothy Williams. *More Than Mercer House: Savannah's Jim Williams & His Southern Houses*. Savannah: Sheldon Group, L.L.C. 2006 reprint. 184 pp.

Klement, Frank L. *The Gettysburg Soldiers' Cemetery and Lincoln's Address*. Shippensburg: White Mane Publishing. 1993. 276 pp.

Kliger, Paul I. "The Confederate Invasion of New Mexico." *Blue & Gray Magazine*. Volume XI, Issue 5. June 1994.

Krick, Robert E. L. *Staff Officers in Gray: A Biographical Register of the Staff Officers in the Army of Northern Virginia*. Chapel Hill: The University of North Carolina Press. 2003. 406 pp.

Krick, Robert K. *Lee's Colonels: A Biographical Register of the Field Officers of the Army of Northern Virginia*. Wilmington: Broadfoot Publishing Company. 2009. 551 pp.

Livingston, E. A. "Bud." "New York City and the Civil War: The City that Lincoln Never Won and the Rebels Couldn't Burn." *Blue & Gray Magazine*. Volume XIV, Issue 2. December 1996.

Magner, Blake A. "The Great Pivot: The Flank Attack of Stannard's Vermont Brigade Against Pickett's Division." *Military Images*. November–December 1984.

———. "The Gettysburg Soldiers' National Cemetery: Yesterday and Today." *Gettysburg Magazine*. January 1996. Issue 14.

———. *Traveller and Company: The Horses of Gettysburg*. Gettysburg: Farnsworth House Military Impressions. 1995. 56 pp.

——— (ed.). *At Peace With Honor: The Civil War Burials of Laurel Hill Cemetery Philadelphia, Pennsylvania*. Collingswood: C. W. Historicals, LLC. 1997. 88 pp.

——— (ed.). *The Gettysburg Encyclopedia*. Unpublished Manuscript.

———. "Hancock's Line at Gettysburg: July 3, 1863. 'This is going to be a hot place.'" *Blue & Gray Magazine*. Volume XXVI. Issue 4. 2009.

Maier, Larry B., and Joseph W. Stahl. *Identification Discs of Union Soldiers in the Civil War: A Complete Classification Guide and Illustrated History*. Jefferson: McFarland & Company, Inc., Publishers. 2008. 212 pp.

Marvel, William. *Lee's Last Retreat: The Flight to Appomattox*. Chapel Hill: The University of North Carolina Press. 2002. 308 pp.

McDonough, James Lee, and Thomas L. Connelly. *Five Tragic Hours: The Battle of Franklin*. Knoxville: The University of Tennessee Press. 1983. 217 pp.

McMurry, Richard M. "Atlanta Campaign: Rocky Face to the Dallas Line, the Battles of May 1864." *Blue & Gray Magazine*. Volume VI, Issue 4. April 1989.

Mertz, Gregory A. "No Turning Back: The Battle of the Wilderness." *Blue & Gray Magazine*. Volume XII, Issue 4. April 1995.

———. "No Turning Back: The Battle of the Wilderness—Part II. The Fighting on May 6, 1864." *Blue & Gray Magazine*. Volume XII, Issue 5. June 1995.

Mewborn, Horace. "Jeb Stuart's Ride Around the Army of the Potomac, June 12–15, 1862." *Blue & Gray Magazine*. Volume XV, Issue 6. August 1998.

———. "The Operations of Mosby's Rangers: Mosby's Confederacy." *Blue & Gray*. Volume XVII, Issue 4. April 2000.

Miller, J. Michael. "The Battles of Bristoe Station." *Blue & Gray Magazine*. Volume XXVI, Issue 2. 2009.

Motts, Wayne E. *"Trust In God And Fear Nothing": Gen. Lewis A. Armistead, CSA*. Gettysburg: Farnsworth House Military Impressions. 1994. 64 pp.

O'Reilly, Frank A. "Slaughter at Fredericksburg: Lee's Most Resounding Victory." *Blue & Gray Magazine*. Volume XXV, Issue 4. 2008.

———. *The Fredericksburg Campaign: Winter on the Rappahannock.* Baton Rouge: Louisiana State University Press. 2003. 630 pp.

Owen, Richard, and James Owen. *Generals at Rest: The Grave Sites of the 425 Official Confederate Generals.* Shippensburg: White Mane Publishing Co., Inc. 1997. 352 pp.

Patchen, Scott C. "The Shenandoah Valley: July 1864—Grant and Lincoln Realize the Need For A New Commander in the Valley." *Blue & Gray Magazine.* Volume XXIII, Issue 3. Summer 2006.

Pfanz, Harry. *Gettysburg: The Second Day.* Chapel Hill: The University of North Carolina Press. 1987. 601 pp.

Potter, Jerry. "The Sultana Disaster: Conspiracy of Greed." *Blue & Gray Magazine.* Volume VII, Issue 6. August 1990.

Quammen, David. *The Reluctant Mr. Darwin: An Intimate Portrait of Charles Darwin and the Making of His Theory of Evolution.* New York: W. W. Norton & Company. 2006. 304 pp.

Quigley, Robert D. *Civil War Spoken Here: A Dictionary of Mispronounced People, Places and Things of the 1860s.* Collingswood: C. W. Historicals. 1993. 199 pp.

Raus, Edmund J., Jr. *A Generation on the March—The Union Army at Gettysburg.* Lynchburg: H. E. Howard, Inc. 1987. 200 pp.

Rayburn, Ella S. "With the Confederate Secret Service: Sabotage At City Point." *Civil War Times.* Volume XXII, Number 2. April 1983.

Richmond National Battlefield Historians. "Grant and Lee, 1864: From the North Anna to the Crossing of the James." *Blue & Gray Magazine.* Volume XI, Issue 4. April 1994.

Robbins, James S. *Last in Their Class: Custer, Pickett and the Goats of West Point.* New York: Encounter Books. 2006. 503 pp.

Robertson, James I., Jr. "Stonewall Jackson: Molding the Man and Making A General." *Blue & Gray Magazine.* Volume IX, Issue 5. June 1992.

———. *Stonewall Jackson: The Man, The Soldier, The Legend.* New York: Macmillan. 1997. 950 pp.

———. *General A. P. Hill: The Story of a Confederate Warrior.* New York: Random House. 1987. 382 pp.

Robertson, William Glenn. "The Chickamauga Campaign: The Battle of Chickamauga—Day 1, September 19, 1863." *Blue & Gray Magazine.* Volume XXIV, Issue 6. Spring 2008.

Roth, Dave. "Grierson's Raid, April 17–May 2, 1863: A Cavalry Raid at Its Best." *Blue & Gray Magazine.* Volume X, Issue 5. June 1993.

Roth, David E. "The Mysteries of Spring Hill, Tennessee." *Blue & Gray Magazine.* Volume II, Issue 2. October–November 1984.

Sallee, Scott E. "The Battle of Prairie Grove: War in the Ozarks, April '62–January '63." *Blue & Gray Magazine*. Volume XXI, Issue 5. Fall 2004.

Sanders, Stuart W. "The 1862 Kentucky Campaign and The Battle of Perryville." *Blue & Gray Magazine*. Volume XXII, Issue 5. Holiday 1995.

Sears, Stephen W. *To the Gates of Richmond: The Peninsula Campaign*. New York: Ticknor & Fields. 1992. 468 pp.

———. *Landscape Turned Red: The Battle of Antietam*. New Haven: Ticknor & Fields. 1983. 431 pp.

Scaife, William R. "Sherman's March to the Sea: Events from September 3 to December 21, 1864, Including the Occupation of Atlanta, More Battles With the Unpredictable John Bell Hood, the Burning of Atlanta, 'Marching Through Georgia.'" *Blue & Gray Magazine*. Volume XII, Issue 2. December 1989.

Sifakis, Stewart. *Who Was Who in the Union*. New York: Facts On File. 1988. 479 pp.

Spearman, Charles M. "The Battle of Stones River: Tragic New Year's Eve in Tennessee." *Blue & Gray Magazine*. Volume VI, Issue 3. February 1989.

Sword, Wiley. "The Battle Above the Clouds: The Fight for Lookout Mountain, Chattanooga, Tennessee, 1863." *Blue & Gray Magazine*. Volume XVIII, Issue No. 2. December 2000.

Tagg, Larry. *The Generals of Gettysburg: The Leaders of America's Greatest Battle*. Campbell: Savas Publishing Company. 1998. 373 pp.

Terdoslavich, William. *The Civil War Trivia Quiz Book: With More Than 1,000 Questions About The People, Places, and Events That Took Place Between The Blue And The Gray*. New York: The Fairfax Press. 1984. 182 pp.

Thompson, James West. "Partisan Comments on Andersonville." *Blue & Gray Magazine*. Volume III, Issue 3, December 1985–January 1986.

Trulock, Alice Rains. *In The Hands of Providence: Joshua L. Chamberlain & The American Civil War*. Chapel Hill: The University of North Carolina Press. 1992. 569 pp.

Urwin, Gregory J. W. *Custer Victorious: The Civil War Battles of General George Armstrong Custer*. East Brunswick: Associated University Presses, Inc. 1983. 308 pp.

Venter, Bruce M. "The Kilpatrick-Dahlgren Raid on Richmond, February 28–March 4, 1864." *Blue & Gray Magazine*. Volume XX, Issue 3. Winter 2003.

———. "Hancock the (Not So) Superb: The Second Battle of Reams' Station, August 25, 1864." *Blue & Gray Magazine*. Volume XXIII, Issue 5. Winter 2007.

Warner, Ezra J. *Generals in Gray: Lives of the Confederate Commanders*. Baton Rouge: Louisiana State University Press. 1959. 420 pp.

———. *Generals in Blue: Lives of the Union Commanders.* Baton Rouge: Louisiana State University Press. 1964. 680 pp.

Weeks, Michael. *The Complete Civil War Road Trip Guide. More Than 400 Civil War Sites, from Antietam to Zagonyi's Charge.* Woodstock: The Countryman Press, 2009.

Welch, Richard F. *The Boy General: The Life and Careers of Francis Channing Barlow.* Madison: Fairleigh Dickinson University Press. 2003. 301 pp.

Wert, Jeffry D. *A Brotherhood of Valor: The Common Soldiers of the Stonewall Brigade, C.S.A., and the Iron Brigade, U.S.A.* New York: Simon & Schuster. 1999. 413 pp.

Where Valor Rests: Arlington National Cemetery. Washington: National Geographic. 2007. 191 pp.

Winschel, Terry. "The Siege of Vicksburg." *Blue & Gray Magazine.* Volume XX, Issue 4. Spring 2003.

NEWSPAPERS

Cavanaugh, Michael A. "Historic Fort Mifflin." *Civil War News.* Volume XXXIII, Number 10. November 2008.

Kaufman, Herb. "Philadelphia Museum Aims To Disperse Holdings for Three Years." *Civil War News.* Volume XXXV, Number 10. November 2009.

Post, Paul. "N.Y. Soldier's Remains Go Home From Antietam For Burial." *Civil War News.* Volume XXXV, Number 10. November 2009.

Wade, Gregory L. "Franklin Pays Tribute For An Unknown Soldier's Burial." *Civil War News.* Volume XXXV, Number 10. November 2009.

PAMPHLETS

The Gettysburg Gun—Battery B 1st RI Light Artillery, Disabled at the Battle of Gettysburg—July 3, 1863. Vertical Files, Gettysburg National Military Park.

Barnard, Sandy. *Custer Burial Revisited—West Point, October 1877.* Custer Battlefield Historical & Museum Association. Sixth Annual Symposium. June 26, 1992. The author's thanks to the memory of Brian Pohanka for this piece.

INTERNET WEB SITES

This author does not like using the Internet as a source because there is so much misinformation on it. However, with our changing world

sometimes we have to bow to technology. Thus, reader, please bear
with me.

Antietam National Battlefield. National Park Service. http://www.nps.gov/
anti/index.htm.
Appomattox Surrender. http://www.nps.gov/apco/the-surrender.htm.
Bull Runnings: A Journal of the Digitization of a Civil War Battle. http://
bullrunnings.wordpress.com.
Civil War Women. http://www.civilwarwomenblog.co.
Elecvillage. http://www.elecvillage.com/juneteen.html.
Fredericksburg. http://www.nps.gov/frsp/fredhist.htm.
History Central. http://www.historycentral.com/navy/CWNavy/America
.html.
Medals. http://www.itd.nps.gov//cwss/history/aa_medals.htm.
Pamplin Park. http://www.pamplinpark.org/park_history.html.
Pennington. http://encyclopedia.stateuniversity.com/pages/23836/William
-Pennington.html.
Smithsonian—National Museum of American History: Kenneth E.
Behring Center. http://americanhistory.si.edu/collections/object
.cfm?key=35&objkey=19.
Yosemite National Park. National Park Service. http://www.nps.gov/yose/
index.htm.

PHOTOGRAPH SOURCES

CWLM	Former Civil War Library and Museum, Philadelphia, Pennsylvania
NA	National Archives, Washington, DC
St. Gaudens	St. Gaudens National Historic Site, Cornish, New Hampshire
USAMHI	Massachusetts Commandery Military Order of the Loyal Legion and the U.S. Army Military History Institute, Carlisle Barracks, Pennsylvania
VHS	Virginia Historical Society, Richmond, Virginia
Washington & Lee	Washington & Lee University, Lynchburg, Virginia

INDEX